Writing Proposals

Writing Proposals

SECOND EDITION

Richard Johnson-Sheehan

Purdue University

PEARSON

Longman

New York   San Francisco   Boston
London   Toronto   Sydney   Tokyo   Singapore   Madrid
Mexico City   Munich   Paris   Cape Town   Hong Kong   Montreal

Publisher: Joseph Opiela
Marketing Manager: Thomas DeMarco
Production Manager: Donna DeBenedictis
Project Coordination, Text Design, and Electronic Page Makeup: Elm Street
  Publishing Services, Inc.
Cover Designer Manager: John Callahan
Art Studio: Burmar Technical Corporation
Senior Manufacturing Buyer: Alfred C. Dorsey

Library of Congress Cataloging-in-Publication Data

Johnson-Sheehan, Richard.
    Writing proposals/Richard Johnson-Sheehan.–2nd ed.
        p. cm.
    Includes bibliographical references and index.
    ISBN 978-0-205-58314-0 (pbk.)
1.   Proposal writing in business.   I.   Title.
HF5718.5.J64   2008
658.15'224–dc22   2007023405

Please visit our website at http://www.ablongman.com

ISBN-13: 978-0-205-58314-0
ISBN-10: 0-205-58314-8

Contents

Chapter Four: Describing the Current Situation   55

Chapter Five: Developing a Project Plan   76

Chapter Six: Describing Qualifications   99

Chapter Seven: Introductions, Costs, and Benefits   117

Chapter Eight: Developing Budgets   141

Chapter Nine: Writing with Style   161

Chapter Ten: Designing Proposals   182

Chapter Eleven: Using Graphics   203

Chapter Twelve: The Final Touches   220

Example Proposals   235

References   267

Index   269

Preface

What is a proposal? In the first chapter of this book, proposals are defined as "tools for managing change." The key words in this definition are tools, managing, and change. By *tools*, I mean proposals are devices that help us do our work. They help us to present our ideas, our plans, and our dreams for the future. *Managing* means taking control of a situation. It means directing people and resources in a way that allows us to achieve specific ends. *Change* is really what life is all about.

As a professional proposal writer and grant writer, I remind myself continually that change is always happening, offering us new opportunities to take action, solve problems, make our world better. Proposals are tools for managing these changes. They are tools for taking purposeful action in a world that never seems to stop moving.

So how do we go about using proposals and grants to manage change? The strategies in this book are rooted in rhetorical theory, a discipline going back at least a few thousand years. Put concisely, rhetoric is the study of what *could be* or what *should be*, not necessarily what *is*. It is a forward-thinking discipline, more concerned with what we are going to *do* in the future than what happened in the past. For this reason, the discipline of rhetoric is particularly helpful writing successful proposals and grants. After all, rhetoric is a discipline that studies change and how humans use communication to mold and shape their social environments.

Premises of This Book

A few important premises set this book apart from other books on writing proposals and grants. Other books offer mostly tips and tricks to write more effective proposals. You will find some of that material here, too. But, you will also find that this book stresses the *process* of writing successful proposals and grants. My aim is to show you how a professional writer of proposals and grants uses a consistent step-by-step process to move from planning to drafting to designing to editing their work.

An initial premise of this book, therefore, is that writing proposals and grants should be approached from a problem-solving point of view. The proposal-writing process should help you and your team sort out complex situations and devise plans that meet specific goals. In this book, it is assumed that a thorough understanding of the situation, a sound plan, and solid credentials will ultimately win contracts and secure grant funding.

A second premise is that you, as a proposal writer or grant writer, need to pay attention to change as you assess situations and develop plans for improving those situations. Put bluntly, proposals are never written in a social vacuum. Rather, they are written in social, political, and ethical environments that are always evolving. What was true today or yesterday may not be true tomorrow. Therefore, the key to writing successful proposals is to first identify what changed to create the current problem or opportunity. Then with these elements of change identified, you can use proposals and grants to shape these forces to your advantage.

The third underlying premise of this book is that proposals should be written "visually." In this multimedia age of television and computers, people tend to think in images rather than in words alone. In this book, you will notice that almost all the techniques discussed employ strategies that take advantage of your and your readers' abilities to think visually. Some of the visual techniques are more apparent, such as the use of logical maps to invent a proposal's content or the use of design principles to guide the page layout of the text. Other visual techniques are subtle, such as the use of similes and metaphors (Chapter 9) to create visual images in the readers' minds. Visual writing allows both writers and readers to develop a strong visual sense of what the proposal is illustrating.

Content and Organization

The ability to write effective proposals and grants is a powerful skill, but the act of writing is only part of the overall proposal development process. In this book, you will also learn the techniques that will

- **Help you tap into your innate creativity to invent the content of your proposals.** Some of the "invention" techniques in this book, such as logical mapping (Chapter 4), may seem a little strange at first. However, these techniques will help you gain unique insights into problems and opportunities. They will help you devise creative strategic plans that use imagination and foresight.
- **Help you organize your ideas in ways that achieve specific goals.** The organizational pattern of a proposal is much more than a convenient structure for presenting your case to the readers. It is a means for helping you formulate your approach and develop your strategy for success. You will learn how to use the proposal genre to generate new ideas and new ways of understanding your or your clients' needs.
- **Help you express your ideas plainly and persuasively.** The use of good style should be a choice, not an accident. You will learn simple, time-tested techniques for clarifying your message for the readers. You will also learn how to amplify your prose by using stylistic techniques that tap into your readers' motives, values, attitudes, and emotions.
- **Show you how to use visual design to clarify and enhance the arguments in your proposals and grants.** In an increasingly visual age, readers are more reliant than ever on visual cues to help them find the important information in proposals. They also expect proposals to include graphics that

illustrate and reinforce the written text. You will learn design principles that will help you devise winning designs for your proposal and include graphics to enhance the text.

The organization of this book will lead you through the process for composing, revising, designing, and editing proposals.

New Material in the Second Edition

The second edition of *Writing Proposals* has been revised from front to back. People who used the first edition have been overwhelmingly positive in their feedback, but I have received excellent suggestions for sharpening some parts of the book and for adding material that readers said they would find helpful.

A major change in this edition is the treatment of grant writing. The first edition addressed grants as a special case of proposal writing. In this edition, grant writing has been centralized and made much more prominent, with additional strategies and a running case study that demonstrates the grant-writing process.

Also, since the release of the first edition, we have seen major changes in the way the U.S. government manages its proposals and grants. This edition explains how the new systems operate and how you can successfully interact with government agencies and foundations.

Overall, readers who are familiar with the first edition of *Writing Proposals* should find this edition much stronger and more comprehensive in its treatment of the proposal-writing and grant-writing processes.

Acknowledgments

A book like this one is never the work of just one person, though there's only one name on the cover. So let me thank the others who helped put this book together. First, I appreciate the help of my colleagues and students at Purdue University and the University of New Mexico who have shaped this text through their suggestions for improvements. At Purdue, Morgan Sousa, Allen Brizee, and Jaclyn Wells helped me strengthen the chapters on strategic planning and teaming. Allen added his expertise on stasis theory. All three were central in the writing of the Cool Campus case study that appears at the end of each chapter. At the University of New Mexico, James Burbank, Karen Schechner, Shannon McCabe, Andrew Mara, Craig Baehr, and Kristi Stewart helped me develop the end-of-chapter questions. Professors Charles Paine and Scott Sanders have offered insightful suggestions to streamline some of the invention techniques described in this book.

I also want to thank the many participants in my grant-writing and proposal-writing workshops over the last fifteen years. Their reactions and comments to the ideas shown in this book have helped me sharpen some concepts and strategies. They have allowed me to test these strategies against a wide range of proposals and grants.

In addition, I want to thank the reviewers of both this and the last edition of this book, who offered immeasurably helpful comments to improve the text: Deborah Andrews, University of Delaware; Elizabeth Birmingham, North Dakota State University; William O. Coggin, Bowling Green State University; Sam Dragga, Texas Tech University; Dean Hall, Kansas State University; Jamie Larsen, North Carolina State University; Roger Munger, James Madison University; John R. Nelson, University of Massachusetts; Elizabeth Pass, James Madison University; Diana C. Reep, University of Akron; and Clay Spinuzzi, University of Texas at Austin.

Finally, this book is dedicated to Tracey, Emily, and Collin, who helped me struggle through the rough spots as the book went from thought to page. In their own ways, they provided the motivation to keep going.

Richard Johnson-Sheehan

Writing Proposals

1 | Introduction to Proposals and Grants

Overview

This chapter will provide an overview of the purpose and importance of proposals and grants. The chapter will meet the following learning objectives:

1. Discuss the importance of proposals in an evolving world and workplace.
2. Define the study of rhetoric and its relation to proposals.
3. Define the genre of a proposal and the sections of a basic proposal.
4. Describe and discuss the proposal writing process.
5. Show how a grant proposal is a business proposal.

Why Do We Write Proposals?

Put simply, a proposal is a tool for managing change. We write proposals because the world around us is endlessly evolving and shifting, creating new opportunities and new problems. We write proposals because, as the old proverb says, "the only constant is change." Even the most successful plans, the strongest buildings, and the securest relationships need to be reimagined, reconsidered, and rebuilt to keep up with a world in flux. Proposals are instruments for managing those changes.

Some people resist change. They worry about losing what they have, so they try to ignore the evolutionary forces around them, attempting to hold back change or slow it down. As a writer of proposals and grants, you should view change as an ally, not an enemy. You should always recognize that a changing world creates new openings and new opportunities that can be used for growing and advancing your business, nonprofit organization, or research. You should look forward to change with optimism, not regret or fear. The sooner you view change as something to be *managed*, not resisted, the sooner you can start using proposals to capitalize on the openings that are created by change. The victims of change are people who fight the currents of reality, eventually drowning or swept away by the advancements in their field. Managers of change, on the other hand, are people who learn how to use proposals to steer and shape reality, riding the currents of change rather than fighting them.

The purpose of this book is to help you write effective proposals and grants by using time-tested rhetorical strategies to identify new opportunities and solve problems. You will learn how to develop plans for action, organize your ideas, improve the clarity of your writing, and persuade your readers to say yes to your ideas. You probably don't need to be told how important proposals are to your career or business. More than likely, you picked up this book because you have an important proposal to write. Perhaps proposals play a significant role in your work life. If so, you already know that proposals are important tools in the workplace, whether you are a CEO pitching a multimillion-dollar design to a client or a manager proposing a new project for your workgroup.

Meanwhile, if you write grant proposals, you already know that securing funding is becoming increasingly difficult as grants from government and private sources become more competitive. Effective writing is essential for grant proposals, whether you are a scientist looking for research funding from the National Science Foundation or a nonprofit organization requesting funding from the McCune Foundation.

In short, proposals and grants are about money and power. They are about who is doing what, for whom, and for how much. Learning to write effective proposals is important to your success in the professional world.

Rhetoric

In this book, we will follow a *rhetorical approach* toward developing proposals and grants. Rhetoric, despite its negative undertones in the mainstream media, is more than empty political promises or amplified speech. Rather, rhetoric is the art of persuasive communication, a rich discipline with more than two thousand years of tradition on which to draw. Aristotle (384–322 B.C.) offered one of the earliest definitions of rhetoric when he wrote, "Let rhetoric be defined as an ability in each case to see the available means of persuasion" (Aristotle 1991, p. 36). In this definition, Aristotle suggests that being persuasive requires you to first "see" or map out the current situation in which you are working. Then, you can develop a persuasion strategy that suits that particular situation.

Until the late nineteenth century, rhetoric was a central study in universities, but today the word *rhetoric* is usually associated with words like *mere, just,* or *empty.* With this demotion of rhetoric as a field of study, it is no coincidence that most people in our society struggle to express themselves in writing and speech. A quick glance at the documents around you should demonstrate how far communication skills have declined. These documents often lack substance, organization, style, and design. They often don't address their readers' needs, and they regularly lack a purpose and a point. Ironically, rhetoric is denounced by a society that desperately needs it most. After all, in this information age, those who can write or speak persuasively are well on their way to success. Those who cannot communicate effectively find themselves imprisoned in their own words.

To help you become a stronger communicator, this book will show you how rhetorical strategies can be applied directly to the development of proposals and grants. Rhetoric is often defined as the "art of persuasion," but it is also the study of change. Rhetoricians see change as the normal condition of reality because rhetoric is the study of what could be, what might be, or what should be. Consequently, an understanding of rhetoric helps us anticipate change, react to it, and then use effective communication strategies to shape the changing world to our own advantage. Rhetoric is a means for gaining power in that uncertain reality.

Rhetoric's emphasis on change is reflected in the two elements of rhetoric, which will be addressed in each chapter of this book: interpretation and expression.

Interpretation

Interpretation involves using rhetorical strategies to ask the right questions and then impose mental frames on situations that are evolving, uncertain, or chaotic. For example, imagine you are a manager who scheduled a staff meeting to help you solve an important problem. As you step into the room, you hear members of your staff arguing, you notice other people walking around the room, and you see papers strewn across the table. Members of your staff seem to be coming at you from all directions, trying to tell you about the "problem."

What would you do? Well, more than likely, your first reaction would be to impose some structure on this chaotic meeting. After telling people to quiet down, you would start questioning each of your staff members to figure out what the current situation really is. As your staff answers your questions, you would find that some of the information they provide is useful. Meanwhile some details and opinions—no matter how emphatically expressed—are not relevant. In most cases, you would also soon realize that some important facts that you need to make a decision are not available. Eventually, as you gather facts, you would start working out a plan for dealing with the problem that created the chaos in the first place.

When writing a proposal, the situation is similar to this chaotic meeting. Usually, when you start writing a proposal, there are thousands of confusing facts, opinions, and concerns floating around in your mind. On your desk, you have reports, notes from meetings, clippings from magazines and newspapers, and your own scribbled comments on pads of paper. At this point, ineffective writers—just like ineffective managers—are often overwhelmed by the sheer mass of information that they need to process. And, like ineffective managers, these writers often fail to achieve their goals because they do not know how to organize the available information into a useful form.

Effective writers, just like effective managers, are quite the opposite: They know from experience that they need to first "interpret" the many available fragments of information. Only then will they be able to grasp the big picture by recognizing what information they already possess and what information they still require before taking action. Experienced writers know that the challenge is not to "discover" order in a chaotic situation, because, frankly, there is no order to be discovered. Rather, effective writers use interpretive strategies to *impose* order on the current situation. A knowledge of rhetoric offers you a basic interpretive structure from which you can take control of chaotic situations and solve problems.

Expression

Expression is the performance side of rhetoric. Once you have properly interpreted the situation you face, then you can begin developing a rhetorical strategy to help you express your ideas persuasively to the readers. Expression involves inventing the content of the proposal by describing the current situation, setting your goals, and promoting the plan. Expression involves using organizational strategies to capitalize on your readers' expectations for the structure of the document. Expression also takes advantage of your readers' psychological tendencies by weaving emotional and authoritative themes into the style of the document. And finally, expression uses visual design to deliver a professional package that will stand above your competitors' efforts. Expression is not simply a means for spinning the facts to your advantage. Rather, it is a way to generate ideas and use the facts effectively to persuade your readers to accept your ideas.

In this book, you will find this interpretation/expression balance used in each chapter to first help you impose order on chaotic writing situations and then use powerful rhetorical strategies to bend each writing situation to your will. In fact, you might find that the strategies you learn in this book go far beyond writing proposals. A knowledge of rhetoric is useful in all situations in which communication is important.

The Proposal Genre

One reason writing proposals and grants is so challenging is that these documents rely on a rather complex *genre*. A genre is a consistent pattern that both you and your readers recognize as a specific type of document. The proposal genre includes a few important elements that your readers will expect:

Current Situation: Your readers expect you to demonstrate that you understand their situation/problem.

Project Plan or Methods: Your readers also expect the proposal to describe a plan for completing the project.

Qualifications: Your readers will expect you to show them that you are qualified and have the capability to complete the project.

Costs and Benefits: Your readers expect you to tell them how much the work will cost and to explain the benefits they will receive for that sum of money.

As shown in Figure 1.1, these are the major sections of a proposal, whether you are writing a business-to-business proposal, an internal planning proposal, or a grant proposal to a funding source.

FIGURE 1.1
The Proposal Genre

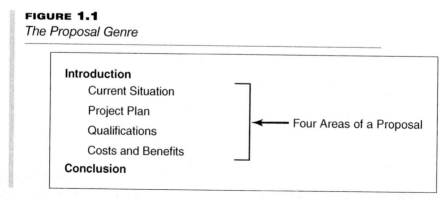

The proposal genre is designed to address some fundamental questions:

- What is the current situation?
- What is needed to improve the current situation?
- What is a good plan for improving the current situation?
- Why is your company or organization best qualified to do the work?
- How much will the work cost?
- What are the tangible benefits of the plan?

This list of questions might make proposals sound complicated, but if you think about it, people use these questions to conduct business all the time. Aren't these the same questions you would expect a mechanic to answer before fixing a problem with your car? Wouldn't you expect a surgeon to answer these questions before she puts you on an operating table? Would you want to do business with a mechanic or surgeon who did not, would not, or could not provide answers to these questions up front? Of course you wouldn't. Just like you, your readers expect your proposal to anticipate and answer these kinds of questions.

Of course, the proposal genre is not a formula into which writers plug and chug content. In fact, proposals often do not always follow the pattern shown in Figure 1.1. Nevertheless, in almost all cases, if a proposal accounts for these four sections, it will have addressed the readers' expectations.

In this book, we will handle each of these areas separately and in some depth. Once you master the basic genre, you will find that you can shape it to suit each unique proposal writing situation.

The Proposal-Writing Process

The best way to write proposals and grants is to follow a repeatable *process* that takes you from your initial ideas to a finished document. In this book, you will learn a process for writing proposals that includes five stages:

- **Stage 1: Planning and Research**—developing your ideas, collecting information, and identifying persuasive strategies that will help you convince the readers to say yes to your project
- **Stage 2: Organizing and Drafting**—arranging your ideas and writing a rough draft of the proposal
- **Stage 3: Improving the Style**—putting your ideas in plain language and strengthening your persuasiveness by appealing to your readers' motives, values, attitudes, and emotions
- **Stage 4: Designing**—using page design and graphics to reinforce your argument and make it more attractive and usable for the readers
- **Stage 5: Revising and Editing**—refining and strengthening the organization, style, and design of the draft.

Professional proposal writers and grant writers rarely follow this process in lockstep. Instead, they move back and forth among the stages as they work on various parts of the proposal.

Writing Grant Proposals

How is writing grant proposals different from writing business proposals? Some researchers and nonprofits mistakenly assume that grant proposals are something quite different from business-to-business proposals. They might believe that a grant is not really *selling* a product or service like a typical business proposal. Rather, grant proposals are only asking for funding to do research, build programs, or solve social problems.

Actually, this way of thinking about grant proposals can greatly hamper your ability to secure funding for important research or projects. Grant proposals *are* business proposals. When writing a grant, always remember that you are promising to do something that the funding source finds beneficial. Funding sources, even the federal government, are not giving away money because they are generous benefactors. They have their own goals and motives, and they only fund people and organizations who will help them reach their objectives.

Let us imagine you have $100 million to start your own foundation. You can give your money to any causes you want. How would you do it? More than likely, you would begin by identifying a set of problems that your foundation would work toward solving (e.g., poverty in rural areas, declining support for the arts, the need for research into diabetes). Then, your foundation would offer funding to people who could do that kind of work on your behalf. But you are not going to give your money to just anyone. Your foundation would only give its money to people who can help you reach your goals. People writing grant proposals to your foundation would be promising to provide a service for your foundation, much as any business provides a service for another business.

What about writing grants to the U.S. federal government, such as proposals to the National Science Foundation (NSF), the National Institutes of Health (NIH), the National Endowment for the Humanities (NEH), or the Department of Defense (DoD)? These funding agencies are *not* simply looking to give away the taxpayers' money. Quite the opposite is true. These foundations only fund projects that help the U.S. federal government achieve its goals. To illustrate, let us say you are a medical researcher writing a grant to the NIH. Your application would be much more attractive to the NIH Board of Directors if it addresses a recognized problem in our society (e.g., cancer, AIDS, terrorism) or your community (e.g., drugs, low birth weight, farm safety). Your proposal will also be much more desirable if it shows how your project moves our society one step further toward solving a problem that is important to the government.

Foundations, governments, and corporations offer grant funding because they have identified important problems that they would like to solve. Even the most altruistic foundations have motives for offering their money, and they want to see how your project will meet *their* goals and objectives. If you do not show clearly how your project addresses the needs of the funding source, you will not receive funding for your research or project.

In the end, grant proposals are a special kind of business proposal. As a grant writer, you should keep in mind that you always need to consider the business side of research when writing a proposal. The sooner you start thinking about grant proposals as business proposals, the sooner you will be successful in securing funding.

Looking Ahead

Proposals and grants are written to manage change. To accomplish your goals as a proposal writer or grant writer, you can use rhetorical strategies to impose intellectual order on chaotic situations. You can then invent the content for your argument, organize your response, craft your text, and deliver a professional document. This book will show you how to use strategies of effective interpretation and expression to write proposals that succeed.

CASE STUDY Writing a Grant for the Cool Campus Project

To illustrate the proposal writing process, each chapter in this book will include a scene from an ongoing case study. The case study will demonstrate how the strategies discussed in each chapter could be used to develop a proposal.

The case study is set on the campus of the fictional Durango University, a mid-sized private university with 12,000 students set in southwestern Colorado. The university was founded in 1912 on an eighty-six-acre campus.

Out of concern for the environment and soaring energy costs, the university's president, James Wilson, recently announced that one of his goals would be to convert the century-old campus into a "green campus" that would eliminate or offset its emissions of greenhouse gases like carbon dioxide, methane, and nitrous oxide.

President Wilson explained that energy costs were severely harming the university's budget, and these costs would likely go much higher as the United States confronted issues involved in global warming. So, he wanted to begin converting Durango University to a "net-zero carbon" campus. He called this initiative the "Cool Campus Project."

Like most campuses built a century ago, Durango University's campus is saddled with aging buildings and a central heating and cooling system that is incredibly inefficient. Converting the campus to renewable forms of energy will not be easy.

Nevertheless, the conversion would need to happen at some point. Plus, as President Wilson pointed out, becoming a green campus would be an attraction to students and potential faculty around the world. Durango University was already an attractive place to study and teach because of its location in the mountains. By converting the university into a green campus, it would become an even more attractive place.

President Wilson delegated the Cool Campus Project to Anne Hinton, the Vice President for Physical Facilities. She immediately began assembling a team of people who could help her write a grant proposal to fund the project. She chose the following people to participate:

- George Tillman is a professor of environmental engineering who researches renewable energy systems, especially geothermal power plants.
- Calvin Jackson is a local contractor who specializes in renovating buildings to make them energy-efficient.
- Karen Briggs is a professor of social science who specializes in human resource issues.
- Tim Boyle is a student who is chair of the Student Environmental Council, a campus organization that advocates for environmental issues.

The five members of the task force bring their own strengths, concerns, and biases to the project. All five of them recognize that their challenge is complex and potentially controversial. Where should they start? How should they proceed with the task of writing the proposal?

In each chapter of this book, you will see how Anne, George, Calvin, Karen, and Tim use the proposal-writing process to help them write a grant that will attract funding for the Cool Campus Project.

Note: *Jaci Wells, Allen Brizee, and Margon Sousa contributed research and text to this case study.*

Questions and Exercises

1. What are some of the problems or opportunities on your campus, in your workplace, or in your community that might be addressed with proposals or grants? List out a few of these problems/opportunities. Under each of these topics, offer some reasons why these problems/opportunities might exist. Then, write down some ways in which you might use proposals to address them.

2. Find a proposal or grant in the library, at your workplace, or on the Internet. Write a memorandum to your instructor in which you study the strengths and weaknesses of the proposal's content, organization, style, and design. Does the proposal address the areas of the proposal genre? Does the proposal include any areas in addition to the proposal genre discussed in this chapter? Are there any areas missing? If so, explain why you think the proposal writer chose to leave out specific areas. Overall, do you think the proposal is effective or ineffective? Why?

3. Using the Internet and e-mail, find and contact a person who writes proposals or grants regularly. Ask what kinds of proposals he or she writes. Ask what kinds of situations require a proposal to be written. Present your findings to your class, highlighting any advice that the proposal writer or grant writer offered to you about writing effective proposals.

4. Identify some situations on your campus, in your workplace, or in society where rhetoric is used to manage change. How is persuasion used to first "identify the available means of persuasion" and then alter that situation to the advantage of the speaker or writer? Who tends to use persuasion in our society? How do they use it?

5. Imagine you have just been assigned to an advisory committee that has been asked to develop ways to reduce the number of cars being driven to your campus or workplace. What information do you have already on this topic? What information would you still need to solve the problem? What are some questions you would need answered before you and your team begin writing a proposal to solve this problem?

2 | Analyzing Problems and Opportunities

Overview

This chapter will show you how to analyze problems and opportunities by using *stasis* questions. The chapter will meet the following learning objectives:

1. Define solicited, unsolicited, external, and internal proposals.
2. Show how to interpret a Request for Proposals.
3. Illustrate how the Five-W and How questions are used to define a problem or opportunity.
4. Explain how the four *stasis* questions are used to answer the *why* question.
5. Discuss how to interact with a Point of Contact.
6. Show how to write a letter of inquiry to a funding source.

Two Basic Reasons for Writing Proposals

Proposals and grants are written for two basic reasons: to solve a problem or to take advantage of an opportunity. In either case, the first question that you, as the writer of the proposal, should ask yourself is, "What changed?" That is, what elements in the current situation changed recently to create this problem or opportunity? For example, if your company's computer network is no longer keeping up with your company's accounting needs, what changed to cause that problem? If childhood obesity is a growing problem in your community, what is different now than in the past? If a client is looking for someone to conduct an environmental impact study, what changed in their situation to cause them to seek out this kind of study? As mentioned in the previous chapter, change is the essence of proposals. So, before you start to develop a proposal, it is critical that you first identify the elements of change that brought about a particular problem or opportunity.

In this chapter, we are going to take our first step toward writing a proposal by discussing how to interpret the *stasis*, or status, of a proposal opportunity. By determining stasis, you can identify the specific problem or opportunity that created the need for the proposal you are writing. Essentially, you first need to figure out *why* the readers are looking for someone to help them solve their problem or *why* they want to take advantage of an opportunity. Similarly, with grant proposals, *why* is the foundation or government agency looking to fund projects in a named area of interest? What has changed recently to create the problem they are trying to solve?

Solicited and Unsolicited Proposals

Proposals are classified according to how they were initiated, where they will be used, and what purpose they will serve. Depending on how the proposal was initiated, it can be either *solicited* or *unsolicited*.

Solicited Proposals

Solicited proposals are requested by clients or funding sources to address needs that they have identified. These proposals are often initiated through an advertisement called a Request for Proposals (RFP). In some cases, solicited proposals result from a direct contact from the client or a funding source.

Unsolicited Proposals

Unsolicited proposals are initiated by you or your company. You can use unsolicited proposals to propose changes, suggest improvements, or pitch ideas for new products or services. Or, as a sales tool, they can be used to pitch existing products or services to another company.

Proposals can also be referred to as *external* or *internal*. An external proposal is one that is used to conduct business between two companies or organizations. External proposals tend to be formal, because they often become interim contracts between two companies. In other words, if an external proposal is accepted by the client, you cannot go back and change the terms without the client's approval.

Internal proposals are used within a company or organization to suggest new strategies, new products, or new ideas. Often, internal proposals are used informally to help people plan out new strategies together. Internal proposals can also be used formally to pitch ideas or projects to the company's management.

Reading RFPs

A solicited proposal is born when a business or government agency publishes or sends out a Request for Proposals (RFP). RFPs are called a variety of names, according to the kind of work or information the client is seeking. An RFP might be referred to as a Call for Proposals (CFP), a Request for Applications (RFA), an Information for Bid (IFB), a Request for Grant Proposals, a Call for Quotes (CFQ), or an Advertisement for Bids (AFB), among other names. Whatever it is called, an RFP is essentially an announcement that a client or funding source is seeking proposals for a specific project. Some RFPs are brief with a few hundred words describing the project and deadlines. Other RFPs, especially from government agencies, can run on for pages and pages, describing in detail the project, goals, and even the kinds of plans that would be acceptable. Requests for Grant Proposals, such as those from government foundations like the National Science Foundation (NSF) or National Institutes of Health (NIH), might include a thick packet of information with forms and guidelines.

RFPs can be found in a variety of places:

- The U.S. government publishes its RFPs on the FedBizOpps website at http://www.fedbizopps.gov. At this site, you can run keyword searches to locate business opportunities with the U.S. federal government.
- State and local governments often publish RFPs in the classifieds section of major local newspapers or on government websites.
- Private corporations usually send their RFPs directly to past bidders or publish RFPs in trade magazines.
- For grant funding opportunities, most government and private foundations list their RFPs on Grants.gov, http://www.grants.gov or the Community of Science website, http://fundingopps.cos.com. These databases are keyword searchable, and they offer both scientific and nonscientific opportunities.

Application packets can often be downloaded directly from a funding source's website, or they can be requested by e-mail, mail, or phone.

An RFP describes the project that a company or an organization wants completed. For example, Figure 2.1 shows an RFP synopsis from the National Oceanic and Atmospheric Administration (NOAA), found on FedBizOpps.gov. The actual RFP would be too long to print here, but the synopsis offers a good overview of the project that is being put out for bid. In this RFP, the NOAA is looking for a supplier who can offer the following service:

> This solicitation will encompass a development phase culminating in the delivery, installation, and testing of a first article wind profiler, followed by the production phase involving delivery and installation of up to 54 wind profilers.

The remainder of this RFP synopsis offers background information on the project and tries to describe the desired capabilities of the wind profilers and the company that will supply them. The end of the RFP synopsis provides information for a Point of Contact (POC).

The RFP in Figure 2.2 is quite different. This RFP from the National Science foundation is soliciting grant proposals for research on nanomanufacturing. The actual RFP (PD-05-1788) is the length of a small book. In this excerpt, you will notice that the request is more open-ended than the one in Figure 2.1. The NSF is looking to fund projects that

> promote fundamental research and education at the nanoscale, and to transfer developments in nanoscience and nanotechnology discoveries from the laboratory to industrial application with prominent societal impacts.

The NSF offers some guidance about how to achieve this goal, but it also leaves a great amount of flexibility about the kinds of research projects that would be appropriate.

The ability to properly interpret RFPs is a valuable skill all its own, whether you are writing a business proposal or a grant proposal. Companies will sometimes hire an RFP manager who coordinates the routing of RFPs within the organization. Similarly, nonprofit organizations hire development officers who search for grant opportunities and stay in close contact with government and private foundations. These professionals look for proposal opportunities by monitoring

FIGURE 2.1

A Sample Request for Proposals

58–Wind Profiler

Solicitation Number: DG133W-07-RP-0005
Posted Date: Oct 16, 2006
Current Response Date: Feb 02, 2007
Archive Date: May 31, 2007
Classification Code: 58-Communication, detection, & coherent radiation equipment
Naics Code: 334511-Search, Detection, Navigation, Guidance, Aeronautical, and Nautical System and Instrument Manufacturing

Contracting Office Address
Department of Commerce, National Oceanic and Atmospheric Administration (NOAA), Acquisition and Grants Office, SSMC4 - Room 7601/OFA61 1305 East West Highway, 7th Floor, Silver Spring, MD, 20910, UNITED STATES

Description
The National Oceanic and Atmospheric Administration (NOAA), National Weather Service (NWS) is upgrading the NOAA Profiler Network (NPN) for improved operations. The existing wind profilers are vertical looking radars, the deployment of which commenced in approximately 1990. The existing wind profilers operate continuously and provide upper air wind data which the NWS uses in a variety of ways. In upgrading the NPN, the NWS expects to improve the resolution of wind phenomena in time and space (horizontal and vertical) and accuracy; enhance end-to-end observing system availability, access, archive, quality assurance, and timeliness monitoring; and to make use of the real-time wind profiles as an integrating sensor for a seamless system of systems. Solicitation DG133W-07-RP-0005 will be issued on or about November 3, 2006 and will close on or about February 2, 2007. This solicitation will encompass a development phase culminating in the delivery, installation, and testing of a first article wind profiler, followed by a production phase involving delivery and installation of up to 54 wind profilers. [It is expected that all installations will take place within the United States.] Additionally, the production phase will provide for initial sparing and initial maintenance of the wind profilers (until the wind profilers are transitioned to Government maintenance). Both the development and production phases will include provisions for associated services, such as training, and associated supplies, including documentation. The solicitation will allow for either the upgrade of the existing wind profilers or the replacement of the existing wind profilers. The solicitation will be structured to allow for up to two awards for the development phase, with a down-select to one contractor for the production phase; however, the Government will not be obliged to make two awards for the development phase. The Government expects that completion of the work called for by the solicitation will take place within five years after award. All responsible sources may respond to Solicitation DG133W-07-RP-0005 by submitting a proposal which shall be considered by NOAA. See Notes 12 and 26.

Point of Contact
Edward Tennant, Contracting Officer, Phone 301-713-0828 x117, Fax (301) 713-0806, Email ed.f.tennant@noaa.gov - Mary Watson, Procurement Technician, Phone 301-713-0828 x146, Fax (301) 713-0806, Email mary.a.watson@noaa.gov

FIGURE 2.2

Summary of an RFP from the National Science Foundation

 NanoManufacturing

Funding Opportunity Number: PD-05-1788
Opportunity Category: Discretionary
Posted Date: Jan 18, 2006
Creation Date: Oct 17, 2006
Current Closing Date for Applications: Feb 15, 2007 Full Proposal Window 01/15/2007–02/15/2007 Full Proposal Window 09/01/2007–10/01/2007
Funding Instrument Type: Grant
Category of Funding Activity: Science and Technology and other Research and Development
CFDA Number: 47.041-Engineering Grants
Cost Sharing or Matching Requirement: No

Eligible Applicants
Unrestricted (i.e., open to any type of entity above), subject to any clarification in text field entitled "Additional Information on Eligibility"

Agency Name
National Science Foundation

Description
The NanoManufacturing Program was established in 2001 to promote fundamental research and education at the nanoscale and to transfer developments in nanoscience and nanotechnology discoveries from the laboratory to industrial application with prominent societal impacts. The program emphasizes scaleup of nanotechnology for high rate production, reliability, robustness, yield, efficiency, and cost issues for manufacturing products and services. NanoManufacturing capitalizes on the special material properties and processing capabilities at the nanoscale and promotes integration of nanostructures to functional micro devices and meso/macroscale architectures and systems, as well as the interfacing issues across dimensional scales. The program covers interdisciplinary research and promotes multi-functionality across all energetic domains, including mechanical, thermal, fluidic, chemical, biochemical, electromagnetic, optical etc. The focus of NanoManufacturing is in a systems approach, encompassing nanoscale materials and structures, fabrication and integration processes, production equipment and characterization instrumentation, theory/modeling/simulation and control tools, biomimetic design and integration of multiscale functional systems, and industrial application. The program places special emphasis in NanoManufacturing education and training of the workforce, involvement of socio-economic sciences, addressing the health, safety, and environmental implications, development of manufacturing infrastructure, as well as outreach and synergy of the academic, industrial, federal, and international community.

FedBizOpps, Grants.gov, trade periodicals, RFP databases, and incoming mail. Then, the RFP manager or development officer coordinates relations between the organization, clients, and funding sources, ensuring that RFPs and any amendments reach the right people.

In some special cases, RFP managers and development officers may even have the opportunity to provide feedback to clients or funding sources on drafts of RFPs. In these cases, a draft of an RFP would be released to solicit feedback. By providing comments on the draft, an RFP manager or development officer can help refine the advertisement, often to the benefit of their company or organization.

Determining the Status, or Stasis, of an Opportunity

Whether you are responding to an RFP or writing an unsolicited proposal, it is important to first determine the *stasis*, or status, of the opportunity. In rhetoric, stasis is the meeting point at which two sides agree to have a discussion. In other words, before negotiation can take place, the two sides need to agree about what exactly is being negotiated.

Using the Five-W and How Questions

The first step in determining the stasis of a proposal opportunity is to analyze the elements of the writing situation. Most people are familiar with the *who, what, where, when, why,* and *how* method that journalists use to develop a news story. Proposal writers can use this journalistic method to sort out the elements needed to understand the current situation:

- Who exactly are the readers, and who else might be involved?
- What do the readers need?
- Where is the work site? Where do we need to submit the proposal?
- When are the deadlines for the proposal, and when does the project need to be completed?
- Why is the client or funding source looking for someone to do this project?
- How should the project be completed?

Even simple answers to these questions will provide an initial understanding of the status of the situation for which the proposal is being written.

Interestingly, you will find that the *why* and *how* questions are rarely answered directly. For example, in the RFP in Figure 2.1, the NOAA never really tells us why it needs to purchase new wind profilers. The RFP only gives us a few ideas about how the wind profiler might be built and installed. As proposal writers, we can initially only speculate about answers to the *why* and *how* questions: Are the current wind profilers obsolete? Have recent major hurricanes and other storms revealed the need for better monitoring of winds? Was a recent law passed by the U.S. Congress that demanded these wind profilers be built? How exactly do they want the wind profilers designed and installed?

Of course, knowing *why* the RFP was written and *how* the client wants the project completed would greatly improve a proposal's chances of winning this contract. And yet, the RFP from the NOAA gives us few hints about why they are asking for bidders to handle this project and how they want it to be completed. Later in this chapter, we will discuss how to address the *why* and *how* questions.

Using Proposal Opportunity Worksheets

Proposal writers and RFP managers will often use a worksheet to help them initially sort out the elements of a proposal-writing situation. The worksheet in Figure 2.3 illustrates how an RFP or other proposal-writing opportunity can be broken down into categories that reflect the Five-W and How questions.

FIGURE 2.3
Proposal Opportunity Worksheet

PROPOSAL OPPORTUNITY WORKSHEET
Instructions: Draw who, what, where, when answers directly from client, RFP, or POC.
If you don't know answers to these questions, write a question mark next to
information you don't know.

Project Title:
Solicitation Number:
Date Advertised or Received:

Client:
Point of Contact (POC):
Deadline for Proposal Submission:
Address for Proposal Submission:

Summary of Proposal Opportunity
(In this area, specify any objectives mentioned by the client, RFP, or POC)

Comments and Recommendations
(In this area, speculate about why the client is requesting the work. Also, speculate
about what kind of projects might meet the client's needs.)

Accept or Reject
(In this area, state whether a proposal should be written or not. Offer a rationale for
your decision.)

Reviewer: Phone Number: e-mail address:	**Reviewer Initials:**	**Date Reviewed:**

Writers of unsolicited proposals can also use the Five-W and How method to help them understand the stasis of a proposal-writing situation. When writing an unsolicited proposal, the elements of the current situation are not stated directly, as they are in an RFP. Rather, unsolicited proposals usually begin with a good idea at a meeting or in a conversation with a client. By working through the Five-W and How questions, you and your readers can come to an initial understanding of the problem or opportunity.

To sum up at this point, when interpreting an RFP, start out by identifying answers to the *who, what, where,* and *when* questions. Then, make some guesses that tentatively answer the *why* and *how* questions. When you are finished answering these questions, you will have a good start toward determining the stasis, or status, of the current situation.

A Description of the RFP Interpretation Process

Lisa Miller is a computer engineer who works for Insight Systems, a consulting firm that specializes in designing local area networks (LANs) and intranet systems. Recently, one of Insight Systems' sales representatives told her that Overture Designs, a growing architecture firm in downtown Chicago, was looking for ways to expand without overextending themselves financially. The salesperson told Lisa that the company would soon be sending out an RFP that would seek plans for helping them manage their growth. He said their deadline for a proposal would be tight, but it might be a project that Insight Systems would want to pursue.

Lisa went to work researching Overture Designs, finding out as much as she could about their principal managers, their typical clients, and their business philosophies and objectives. A couple weeks later, the sales representative faxed her the RFP (Figure 2.4).

Lisa noticed that the RFP left a good amount of room for interpretation. As you can see in Figure 2.4, the RFP could not possibly fill all the gaps in Lisa Miller's knowledge of Overture's situation. Specifically, it does not say exactly *why* the proposal is needed, though it does offer some hints that might help answer the *why* question. There are also many missing details about the current situation. Nevertheless, Lisa turned to her computer and began filling out a Proposal Opportunity Worksheet (Figure 2.5).

As usual, using the RFP to identify answers to the Five-W and How questions only brought up more questions for Lisa to answer. So, after e-mailing her completed Proposal Opportunity Worksheet to her boss and co-workers, Lisa continued researching Overture Designs through the Internet, trade magazines, and past editions of the business section of the *Chicago Tribune*. Later that week, she scheduled the tour of Overture's office and had a good talk with Grant Moser, the office manager and Point of Contact for the proposal.

While touring the Overture Designs' office, Lisa saw immediately why the company sent out the RFP. Their employees were already tightly packed into the current office space. Until recently, according to Mr. Moser, there was more than enough space, but the latest boom in construction around Chicago had doubled

FIGURE 2.4
Overture Designs' RFP

Overture Designs
300 S. Michigan Ave., Suite 1201
Chicago, Illinois 60001
800-555-9823

March 29, 2007

RE: Request for Proposals for Managing Office Growth
Contact Person: Grant E. Moser, Office Manager

Overture Designs, one of the top ten architecture firms in Chicago, invites pre-proposals from qualified consultants to develop plans for managing the physical growth of its architectural design operations. Due to growth in business, we find ourselves needing more room for our architects and their staff. From the pool of submitted pre-proposals, we will choose three finalists who will be invited to submit full proposals and deliver a presentation on the merits of their plan.

Overture is open to innovative approaches to managing the growth of its office needs. A premium will be placed on proposals that cause the least disruption to our current operations. Our architects and staff are fully engaged in complex projects, so we cannot accept any proposal that suggests we shut down our operations, even temporarily.

Cost is an important issue but not the most important issue for the successful pre-proposal. At this stage, exact cost estimates are not expected; however, pre-proposals should include a general cost estimate. Overture will negotiate for a final fee with the firm that submits the most feasible final proposal.

Pre-proposals should not exceed 10 standard pages, including any diagrams. They should be addressed to Grant E. Moser, Office Manager, and should arrive at Overture Designs by April 30, 2007, by 4:00 P.M. If you would like to tour our current facilities or have any questions about this project, please contact Mr. Moser at 1-800-555-9823. Ask for extension 284.

their business. Mr. Moser proudly told Lisa that the award-winning interior of the office was designed by Overture's president, Susan James. The view of Lake Michigan was stunning. With a sour look, Mr. Moser confided to Lisa that most of the people who had scheduled tours were contractors and owners of office buildings in the Chicago suburbs.

While visiting Overture Designs, Lisa picked up as many of their promotional materials as she could, and she jotted down some measurements of their current office space. She asked Mr. Moser if there was a diagram of the office available. He gave her an old diagram that showed the office layout before Overture's recent hiring growth.

Lisa Miller's Assessment of Overture Designs' RFP

PROPOSAL OPPORTUNITY WORKSHEET
Instructions: Draw who, what, where, when answers directly from client, RFP, or POC.
If you don't know answers to these questions, write a question mark next to
information you don't know.

Project Title: "Request For Proposals for Office Expansion"
Solicitation Number: None Given
Date Advertised or Received: March 29, 2007

Client:
Point of Contact (POC): Grant E. Moser (800-555-9823 ext. 284)
Deadline for Proposal Submission: Pre-Proposal Due by 4:00 on April 30, 2007
Address for Proposal Submission: 300 S. Michigan Ave., Suite 1201, Chicago, Illinois
60001

Summary of Proposal Opportunity
The RFP requests a pre-proposal that helps the client "manage the physical growth
of its architectural operations." The client has experienced recent growth in business,
allowing them to hire more architects and staff. With this hiring, though, their office
space is becoming a bit cramped.
The RFP names two goals: (1) manage their need for more office space, and (2)
cause the least disruption in their current operations.

Comments and Recommendations
I think the client is experiencing some growing pains in this strong market. They want
to keep growing their business, but they don't want to overextend themselves in case
the market drops again. Also, looking at their Website (www.overturedesigns.net), I
notice they seem to take a great amount of pride in their current office, which they
designed and which has won several interior design awards. Also, since business is
hot, they don't want to disrupt their current projects. Frankly, I think they want to stay
in their current office, but they cannot figure out how to do so.
   They probably aren't thinking about telecommuting right now, but my hunch is that
we could sell them a plan that employs a LAN and an intranet, allowing some of their
architects to work at home. Telecommuting might free up the office space they need.
Also, architects, being "creative" people, might like to work at home where it's quiet.
They are offering a tour of their facilities. I will take the tour and report back.

Accept or Reject
We should write a proposal for this project. We are taking a small chance by
proposing something they might not expect. But, I think we can meet their goals.

Reviewer: Phone Number: 5-4144 e-mail address: lmiller@insight_system.com	**Reviewer Initials:** *LM*	**Date Reviewed:** 3/30/07

When Lisa returned to her office, she did more research on Overture Designs, its principal owners, its mission statement, and their architects' current and past projects. Her research gave her the strong feeling that these people would not be happy in some bland, cubicle-filled office in the suburbs. After talking over the project with her boss, she decided to write the pre-proposal.

Most of Lisa's activities up to this point had been devoted to answering the Five-W and How questions that will help her define the stasis of the current situation. Even though a typical RFP provides basic answers to most of the *who, what, where,* and *when* questions, most proposal writers will research much further to gain a better understanding of the factors and people involved. After all this research, Lisa is just starting to answer the *why* and *how* questions: Why is this project out for bid? What changed? How can we help Overture Designs solve this problem? In this chapter and future chapters, we will see how Lisa wrote a pre-proposal to bid for the project at Overture Designs.

Defining the Problem or Opportunity

It is almost a cliché for consultants to say, "There are no problems, only opportunities." And, in the eternally optimistic world of business-speak, that's probably true—a problem *is* just an opportunity to improve. The word *problem,* though, lends a sense of urgency and importance to a project. Moreover, "problem-solving" or "working the problem" are positive, action-oriented ways to look at the proposal-writing process. Proposals are problem-solving tools. This statement is true whether you are pursuing a golden opportunity or proposing a way out of a tricky situation.

The writing of a successful proposal begins with a clear understanding of the underlying problem. So, before starting to write, you should first use the clues offered by the client, the funding source, and your own research to start determining *why* the problem exists. When you put all those clues together, you will be able to accurately define the stasis, or status, of the problem. To help you answer the *why* question, you might try out another stasis tool from rhetoric. Answer the following four stasis questions:

1. Is there a problem? (Fact)
2. What exactly is the problem? (Definition)
3. How serious is the problem? (Quality)
4. What kind of proposal would solve the problem? (Policy)

When you can answer each of these questions confidently in detail, you will have a clearer notion about how to start the proposal-writing process.

Is There a Problem? (Fact)

This first question might seem a bit odd until you realize that sometimes the best proposal is no proposal. At your office, for instance, business is going so well that your boss is growing anxious. So, at the first sign of a dip in sales, your boss suggests that you write a proposal to completely restructure the manufacturing operations. In this case, perhaps there really isn't a problem at all. Your best move might be to first propose a research study that determines whether the dip in sales is just a natural fluctuation in the market.

Another situation in which you might first ask "Is there a problem?" is when you are seeking new clients. Often, in the rush to drum up new business, we are tempted to sell our clients products or services they really don't need. But, an old saying among consultants is, "You can only sell an empty box once." In other words, it is wise to only write proposals that solve real problems at a client's company. After all, the short-term gain is soon more than offset by the loss of future opportunities, especially when your clients realize you misled them. It is best to honestly answer no to the question "Is there a problem?" than lose future sales.

What Exactly Is the Problem? (Definition)

Before writing a proposal or grant, the second stasis question—"What exactly is the problem?"—is usually the most important question to answer. In most cases, when you answer this question, you will confirm the readers' gut feelings about the current situation. By defining the problem for the readers, you will develop a common ground on which you and they can begin negotiating the project plan and even the costs.

In some cases, though, your readers believe they have one problem, but the actual problem is something a bit deeper. In these situations, the surface problem is only a symptom of a deeper, underlying problem. For example, let us say a school district in an affluent community is having trouble attracting top-notch teachers. The school board wants you to come up with a plan to entice strong teachers to the district. As you research the problem, however, you soon discover that some of the best teachers left the district because they could not afford to live in the community. When you interview these former teachers, they tell you that they wanted to stay, but housing is too expensive in the area. Meanwhile, they say, the commute from other areas was grueling and dangerous. You quickly see that the root problem might not be attracting good teachers; it is retaining good teachers. Of course, your proposal would most likely include a plan to attract strong teachers, but you could also enhance your proposal by addressing the root problem of affordable housing for teachers.

As stated before, the secret to defining the problem is to ask yourself "What changed?" When you look over the *who, what, when,* and *where*, pay special attention to any of these elements that have shifted recently. Ask yourself: In an affluent community that is having trouble attracting and retaining teachers, what changed in this community that created this problem? Have housing costs increased suddenly? Have property taxes gone up? Are the more experienced teachers retiring? By paying attention to changes, you can usually identify the specific problem that needs to be solved.

This second stasis question—"What exactly is the problem?"—urges us to look for a root problem beneath the obvious. After all, the apparent problem might be merely a symptom of a deeper problem. Addressing these symptoms may provide a short-term fix, but the problems will return if the root problem is not addressed, too.

How Serious Is the Problem? (Quality)

The third question—"How serious is the problem?"—helps you determine what needs to be done first. After defining the problem, you may determine that some issues need to be addressed right away. Other parts of the problem can wait while these high-priority issues are handled. By determining the seriousness of the situation, you can focus your efforts on the most pressing issues, especially as you define the scope of your work, develop your project timeline, and estimate costs.

A good rule of thumb when determining the seriousness of a problem is to "put first things first." In other words, the most urgent part of the problem is likely the part that needs to be solved first. Once that part of the problem is solved, you can then work on the next thing that needs to be handled. By putting first things first, you can avoid being overwhelmed by the size and scope of the project.

In a proposal or grant, a good strategy might be to propose solving only one part of the problem at a time. The client or funding source may want the whole problem solved right away, but you might point out that handling the most urgent issues first will give you a better sense of how to handle remaining ones. Then, you can write a follow-up proposal that addresses the rest.

What Kind of Proposal Would Solve the Problem? (Policy)

The final question—"What kind of proposal would solve the problem?"—helps us identify what kind of proposal is needed in a particular situation. Proposals tend to fall into the four categories shown in Figure 2.6.

The type of proposal you need to write depends on two things: the problem or opportunity you are trying to address and the deliverables you are expected to provide the clients when the project is completed. Deliverables are the tangible objects or services that result from the project. In other words, deliverables are the things (e.g., reports, plans, products) that are handed over to the readers during the project and when it is finished.

Let us look more closely at the four types of proposals and their deliverables.

Research Proposals

Research proposals describe methods for gaining insight into a particular problem or opportunity. Scientists often use research proposals to request funding and approval to conduct an empirical study or develop a prototype. An electrical engineer, for example, might write a research proposal to figure out why an undersea robot shuts down when it reaches five hundred meters below surface. A biologist, meanwhile, might write a grant proposal to the National Science Foundation in order to study the yearly migration of a sandhill crane population. The intent of a research proposal is to propose a study that will generate data or observations

FIGURE 2.6

Four Types of Proposals

Type of Proposal	Problem	Purpose	Deliverables
Research Proposal	Needs insight or empirically produced facts	Proposes a research project; often requests funding	Report or publication that describes and analyzes results of study; might offer recommendations
Planning Proposal	Needs a plan that outlines a general strategy	Proposes to develop a strategic plan for addressing a problem/opportunity	Plan that describes a general strategy for solving the problem or taking advantage of the opportunity
Implementation Proposal	Needs to implement a strategic plan	Offers a detailed plan for implementing a project	Completion of the project and a completion report that demonstrates and measures results of project
Estimate Proposal (Sales)	Needs to provide costs for a product or service	Provides a cost estimate for a product or service	A product or service

and fill a gap in our understanding. The deliverable for a research proposal is typically a report or article that explains the results of the research. In some cases, a prototype machine or service is also a deliverable.

Research proposals are also written for clients who need an understanding of a situation, problem, or opportunity. For instance, perhaps a client has experienced the sudden loss of key employees to its competitors. A research proposal would propose a study to determine the causes (e.g., salaries, morale, benefits, stress) of this problem. This type of research proposal would describe the methodology that would be used to gather information (e.g., marketing studies, legal research, environmental impact testing, customer surveys, audits, or product quality studies). The "deliverable" for this kind of proposal would be a final report in which the findings are presented and explained. In some cases, research proposals might conclude with recommendations for taking action.

Planning Proposals

Planning proposals offer plans for improvement or recommendations for taking action. A planning proposal might be used to devise strategies to increase sales, describe new manufacturing techniques, or suggest changes to current business practices. For example, a planning proposal might be used to design a new bridge or suggest a better way to handle toxic waste. In most cases, the deliverable is the project plan contained within the proposal itself. In other cases, the deliverable is an *implementation plan* that describes in detail (i.e., dates, times, personnel) how the project will be completed.

Implementation Proposals

Implementation proposals are written when the readers already have a plan that needs to be implemented. Contractors often write these kinds of proposals, showing how they would turn an architect's drawings (the project plan) into an actual building. In this kind of proposal, the clients are looking for specific timelines, the names of involved personnel, a list of materials, and an itemization of costs. The deliverables for an implementation proposal are the promised final products or services and a "completion report" that documents the implementation process and describes any deviations from the original plan.

Estimate Proposals (Sales)

Estimate proposals, often referred to as *sales proposals*, offer a product or service for a specific cost. In these cases, the clients know what product or service they need. They simply want you to tell them how much you would charge for that service or product. Estimate proposals offer bids for standard services, like legal representation, janitorial services, maintenance work, or clerical services. When used for sales purposes, estimate proposals are often unsolicited. They describe your company's products and services, showing the customer why these products or services would be beneficial to them. The deliverable for these proposals is the product or service itself.

Of course, these proposal types overlap, and in many cases two different types of proposals might be merged. For instance, a planning proposal might include both a research phase in which an empirical study will be conducted and a planning phase that develops a strategic plan after the assessment is completed. It is often prudent, though, to urge the client to accept one type of proposal at a time. Let us say you discover that the clients lack a clear understanding of their current situation; yet they want your company to write a proposal to implement a solution. The client is essentially telling you, "We have no idea what is wrong, but we want you to fix it." In these cases, you are being asked to implement a plan when you are not even sure what the problem is—always a bad idea. Instead, you should urge the clients to accept one type of proposal (i.e., a research proposal or a planning proposal) for the time being. Then, promise them a follow-up implementation proposal when you have isolated the problem or developed a strategic plan.

Similarly, before expending the effort to write an implementation proposal, it is usually best to write a planning proposal that offers a more general strategic plan. Once you and the clients agree on the strategic plan, you can write an implementation proposal. As you might have noticed already, proposals sometimes become stepping stones to future proposals. Research proposals often lead to planning proposals. Planning proposals lead to implementation proposals.

Applying Stasis Questions

As mentioned earlier, one of the main reasons proposals fail is because their writers misinterpret the stasis of the problem. The four stasis questions discussed earlier in this chapter should help you determine the problem or opportunity that brought about the need for a proposal. These questions offer you a place to start writing the proposal by helping you to answer the *why* question.

Let us return to Lisa Miller's proposal to Overture Designs. After finding answers to the *who, what, where,* and *when* questions, she was ready to start tackling the *why* and *how* by working through the stasis questions. First, she asked herself, "Is there a problem?" Her visit to Overture Designs only confirmed that the client had a problem that needed to be solved. At the Overture Designs' office, people, desks, computers, and copiers seemed to be stacked on top of each other. The employees had little room to operate comfortably. Yes, there certainly was a problem.

Second, she began answering the question, "What is the problem?" The RFP seemed to be suggesting that Overture Designs needed more office space. But she sensed a reluctance from Mr. Moser to leave their current Michigan Avenue office. So, to answer the *why* question, Lisa tried to think beyond the surface problem (lack of physical space) toward identifying a deeper, underlying problem. She asked herself, "What changed to create this problem?" She remembered that the office manager, Mr. Moser, said a recent surge in construction in Chicago forced them to hire more architects and staff. He called it the "usual boom and bust cycle" in the Chicago market, and he complained that two years from now, when the market goes down, they might need to let some of these extra people go. The problem, Lisa concluded, is indeed a lack of office space, but the problem might be only temporary. If the market went down, Overture Designs would not want to be financially overextended with a larger facility.

Third, she answered the next stasis question, "How serious is the problem?" The problem seemed serious in the long-run, but Lisa could see Overture was not immediately threatened by the office space shortage. However, if the problem was allowed to continue, they might reach a tipping point where their architects and staff would start leaving. The office-space problem could become serious quickly, though, if Overture suddenly took on a surge of new business in a boom time. Lisa felt these factors were working in her favor. Overture needed a solution that would solve the problem quickly and flexibly. Some immediate relief would be very welcome to the current employees. In the long run, though, they needed a solution that allowed them to scale their office space needs to the ups and downs of the Chicago market.

Finally, she began thinking about what kind of proposal she would need to write. It seemed as though the people at Overture Designs had a pretty good grasp of their problem. They wanted a plan for solving that problem. So, a planning proposal seemed like the best option for this project. Lisa's pre-proposal would sketch out a general plan. If her pre-proposal was accepted, then she would write up a more detailed planning proposal for creating new space in their current office. As she noticed in the RFP, the clients did not want an implementation proposal or even an estimate proposal. In other words, they were not looking for specific times and dates when the workers would show up to start redoing their offices. Instead, they were looking for a general strategy for addressing their growth problem.

By working through the stasis questions systematically, Lisa gained a deeper understanding of the client's problem and she figured out that the clients needed a planning proposal.

Talking to the Point of Contact

Once you have worked through the Five-W and How questions and you have answered the four stasis questions, you are probably ready to contact the Point of Contact (POC) listed on the RFP. In most cases, you will find that POCs, especially those who handle government projects, are not as forthcoming as you would like with additional details. POCs usually want to give the impression that they are impartial, fair, and not playing favorites among bidders.

Nevertheless, once you have worked out the status, or stasis, of the situation, you can ask the POC specific questions that will confirm or challenge your understanding of their problem or opportunity. At this point, the POC can usually confirm or deny your answers to the *why* question, sometimes offering further information that will help you understand the situation. You should also ask about the expected deliverables. Finally, confirm with the POC that your proposal will offer the kinds of results that the readers are expecting.

Of course, there is no script that you can use to talk with a POC. Figure 2.7, however, shows how statements and questions to the POC might be phrased to gain the most valuable feedback.

The ability to ask the POC specific questions is one of the great benefits to determining stasis up front. When talking to the POC, you will often receive only yes and no answers to your questions. So, if you have not developed a reasonable answer to the why question before calling, the POC will likely offer only unhelpful and agitated responses to your clumsy questions. However, if you are prepared with informed, specific questions, the POC will tend to be more helpful, often giving you even more insight into the problem the company or funding source is trying to solve.

Writing a Letter of Inquiry (Grant Writing)

Increasingly, private foundations are asking nonprofit organizations to submit two- to three-page *letters of inquiry* before submitting full-length grant proposals. The purpose of a letter of inquiry is to offer an overview of the proposed project without the detail of a longer proposal. Then, if the reviewers at the foundation like the project, they will "invite" the nonprofit to submit a full proposal. In a few cases, especially when the requested amount is small, the reviewers might decide to fund the project based on the letter of inquiry alone, without asking for a full proposal.

A letter of inquiry is *not* a letter that says, "Hi, how are you? We would like to submit a grant proposal for funding." Instead, a well-written letter of inquiry

FIGURE 2.7

Talking to the Point of Contact

Comment or Question	Intent of Comment or Question
"Here is our understanding of your current situation."	Allows you to confirm your answers to the *who, what, where,* and *when* questions. Here is also your opportunity to clarify any uncertainties about the details of the project.
"What created the need for this RFP?"	Essentially, you are trying to find out two things with this question. First, what *changed* at the client's company or organization to create this proposal opportunity? Second, *why* are they asking for proposals?
"Here is our understanding of why you are looking for someone to do this work."	Allows you to test your best answer to the *why* question. Talk about how changes in the current situation brought about this opportunity for the client. Also, in most cases, phrase your answer to the *why* question as an "opportunity," not a problem.
"What are the specific deliverables you expect when the project is complete?"	This question has two purposes. First, the POC's answer may give you an idea about what the clients expect bidders to propose. Second, the answer should tell you what kinds of documentation the clients expect when the work is finished.
"Are there any other sources of information we might access to help us write a proposal that fits your needs?"	In some cases the POC has a packet of information that is available if you ask. Also, published reports or websites may be available that refer to their current situation.
"Do you have a price range into which the project must fit?"	This question is somewhat risky. Most POCs will not offer specific numbers. However, they may give you a range in which the clients are expecting the project to cost.

summarizes the project being proposed. Essentially, a letter of inquiry is a full proposal in miniature, addressing the four major sections found in a typical grant proposal: Current Situation, Project Plan, Qualifications, and Costs and Benefits. When writing a letter of inquiry, you should devote a solid paragraph to each of these areas. The Project Plan should receive an additional paragraph or two because it is the most important part of the letter. Figure 2.8 shows an outline of a typical letter of inquiry.

FIGURE 2.8

Outline of a Letter of Inquiry

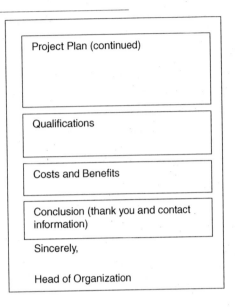

There are pros and cons to letters of inquiry. On the pro side, the foundation is doing grant writers a favor by asking for only two to three pages. A brief letter of inquiry gives grantseeking organizations an opportunity to describe their projects without spending all the time required to put together a full-length proposal. Then, after considering the letter, the reviewers at the foundation can offer feedback on projects they might support, and they can turn away projects that they would never consider funding.

The con side is that your letter of inquiry needs to describe fully the project for which you are seeking funding, but you only have a few pages to make your case. Moreover, at this point in the process, you might not have done enough thinking and planning to describe your proposed project in depth.

The secret to writing a successful letter of inquiry is to treat it like a real proposal, albeit a very small proposal. You are not writing a personal letter of introduction. Instead, you are writing a small proposal in letter form that summarizes your project ideas. To write this miniature proposal, you should go through all the steps described in this book. They will help you compose a richer, more persuasive letter of inquiry. Then, if the foundation invites you to submit a full proposal, your letter of inquiry can serve as a summary that will guide the proposal's development.

New grant writers often ask whether they can send the same letter of inquiry to multiple foundations. The answer is yes, but you should carefully personalize each letter to match the characteristics of each foundation. Then, double-check each letter of inquiry to ensure that you properly changed any names to match the foundation that will receive the letter. Nothing sours reviewers more than finding another foundation's name in a letter of inquiry that is addressed to them.

Your letter of inquiry needs to be especially well written if it is your organization's first formal contact with a foundation. If you compose a strong letter of inquiry, you will make a lasting positive first impression. Sloppy or poorly written letters of inquiry, on the other hand, can harm your organization's reputation with any foundations that receive them.

Looking Ahead

In a proposal, you need to initially agree with your readers about the elements of the current situation. You need to agree about the who, what, where, when, and—with some solid research—the why and the how. You also need to agree that there is a problem, what the problem is, and what kind of proposal is needed to solve that problem. Only then will you be able to write an effective proposal. In this chapter, you learned how to interpret RFPs and you learned two important steps for determining the stasis of the proposal writing opportunity (i.e., the Five-W and How questions and the four stasis questions). In the next chapter, we will build on this understanding of stasis by defining the rhetorical situation in which you are submitting the proposal.

CASE STUDY What Is the Problem?

At their first meeting in the Durango University Student Union, Anne Hinton, George Tillman, Calvin Jackson, Karen Briggs, and Tim Boyle started to discuss the Cool Campus Project. They were all excited about the project and were looking forward to working with each other.

After introducing themselves, they spent some time discussing their backgrounds and their expectations for the project. They looked over a Request for Proposals from the Tempest Foundation, which was forwarded to them by the university president (Figure 2.9).

"I know why President Wilson is interested in this grant," said Anne Hinton, the VP for Physical Facilities. "He is concerned about the university's bottom line. Energy costs are eating up a major part of the university budget, and it's only going to get worse. So, the president is trying to put energy conservation projects in the pipeline that will pay off later."

George Tillman, a professor of environmental engineering, said, "Listen, I'm as excited about this project as anyone, but we're talking about a whole change in the way we do things on this campus. We won't be able to just set up

a wind generator or a few solar panels and call it a success."

"Of course not," said Anne, "I think we all know that there is no silver bullet that will solve this problem. I'm sure there are some smaller changes we can make right now, like encouraging people to conserve energy, but some changes are going to need to occur over years, maybe decades."

Professor of social sciences Karen Brigg added, "These things do take time, but I find that people are rather adaptable if they believe in the cause. Fortunately, on a college campus, there are plenty of people who want us to work toward a campus that is good for the environment. And, we have economic reasons for making this happen. Those are some strong motivators."

Tim Boyle, the Chair of the Student Environmental Council, nodded. "I know the students would like to do this. A project like this one offers lots of opportunities to do something good for the university and the planet, while picking up some work experience."

Calvin Jackson, the local contractor, said, "Hey, those of us with local construction companies are

FIGURE 2.9

The Request for Proposals from the Tempest Foundation

Tempest Foundation

Sustainable Development and Conservation: Guidelines for Grants
Following a strategic review of the Foundation's previous support for conservation issues, the Tempest Foundation has decided to focus its grantmaking on issues involving climate change caused by humans. We believe strongly that climate change is the greatest threat to the planet's ecosystems and human survival. The core of the Foundation's grantmaking will be devoted to support for research and projects that will promote long-term environmental sustainability.

In the past, we have supported a wide range of conservation projects. We will now be focusing our grantmaking on projects that have the greatest potential for lasting impact on this planet. Therefore, the Tempest Foundation will concentrate its grants on projects that promise real change. We do not need studies to re-affirm that climate change is a dire threat to the planet's ecosystems. We consider the facts of climate change to be settled science. Instead, we want to fund research and projects that will take purposeful steps toward solving the problem of human-caused climate change. The most attractive projects to the Foundation will be ones that inspire other projects. Our intent is to use our funding to generate other initiatives that go beyond the initial funding. We are especially interested in projects that can be transferred and repeated elsewhere.

Annual support for individual projects typically ranges from $10,000 to $250,000. The Foundation is especially attracted to projects that can attract funding from other sources.

Application Process
The Foundation meets to consider grant proposals four times a year. As described in the section "How to Apply for Grants" (http://itempestfoundation.org/howtoapply), the Foundation will only consider brief proposals with narratives under fifteen pages. After the review, the board of directors will decide a) whether funding can be extended based on the proposal or b) whether a more detailed proposal will be requested. Grants with narratives of more than fifteen pages will be considered by invitation only.

Questions about the Foundation and its grantmaking can be directed to John Philips, Tempest Foundation Administrator, at forinfo@itempestfoundation.org. Inquiries by phone can be made to 312-555-1228.

interested too. Of course, we're interested in doing the work, but many of us also want to stay on top of these issues involving renewable energy."

The members of the team seemed to all understand that the problem they were trying to solve was very complex. Fortunately, the writing of the grant proposal would help them put their ideas on paper and focus their efforts.

George read the RFP from the Tempest Foundation out loud to the group. Then, they began answering the Five-W and How questions. On his laptop, George began typing their answers to the *who, what, where,* and *when* questions, putting question marks in places where they were unsure about the answers (Figure 2.10).

Afterward, they turned to the *why* question. Anne asked, "Why do you think the Tempest Foundation decided to start offering this funding? What has changed recently that created this opportunity?"

Karen spoke up, "Well, I did a little research into the Tempest Foundation. The foundation has always been interested in conservation issues. But recently, the foundation's board of

FIGURE 2.10

Answers to the Five-W and How Questions

Questions	Answers
Who?	Reviewers at the Tempest Foundation. Students, faculty, staff, administrators, the city government (?), news media (?), alumni (?), local citizens (?)
What?	Saving money on energy, global warming issues, converting the campus into one that is viable in the future, renewable energy sources
Where?	Tempest Foundation offices, meetings on campus, public forums (?)
When?	The Tempest Foundation's next submission deadline, President Young's annual address at the beginning of the Fall Semester (?)
Why?	The Tempest Foundation sees global warming as the greatest threat to life on this planet. They are looking to fund projects that do something about it.
How?	From RFP: "purposeful steps toward solving the problem," "projects that inspire other projects," "projects that can be transferred and repeated elsewhere"

Directors decided that global warming is the single-most important threat to life on this planet. So, they shifted the majority of their funding into research and projects that will address that issue."

George frowned. "OK, so why would they give *us* money? We just want to make changes to our own campus. We're not proposing high-level research here."

"That might be the key to persuading them," replied Tim. "We need to show them that our project at Durango University can be used as a model for transforming other college campuses. That might make funding our project more attractive to the foundation."

The others agreed. Anne said, "That seems to be a good way to address the *why* question. I'll call the Point of Contact to see if our project would work for them. For now, let's work on defining our problem here at Durango University."

Using the four stasis questions, they began to isolate and identify the problem they faced. They started by tackling the first stasis question, "Is there a problem?"

Karen answered, "Of course. Energy is the worldwide problem that will likely be the defining challenge of the twenty-first century. Energy issues affect just about everything from climate change to political stability."

"Yes, but that's not a problem we can solve," said George. "Our problem is that our campus is totally reliant on nonrenewable energy sources, like coal and petroleum."

Anne said, "OK, we agree there is a problem. Let's answer the second stasis question, 'What exactly is the problem?'"

Tim spoke up, "Well, people need to conserve and make a conscious effort to reduce their use of energy. People don't recycle enough and they don't take public transportation."

"Tim, I don't mean to be cynical here," responded Karen, "but the majority of people on this campus won't change their ways, even if they support the project. They might try recycling and public transportation, but most will eventually revert back to their wasteful ways. People do what is most convenient. They don't really think about how much energy they are using."

Calvin jumped in. "Maybe we need to do something that will get people to conserve energy whether they want to participate or not. For example, if we put solar panels on all the buildings, we could generate a significant amount of electricity without changing the way people do things around here."

George said, "But that's not going to solve our problem with the university's fleet of gas guzzling trucks. The university can't function without those trucks."

"Of course not," Karen responded, but again, we can make strategic changes, perhaps over several years, that would eventually wean the fleet off gasoline. Each time a truck needs to be replaced, perhaps it could be replaced by something that uses biodiesel or propane. Perhaps fuel cell vehicles might be available in the next couple decades. We can do this gradually."

Anne looked up from her notes. "I think I'm beginning to understand our real problem. Our problem is that this campus is reliant on nonrenewable energy sources, and we don't have a realistic long-term strategy that will gradually lead us to 'sustainable' uses of energy and other resources. We can ask people to conserve until we're blue in the face, but they will only do so much. Instead, the university needs to see sustainability as a strategic goal that will be accomplished over many years. Of course, we can ask people to make changes to their lifestyles right now, like using less water, recycling, and taking public transportation. We can use incentives to encourage them not to drive their cars to campus. But, in the end, the university needs to commit itself to making strategic infrastructure changes over a longer period of time."

The others agreed with Anne's definition of the problem. The problem wasn't that people on campus were making the wrong decisions about their energy usage and their use of other resources. The problem was that the campus infrastructure was dependent on nonrenewable sources of energy. The campus was not designed in a way that made the sustainable use of energy possible.

Feeling like they accomplished something by isolating the problem, the taskforce decided to tackle the third stasis question, "What kind of problem is it?"

George started out, "I don't know about you folks, but I still don't feel like I have a very good grasp of the problem at this point. But, I also don't want to just spin our wheels, getting nothing accomplished. I feel like we need to make some short-term changes and set longer-term changes in motion."

"I agree," said Tim. "I think we're talking about creating a strategic plan of some kind. So, we're really looking at writing a *planning* proposal."

"Is that what the grant would pay for?" Karen asked.

"In a way." said Tim. "Our grant proposal would sketch out a general description of the full plan. We would ask for money to do more research and develop a master plan."

"That makes sense," said George. "We're all smart people, but there's no way the five of us are going to come up with that master plan. We need to get more people involved. The grant would pay for us to research the current energy use of the campus. Then, it would pay for the university to put together the master plan."

Calvin was looking a little disappointed. "I was hoping the grant money would at least buy a few solar panels or something."

Anne looked over at him. "I feel the same way, Calvin," she said, "but I think Tim and George are right. Our problem is that we don't have a comprehensive plan in place. Creating that kind of plan is the only way we are going to make lasting, long-term changes to this campus. If the grant money allows us to do some research and develop the master plan, then the university can begin using that plan to make strategic changes to the campus. Short-term changes won't get us very far, but a long-term strategic plan could guide the transformation of this campus.

They decided to write a *planning* proposal. Their grant proposal to the Tempest Foundation would first describe their research methods for gaining insight into the problem. Then, the proposal would sketch out the boundaries of a strategic plan. They would use the grant to pay for developing a full strategic plan.

By the end of the meeting, they felt like they were making some headway. They agreed to meet again the next Friday to work on the proposal.

Questions and Exercises

1. Find an RFP in FedBizOpp, Grants.gov, a grant RFP database, or the newspaper classifieds. Write a memo to your instructor in which you use the Five-W and How questions to summarize the RFP. Then, discuss *why* you think the client is looking for someone to do the work described in the RFP. Specifically, discuss what might have "changed" to create this proposal opportunity. And finally, discuss some possible projects that might be suitable for this RFP.

2. Analyze an RFP in your field or area of interest by using the Proposal Opportunity Worksheet shown in Figure 2.3 of this chapter. According to the Worksheet, what kinds of information would you still need to gather if you were to respond to this RFP? What questions would you need to ask the Point of Contact in order to clarify what kind of work is needed and why it is needed?

3. Research a problem or opportunity on your campus, in your workplace, or in your community, such as parking, health care, or safety. What has changed recently and brought about these problems/opportunities? What are the underlying problems that created these problems? Write a memorandum to your instructor in which you discuss how change has created these problems/opportunities. In your memo, speculate about some of the reasons why these problems/opportunities have not been addressed yet.

4. Apply the four stasis theory questions to a problem on your campus, in your workplace, or in your community. Is there really a problem that can be addressed? What exactly is the problem? How serious is the problem? What kind of proposal (research, planning, implementation, or estimate) would be needed to address this problem?

5. Call a Point of Contact listed on an RFP. Politely tell the POC that you are learning how to write proposals and grants. Then, if allowed, interview that POC, asking what kinds of questions might be appropriate for a proposal writer to ask. Ask what kinds of answers the POC is allowed to give to proposal writers who call. Report your findings to your class.

6. With a team, analyze the following RFP using the Five-W and How questions and the four stasis questions.

> RFP: Campus Safety Assessment. SOL 45-9326. DUE 10/10/07. POC James Sanchez, Assoc. VP/Student Affairs (318) 555-4503. Bentworth University, a research university serving more than fifteen thousand on-campus and commuter students and located near downtown Bentworth, is soliciting proposals for an assessment of safety on campus. The objective of such an assessment would be to determine the causes for a recent increase in reported crime on campus. We are especially interested in addressing forms of crime like assault, graffiti, and theft. Depending on the outcome of the report, special priority will be given to those consultants who can also help develop a plan for reducing the amount of crime on campus. Also, special consideration will be given to proposals that offer non-intrusive methods for collecting data and information. Interested parties should submit a five-to seven-page pre-proposal that offers a general sense of how they would go about assessing crime on campus. The Student Affairs office will select five parties to submit full proposals. At that point, more information will be offered. Due date for pre-proposals is October 10, 2007. Full proposals will be due on December 1, 2007.

7. Answer these questions: What might be the problem underlying the current situation? What might have changed to create this opportunity? How serious is the problem and what are its most urgent parts? What kind of proposal is the client looking for the bidders to write? What information do you still need to write the proposal? What are some questions you would need to ask the Point of Contact?

Strategic Planning for Proposals and Grants

Overview

This chapter will show you how to begin planning a project and developing the content of a proposal or grant. The chapter will meet the following learning objectives:

1. Define what is meant by *strategic planning*.
2. Discuss subject, purpose, readers, and contexts of proposals.
3. Show how to analyze readers.
4. Show how to analyze contexts.
5. Discuss how understanding the rhetorical situation can be used to focus proposal writing teams.

Elements of Strategic Planning

Strategic planning is a process of setting objectives and developing a project plan for meeting those objectives. When writing a proposal, including grant proposals, you need to identify (a) what you are trying to achieve, (b) why you want to achieve it, and (c) who can help you achieve your objectives. Effective strategic planning can save you a great amount of time when writing a proposal. Of course, we are all tempted to just jump in, drafting the proposal from beginning to end. Time devoted to good planning, however, will focus your writing efforts, thus saving you time later and helping you avoid dead ends.

In this chapter, you will learn how to use strategic planning to clarify what you want your proposal to achieve. You will learn how to set objectives, clarify your purpose, and develop useful profiles of your readers. With this information in place, you will find that drafting the proposal or grant will be much easier and more efficient.

Setting Objectives

When planning out a proposal or grant, your first step should be to set some objectives for the project you are proposing:

1. *List all your project's objectives, including the most and least significant goals.* If the project you are proposing is small or simple, you might have only a

few items on your list. If your project is complex, you might fill the whole page. Keep in mind that you can always remove items from your list, so put down anything that comes to mind.

2. *Rank your project's objectives from most important to least important.* If you are writing your proposal with a team, this activity of ranking objectives offers an excellent opportunity to discuss the complexities and issues involved.

3. *Identify the project's top rank objective (TRO).* The top rank objective is the paramount goal of your project. It is the one goal you and your team most want to achieve.

Your top rank objective will be used to guide your project and the proposal-writing process. It might look something like the following statements:

- To develop a prototype of a hybrid vehicle that runs on ethanol
- To develop a nonhazardous decontaminating foam that neutralizes chemical and biological agents on humans
- To study the effects of depression on teenagers who are the children of alcoholics
- To implement a Radio Frequency Identification (RFID) system that allows our company to track inventory

To clarify, your top rank objective is not something like, "We want to raise $3.2 million for our project." The funding for your project is only the means to achieving the top rank objective; it is not the main objective of your proposal.

The Rhetorical Situation

Now that you have identified your top rank objective, you are ready to start researching the *rhetorical situation* in which your proposal will be used. The rhetorical situation includes all the elements that will influence how your readers interpret your proposal.

There are several approaches and analytical tools available to help you define the rhetorical situation. One of the most flexible of these analytical tools is the following list, which will prompt you to consider four issues:

- **Subject**   What is my proposal about? What is it not about?
- **Purpose**   What is my proposal supposed to achieve?
- **Readers**   Who will read my proposal?
- **Context**   Where will my proposal be read, and how does that context shape the reading?

When preparing to write a proposal, you should answer these questions up front to fully understand the situations in which the proposal will be used. Let us look at these four issues in more depth.

Subject

Essentially, the *subject* is what your proposal or grant is about. In Chapter 2, you learned how to determine the stasis of a problem or opportunity. Answers to the four stasis questions (i.e., Is there a problem? What exactly is the problem? How serious is the problem? and What type of problem is it?) will already provide you with a large amount of insight into the subject of your proposal.

Now that you have a good idea of the problem you are trying to solve, you should start thinking about the boundaries of that problem. Specifically, ask yourself two questions:

- What do my readers "need to know" to make a decision about my proposal?
- What information, no matter how interesting to me, is *not* needed to make a decision about my proposal?

These questions are important because readers tend to evaluate proposals from a "need-to-know" perspective. In other words, they only want to spend time processing information that will help them make an informed decision. Writers, on the other hand, often approach a text from a "want-to-tell" point of view. That is, after spending weeks, perhaps months, collecting information on the subject, writers very much want to tell the readers everything they collected, no matter how insignificant.

As anyone who has struggled to read a bloated proposal or grant will agree, readers quickly grow frustrated with all the tidbits of want-to-tell information. The seemingly endless string of details can distract the readers from the more important need-to-know issues in the proposal. As a result, a thirty-page proposal that includes want-to-tell information is much less effective than a leaner fifteen-page proposal that is limited to need-to-know information, because the leaner proposal highlights the crucial points for the readers. The bloated proposal, meanwhile, blurs the crucial points by hiding them among noncrucial details.

To help you sort out the need-to-know from the want-to-tell information, you should pay close attention to the boundaries of your proposal's subject. First, ask yourself what is *inside* the subject (i.e., what do the readers need to know?). Then, ask yourself what is *outside* the subject (i.e., what don't the readers need to know?). In some cases, this second question can be most useful for defining the boundaries of the subject. By consciously deciding what topics will *not* be discussed in the proposal, you can better define what information should be included.

Purpose

The purpose of the proposal is what you want the proposal or grant to achieve. More than likely, your purpose will be similar to the top rank objective you developed earlier:

- The purpose of this proposal is to offer a plan for developing a nonhazardous decontaminating foam that neutralizes chemical and biological agents on humans.
- Our aim is to secure funding from the National Institutes of Health to study the effects of depression on teenagers who are the children of alcoholics.

One of the most common reasons why reviewers reject proposals is that the writers were not absolutely clear about their purpose.

Of course, proposal writers usually have a good grasp of what they are trying to achieve. But, when they are asked to state their purpose, they sometimes ramble for a couple minutes with a laundry list of items: "Well, it should do this, this, and this . . . and, oh yes, it should do that, too." This kind of shotgun approach to the purpose almost guarantees that the proposal will sound unfocused and vague to the readers. After all, if the writer cannot articulate the purpose of the proposal succinctly, the readers certainly will not be able to articulate the purpose, either.

The secret to writing a good purpose statement is to limit yourself to expressing the purpose in one sentence: "The purpose of this proposal is to. . . ." If you cannot squeeze your purpose into one sentence, then your proposal might not be focused enough for the readers.

Fortunately, once you have hammered down your proposals' purpose into a one-sentence statement, you will have set a cornerstone for the entire proposal. As you write, you can look back at your statement of purpose to see if your proposal is indeed achieving what you set out to do. Meanwhile, you can use that purpose statement to help you carve away all the distracting, non-crucial information that tends to creep into the writing of larger documents. A good purpose statement acts like a knife to help you cut away the fat.

Readers

Experienced proposal and grant writers will tell you that developing a complete understanding of the readers is the most important part of the proposal-writing process. In fact, some professional proposal writers and development officers collect whole dossiers of information on their readers, trying to find out what motivates them to say yes to a proposal or grant. The methods offered here are a bit less thorough, but they will provide you with great insights into your readers' thought processes.

When analyzing your readers, you should first recognize that there are different levels of readers who will pick up your proposal: primary readers, or decision makers; secondary readers, or advisors; tertiary readers, or evaluators; and gatekeepers, or supervisors.

Primary Readers (Decision Makers)

The primary reader is the person or persons to whom the proposal is addressed. In most cases, the primary readers are the people who can actually say yes to your proposal. They are the *decision makers* in the proposal process, because they are most responsible for assessing the merits of your ideas. If you are unsure who your primary readers are, ask yourself who actually has the power to accept your proposal. Who can say yes?

Secondary Readers (Advisors)

There are also numerous secondary readers who will influence the acceptance or rejection of your proposal. Think of secondary readers as the people to whom your primary readers might turn for advice. They could be supervisors, experts, accountants, or lawyers who check over the methods, facts, and figures of the proposal or grant. Compared to the primary readers, these secondary readers often have different motives for reading the proposal. As experts, they are usually looking for more specialized information than the primary readers. For example, as an advisor, the senior engineer at a company could significantly influence whether a proposal is accepted, because he will study the technical feasibility of your ideas. As you write the proposal, you should keep that senior engineer in mind, even though he may not be the person who can say yes to your ideas.

Tertiary Readers (Evaluators)

Tertiary readers are the people who you do not expect to read your proposal but who would have a stake in what you are proposing. For example, tertiary readers could include reporters, hostile lawyers, program assessors, historians, politicians, the public, or your competition. At first, it might seem odd to keep the interests of these distant readers in mind, but tertiary readers often prove to be people who can unexpectedly sabotage (or support) your plans. You should always identify these potential readers to make sure that you are not writing something that would make you or your organization vulnerable to their challenges.

Gatekeepers (Supervisors)

Gatekeepers are the readers who have the most direct influence over you. They could include your supervisor, the CEO of your company, an accountant, or your company's legal counsel. They might include the board of directors of your organization. Gatekeepers are the readers who need to endorse your proposal before it is sent to the primary readers. Again, it might seem strange to keep the needs of these readers in mind as you invent your ideas. But if your proposal or grant is not acceptable to your boss or the legal department, then the primary readers will never have the chance to say yes. You need to make sure you understand what these gatekeepers want to see in the proposal before you start writing it. Otherwise, the proposal may end up in an endless loop of revisions as various gatekeepers ask for further changes.

If you haven't noticed already, these four classes of readers represent a variety individuals who will influence the development of the proposal. How can you identify all these different people and their interests? One way is to use a *writer-centered worksheet* to help you identify and sort out all these different readers (Figure 3.1).*

Here is how the worksheet is used:

1. Place yourself and/or your organization in the half-circle labeled *Writer*.
2. In the arch labeled *Primary*, write down the primary readers, preferably by name, who will be directly responsible for making a decision on your

---

*The audience worksheets in Figures 3.1 and 3.2 are similar to those provided by J. C. Mathes and Dwight Stevenson in their book *Designing Technical Reports* (pp. 15–23). The worksheets used here, however, are designed differently to focus on the audience issues that are important to proposals.

FIGURE 3.1
Writer-centered Worksheet

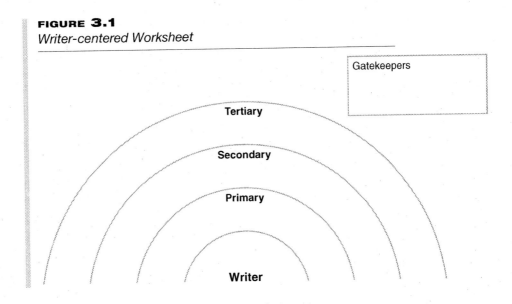

proposal. You should list only one or two primary readers, because only a few people will have the power to say yes or no to your proposal.

3. In the *Secondary* arch, write down all the readers who might serve as advisors to the primary readers. Think about the people to whom the primary readers might turn for information or advice. In most cases, you will find that there are many more secondary readers than primary readers.

4. In the *Tertiary* arch, try to imagine anyone else, no matter how remote, who might have a stake in your proposal. Write down the people who might use your proposal, even if you never intended for them to possess a copy.

5. In the *Gatekeepers* box, list your supervisors. As you think about gatekeepers, write down people who need to approve your proposal before it is sent to the primary readers.

The writer-centered worksheet helps you visualize your potential readers by spatially viewing their relationship to you. Your primary readers are usually the most important part of your audience, so they occupy the circle closest to you. The secondary and tertiary readers occupy places a bit further away. The gatekeepers are off to the side because they are not really the intended readers of the proposal, but they will supervise your work.

What about the readers of grant proposals? The process is the same. You may not know the names of the readers, but you can make some guesses about the types of people who will be reading the proposal. Put your best guesses in the writer-centered chart. That said, at many foundations you should be able to find out the names and backgrounds of the people who will review your grant proposal. Once you identify who will be reading the proposal, you can use the Internet to find out more information about them.

Now it is time to consider the psychology of the people you identified in the writer-centered worksheet. It is time to get inside their minds to figure out why they might say yes or no to your proposal. To begin, keep in mind that readers of proposals and grants react positively or negatively on four levels: motives, values, attitudes, and emotions.

Motives

Readers are motivated to take action when they think a plan will improve their personal, professional, or organizational lives. For example, perhaps a particular reader is motivated by a higher profit margin. A successful business proposal would address that motivation by stressing the enhanced profit margin created by the proposed project. Another reader might be motivated to fight poverty, so a successful grant proposal written to this reader might show how the project will lift people out of poverty. In our culture, the word *motives* has a slightly negative undertone, as though people with motives have hidden reasons for behaving a particular way. Here, we are using the word to suggest that people always have motives for taking action. When you identify someone's motives, you will know what moves them to act.

Values

Readers often react positively or negatively because an idea or plan touches their personal, professional, or organizational values. Usually, it is not hard to find out your readers' values. Often, companies and funding sources publish documents like mission statements, policy statements, and ethics policies that spell out the values that the organization publicly holds. An individual reader's professional or personal values can often be found in biographical statements, speeches they have made, or their past actions. The Internet is a great place to figure out your readers' values, because people often reveal more in their corporate and personal websites than they would be in person.

Attitudes

Readers typically start out with a positive or negative attitude toward a given proposal. In some cases, they are looking forward to moving into new markets or solving a long-standing problem in society. In other cases, however, readers will approach a proposal with a negative attitude, because the proposal resulted from a personal or organizational failure. For example, the in-house experts at a client company might have a negative attitude toward your proposal because they think their managers' decision to solicit proposals implies a lack of faith in the experts' ability to solve the problem themselves. Of course, readers' attitudes are always hard to judge, but you should pay close attention to what the readers say and how they say it. Sometimes the readers' language or tone can tell you a great amount about their attitude toward you, the project, and your proposal.

Emotions

Readers also react to proposals in emotional ways that go beyond the simple logic or costs of your proposal. For instance, if you are proposing to renovate a landmark building, the readers may have strong positive or negative emotions. They may feel joy, frustration, pride, or even anger. You should always take these emotions into account as you write the proposal. Positive emotions can be used to energize your proposal, while negative emotions should be addressed by stressing the benefits of taking action.

Again, a worksheet can help us sort out all the complex motives, values, attitudes, and emotions of the various readers. By listing the different readers in a *reader analysis worksheet* (Figure 3.2), you can start anticipating the psychological factors that will affect their reactions.

Using the reader analysis worksheet is a simple process. First, in the left-hand column, list the readers you identified in the writer-centered chart. Then, working from left to right, fill in what you know about each reader's motives, values, attitudes, and emotions. If you do not know something about the readers, just put a question mark in that space. Question marks signal places where you need to do more research on your readers. Of course, you cannot know everything about your readers, but eventually you should be able to put notes of some kind inside each of the spaces in this worksheet.

Some writers may mistakenly believe that all this reader analysis is not necessary for writing a proposal. And perhaps, for smaller proposals and grants, such detailed analysis might be too much. However, as proposals and grants grow larger and more complex, the stakes start to grow higher and the competition more intense. The more important the proposal, the more critical it is that you develop a high awareness of how and why your readers react in specific ways. Try using the writer-centered worksheet and reader analysis worksheet, and you will almost certainly feel more able to shape your proposal specifically to the needs of the readers. In most cases, your deeper understanding of the readers will increase your chances of winning the contract or funding.

Context

Analysis of the context is strongly related to your analysis of the readers, because context involves the physical, economic, ethical, and political environments in which the readers will evaluate your proposal or grant. If, for example, you know that the decision on a contract will be made by a large committee that will receive several other fifty-page proposals, you might want to find a way to use executive summaries, lists, and graphs to highlight your main points. After all, you can safely predict that committee members will first scan all the proposals and choose only a few to study in greater depth. By recognizing the readers' physical context, you can highlight your main points, thereby increasing the odds that your proposal or grant will make it into the "keep" pile and away from the "reject" pile.

But there are also more complex contextual factors to consider when writing a proposal or grant. In addition to physical constraints, you should also consider the economic, ethical, and political issues that shape the reading of your proposal.

Physical Context

Professional proposal writers and grant writers will often try to visualize the physical context in which their document might be used. Do the readers expect a

FIGURE 3.2
Reader Analysis Worksheet

Readers	Motives	Values	Attitudes	Emotions
Primary Readers				
Secondary Readers				
Tertiary Readers				
Gatekeepers				

large document or a smaller document with appendices? Will they be reading many proposals at the same time? How will the proposals be discussed? Will the proposal be read in a large meeting or at someone's desk? These elements of the physical context will influence how you organize and design your proposal.

Economic Context

Of course, the bottom line *is* the bottom line for any proposal. You should always consider the economic status of the client or funding source. In some cases, an expensive plan might solve all of their problems, but the client or funding source is only able to afford something modest. On a larger scale, the economic context might involve studying forecasts for the client's industry or developing an understanding of the health of the current market for the client's products or services. In a grant proposal, you should find out how much money the funding source has given to similar projects in the past. Overall, you should always pay close attention to the money issues in a proposal. You can be certain that your readers will.

Ethical Context

Clients often shy away from proposals that sound ethically questionable. In an increasingly litigious society, the ethics of any project are critically important. Therefore, you need to be mindful of plans that might leave the readers facing ethical pitfalls, harming their image or leaving them open to liability lawsuits. Moreover, short-term gains at the expense of the environment or society might sound tempting, but these ethical transgressions have a way of returning later to hurt the client and yourself. As a result, proposals should always evaluate the risks of litigation and public condemnation. As you analyze the context, try to identify any potential ethical problems, even the most obscure.

Political Context

In proposals, political issues come into play on two levels. First, as corporate citizens, most company executives and boards of directors are well aware of the national, local, and industrial political issues that might affect their business or organization. Proposal writers should be well aware of the politics in a particular industry and how they play out in the local, state, and federal sectors. Grant writers should consider how the project they are proposing will affect the political status quo. The second level of politics involves the office politics that influence the review of proposals. It is important to recognize that proposals are usually treading on someone's turf or offering ideas that other people in the company believe they could have provided. In some cases, the good-old-boy or good-old-gal network might give one proposal an edge over others. These office political issues are unavoidable, but you should be aware of them so you can better plan your proposal-writing strategy.

Figure 3.3 shows a *context analysis worksheet* that can be used to help you sort out all these complex contextual issues. It is divided into three different levels, primary readers, industry/community, and writers, to represent the various levels on which these contextual issues tend to influence the readers. The *primary reader* level is for your notes about the different contexts that face your primary readers. As you think about this level, imagine any outside influences that will impact

FIGURE 3.3
Context Analysis Worksheet

	Physical	Economic	Ethical	Political
Primary Readers				
Industry/ Community				
Writers				

how your readers make their decision about your ideas. The *industry/community* level is for observations about current trends in the readers' industry or community. This part of the chart might also include the concerns of the secondary or tertiary readers described in the reader analysis worksheet. And finally, the *writer* level concerns your company's or organization's context. It is important not to forget that many of the same contextual factors that are influencing your readers and their industry/community are also the factors that influence your company or organization. You may need to modify your proposal to fit your own contextual-based interests.

Put question marks in spaces where you do not know enough about the readers' context. These question marks signal places where you may need to do more research on your readers.

The Situation at Overture Designs

In the last chapter, we saw how Lisa Miller used stasis techniques to identify the who, what, where, and when of the RFP sent out by Overture Designs. We also saw how she used the three stasis questions to isolate Overture's problem. Lisa was now ready to list the project objectives and start developing a deeper understanding of the rhetorical situation in which her proposal would be used.

Objectives

Lisa began by listing all the objectives she could gather from Overture's request for proposals and her visit to the firm's offices. She then ranked them, allowing her to identify the top rank objective.

Objectives	Objectives When Ranked
• Stay among the top ten architecture firms	1. **Create more space in the office (TRO)**
• Manage growth of design operations	2. Manage growth of design operations
• Create more space in the office	3. Make more room for architects and staff
• Make more room for architects and staff	4. Plan that causes least disruption to current operations
• Innovative approaches welcome (desired?)	5. Prefer to stay in current office (?)
• Plan that causes least disruption to current operations	6. Stay among the top ten architecture firms
• Cost an issue, but not most important	7. Innovative approaches welcome (desired?)
• Not overextend themselves	8. Cost an issue, but not most important
• Prefer to stay in current office (?)	9. Not overextend themselves

After listing the objectives and identifying the top rank objective, Lisa turned to defining the subject, purpose, readers, and context for the proposal.

Subject

From her notes on the RFP, Lisa knew that her subject was the lack of office space at Overture Designs. This subject, Lisa decided, called for a planning proposal in which she would suggest that Overture use a local area network (LAN) and an intranet site to free up some office space. Specifically, she was going to propose that some of Overture's employees be asked to telecommute from home at least a few days a week, using the LAN and intranet site.

Along these lines, she wrote, "The subject of this proposal is the use of a LAN and intranet site to free up office space at Overture by allowing some employees to telecommute." This sentence itself already hinted at what the readers would need to know in order to make a decision. First, the proposal would need to define LANs and intranet sites, while showing how these communication tools could be used to conduct the firm's business. Second, she would need to show the readers how telecommuting works and why it would be beneficial to their company. And most important, she would need to show the readers exactly how much office space would be freed up by her plan.

Purpose

The purpose of the proposal was tough to write, but Lisa ended up stating, "The purpose of this proposal is to persuade Overture Designs that telecommuting will free up space in their office, allowing the company to avoid the disruption and cost of moving to a new location." Of course, this purpose statement was rough and it would need to be modified for the proposal itself; nevertheless, it seemed to sum up what Lisa wanted the proposal to do. This sentence was fine as a working statement to guide her planning and writing of the proposal. It would help keep her on track as she drafted the proposal.

Readers

She then analyzed the readers, using a writer-centered worksheet and a reader analysis worksheet. Her research on the Internet and her discussion with Grant Moser, the office manager, confirmed that the primary readers for the proposal would be the two principal architects in the firm, Susan James and Thomas Weber. From Overture's website, Lisa discovered that Susan James was a progressive, modernist architect who preferred simplicity when she designed buildings. Lisa noticed that Ms. James's designs and a couple of speeches published on the firm's website showed a strong preference for innovation and creativity above all else. Thomas Weber was a bit more conservative, though still a modernist in approach. He seemed more responsible for the day-to-day functions of the firm, though he was also the principal architect on the standard projects handled by the firm. From her conversations with Mr. Moser, Lisa came to believe that both primary readers wanted to stay in their current Michigan Avenue office. They were also concerned about the disruption in business created by a move to a new building.

On her writer-centered worksheet, Lisa noted that the secondary readers were the financial officers, staff, public relations agents, and clients associated with the firm. She knew the financial officers would probably not want to spend a great amount of money on moving or renovation, because these expenses might overextend the firm's resources. Staff and PR agents, she guessed, would also resist a move to the suburbs. Most members of the staff lived downtown, so relocating to a suburban office would require more commuting. Meanwhile, Lisa guessed that Overture's PR agents would regret their client giving up such a posh address in Chicago. The firm's clients, too, would probably react negatively to a move to the suburbs. After all, one of the advantages of hiring Overture was the accessibility of their offices and—to be honest—the appeal of having a "Michigan Avenue" architecture firm drawing up the plans.

Tertiary readers included the press, local politicians, and the competition. The press and local politicians, Lisa felt, would react positively to her idea for telecommuting, because it kept an important architectural firm downtown. Lisa's competitors for the project, of course, would not like her proposal. They were motivated by larger, more expensive solutions that would put their people to work and more money in their pockets. Certainly the competition would work hard to undermine her project if they received a copy of the proposal. They would probably point out that telecommuting is new and unproven as a work environment.

Gatekeeper readers included Lisa's boss and the chief engineer at Insight Systems. Lisa's boss, Hanna Gibbons, would be enthusiastic about the project. Lisa knew Hanna valued these higher-profile cases, because they seemed to attract business from other affluent customers. In the proposal itself, Lisa's boss would want the biographies of key employees at Insight Systems to play a prominent role. Her boss believed high-profile clients put added emphasis on relationships, so extensive biographies would be important. The chief engineer at Insight Systems, Frank Roberts, was far more interested in the technical details of a proposal. He would, as always, insist that the technology be clearly explained in the greatest detail. In fact, his insistence on "full disclosure," as he termed it, had almost sabotaged Lisa's last proposal because the clients could not comprehend some of the technical parts of the project plan. This time, Lisa would need to figure out another way to satisfy Frank's need for detail.

Context

The proposal's context was complicated also, so Lisa pulled out a context analysis worksheet to help her sort out the outside influences on the readers. The primary readers at Overtime Designs would certainly feel a great amount of political pressure inside and outside the firm to stay in downtown Chicago. After all, both employees and clients would be trying to influence them to keep their current office. Economic concerns were also important, because it was not clear whether the current growth in Overture's business could be sustained in the long term. Lisa also considered the physical context in which her proposal would be read. The primary readers were certainly very busy people, so she needed to make her proposal highly scannable and visual. She would also need to keep sections and paragraphs short and simple, so the primary readers could look over the proposal even when they were being interrupted.

Lisa also did some research into the industry/community issues that might influence the reading of the proposal. Recent stories in the business sections of the Chicago papers talked about the "explosive" rebirth of downtown Chicago. It seemed like this rebirth was leveling off, though, and there was good reason to believe the fast pace of downtown renovation and construction would be slowing down. Of course, local politicians were taking a great amount of credit for bringing people and businesses back to Chicago. The local alderman would probably call Overture as soon as he heard rumors that the firm might leave his ward.

As you can see, by working methodically through the rhetorical situation, Lisa discovered a great amount about her purpose, her readers, and the contextual factors that will influence her readers. Already, some important themes, like the internal and external politics of moving, were becoming clearer to Lisa. She was also discovering ways she might try to match the proposal to the personalities and values of her primary readers. Of course, Lisa could have just jumped into the writing of the proposal, but she more than likely would have missed many of these subtle influences on the readers. The time she invested toward defining the rhetorical situation would pay off later with a much more informed proposal.

Focusing a Writing Team

Up to this point in the chapter, we have discussed setting objectives and using the four areas of the rhetorical situation (subject, purpose, readers, and context) as strategic planning tools. These items might sound a bit abstract, and, with the deadline looming for your proposal, you might be tempted to just jump ahead to writing a draft. In most cases, though, skipping the analysis of the rhetorical situation only leads to a shallower, less creative proposal. Skipping ahead also wastes your time, because your supervisor, your co-workers, and unforeseen circumstances will send you off on tangents and wild goose chases. Moreover, if you have not clearly defined your objectives, purpose, readers, and context, you are almost certain to misread many of the clients' suggestions about what they are looking for in the proposal.

Perhaps the most effective use of strategic planning is to help you organize team projects. All too often, when writing with a team, co-workers discuss a project at a meeting and agree verbally about what needs to be done. But then each person walks away from the meeting with a slightly different idea of what the project involves. We have all found ourselves in these kinds of situations. As time passes and the project moves forward, each member's ideas grow further apart. Soon, your co-workers and you find yourselves trying to patch together a Frankenstein proposal that was written to multiple audiences for multiple reasons.

If you sit down with your co-workers before writing a proposal and simply agree up front on the objectives, subject, purpose, readers, and context, you are well on your way to writing an effective proposal. Try identifying your objectives and then working through the four-part analysis of the rhetorical situation with them:

- **Subject:** Use the stasis questions to figure out (a) if there is a problem, (b) what the exact problem is, (c) how serious the problem is and (d) what type of proposal will solve that problem. Then, discuss what information the readers need to know to make a decision on your ideas. Also, try to identify information the readers do not need to know.
- **Purpose:** State the purpose of the proposal in one sentence. Period. That is, complete the following phrase, "The purpose of this proposal is to. . . ." If you need two or more sentences to state your purpose, your ideas might not be focused.

- **Readers:** Identify the various readers (primary, secondary, tertiary, gate-keepers) and their individual characteristics (motives, values, attitudes, and emotions). To identify the readers and their characteristics, fill out the writer-centered worksheet (Figure 3.1) and the reader analysis worksheet (Figure 3.2).
- **Context:** Identify the various contextual issues (physical, economic, ethical, and political) that influence the writing and reading of the proposal. Fill out the contextual analysis worksheet to sort these issues into levels that influence the primary readers, the industry/community, and you and your organization (Figure 3.3).

More than likely, you will find that this analysis will start your proposal-writing process off on the right foot.

Looking Ahead

This chapter and the previous chapter were designed to help you start thinking about the problem/opportunity your proposal or grant is pursuing. You learned how to clearly define the problem and anticipate the rhetorical situation in which your document will be used. Now it is time to start learning how to write the proposal itself. In the next chapter we are going to discuss how to write the Current Situation section.

CASE STUDY Defining the Rhetorical Situation

In their previous meeting to discuss the Cool Campus Project, Anne, George, Calvin, Karen, and Tim agreed that Durango University's problem was that it lacked a long-term strategy for eliminating or offsetting the greenhouse gases produced on campus.

They agreed that most people on campus would not voluntarily change their amounts of energy consumption in a significant way—even if these people supported the Cool Campus concept. Therefore, the university itself would need to renovate the campus infrastructure in ways that would lead to more conservation and use of renewable energy sources.

"All right," said Anne, as she grabbed a dry-erase marker and went up to the whiteboard in the room, "let's start listing out our objectives for the project." The others brainstormed some objectives:

- Use alternative fuels and/or hybrid engines in the campus trucks
- Heat buildings with solar energy
- Generate electricity with solar power and wind power
- Use geothermal heat pumps to heat and cool buildings
- Develop a comprehensive strategic plan that guides decisions about conservation and sustainability
- Encourage people to walk or ride their bikes to campus
- Plant more trees to offset greenhouse gas emissions
- Maximize recycling
- Introduce composting
- Support research on fuel cells
- Raise awareness of energy conservation on campus
- Raise awareness of climate change/global warming
- Encourage faculty and students to see campus as a research site for conservation and alternative energy

"This is a good start," said Anne. "I'm sure we'll be adding and subtracting items from this list. Now, what is our top rank objective?"

Everyone looked over the list. Then George spoke up. "Well, it seems like all of these objectives point to the need for a comprehensive strategic plan."

Calvin added, "Yeah, the strategic plan seems to be the one thing that holds all these other pieces together." The others agreed.

Anne wrote "TRO" next to "Develop a comprehensive strategic plan." "All right, let's move on," she said. "Let's look at the subject, purpose, readers, and context of this proposal."

Keeping their objectives in mind, they began filling out the rhetorical situation in the following way:

Subject: Transforming the Durango University campus into a "Cool Campus" that produces net-zero carbon emissions

Purpose: The purpose of the Cool Campus Project is to develop a strategic plan that guides the long-term conversion of the campus to renewable and sustainable sources of energy.

Readers: Tempest Foundation Board of Directors

Context: Offices of Tempest Foundation, and perhaps a campus visit?

With these elements of the rhetorical situation tentatively defined, they then studied each individually.

Subject

Defining the subject of the proposal was a bit more difficult than they expected. They all agreed that issues involving renewable energy sources, like solar power, wind power, and geothermal heating, were part of the proposal. They had trouble deciding whether issues like improved campus recycling programs should be part of the plan also.

Karen said, "I think it is important that we add in a few goals that are reachable in the short-term. Better recycling and encouraging people not to drive their cars to campus are things we can do right now."

Calvin was skeptical. "I'm just concerned that these smaller items might distract from our larger goals," he said. "You know how these

things happen. We'll see some extra recycling bins and a few signs about taking the bus. The rest will be forgotten over time."

"That's why we need to find ways to make this strategic plan an integral part of the infrastructure and mission of this university," said Anne.

George added, "Yeah, it needs to be more than just a plan. It needs to be a core objective of the university—how the university does business."

"I'm reluctant to say this," said Tim, "but I think we need to narrow our subject to energy issues, cutting out non-energy issues like recycling."

"What?" said Karen. "Recycling is very important."

"I agree," said Tim, "but energy issues seem to be our main issue in this proposal. I believe we need to focus on issues that directly involve converting the campus to renewable energy sources."

The group debated whether non-energy issues like recycling should be included in the grant. They decided that Tim was probably right, so they crossed out all the objectives that didn't directly address energy-related issues.

Karen then said, "Something else I think we should avoid is looking outside of campus. As much as I care about the Amazon rain forests or sustainable farming practices in Africa, we should keep our focus on campus."

"I agree," said George. "The strategic plan should only be concerned with issues that directly impact the Durango University campus. Other issues are important, but they make our subject seem less focused."

Purpose

They then defined the purpose of the Cool Campus Project. What did they want the project to do? Confining themselves to one sentence, they hammered their purpose down into a clear, crisp statement: "The purpose of the Cool Campus Project is to develop a strategic plan that guides the long-term conversion of the campus to renewable and sustainable sources of energy."

This statement of the purpose, though generic, offered them two immediate tools for writing the proposal. First, it specified the overall purpose for the proposal itself. Second, it offered them a knife to cut away the nonessential details so they could focus on the need-to-know information.

FIGURE 3.4
Cool Campus Proposal's Writer-Centered Worksheet

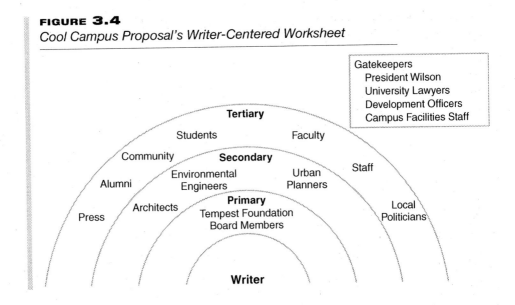

Readers

They then turned to the writer-centered worksheet to identify their other potential readers (Figure 3.4).

The primary readers would be the Tempest Foundation board of directors, who would decide whether to fund the grant. These readers, after all, were the people who could actually say yes to their ideas and fund their project. They would be the decision makers.

They weren't sure who the secondary readers might be. More than likely, the Tempest Foundation would hire advisors or consultants to determine whether a project was feasible. These secondary readers might be engineers, architects, or urban planners who specialize in environmental projects.

The tertiary readers, at first, seemed a bit more problematic. Who else might be interested in obtaining a copy of the proposal? Karen immediately pointed out that the media might be interested in a copy. "They will probably receive a copy, whether we send it to them or not. We need to keep them in mind as we're writing."

Calvin pointed out that local contractors would also be interested in a copy of the proposal, because they would want to bid on any future contracts. Tim mentioned that other universities might want a copy to use as a model for writing similar grants.

George added, "Don't forget the alumni. The Alumni Association is going to be very interested in this project. We need to always remember that concerns from alumni can scrap a project like this one."

Finally, they listed several gatekeepers. Anne pointed out that the President Wilson was probably the most influential gatekeeper. "And, as VP for Physical Facilities, I guess I'm a gatekeeper, too." They also wrote down the university's accountants, legal counsel, and development officers. All of these people would need to see the grant proposal before it went to the Tempest Foundation.

Having identified their various readers, they filled out a reader analysis worksheet, as shown in Figure 3.5.

Context

With their readers identified and described, the group decided to use a context analysis worksheet to look more closely at the situations in which the proposal would be used. It wasn't long before they realized that the context for the proposal was very complex.

The context analysis worksheet seemed to highlight the economic and political issues that would influence how the readers interpreted the proposal (Figure 3.6). On one hand, they felt the directors of the Tempest Foundation would be

FIGURE 3.5

Cool Campus Proposal's Reader Analysis Worksheet

Readers	Motives	Values	Attitudes	Emotions
Primary Readers (Board Members of Tempest Foundation)	• Address global warming issues • Fund environmental causes	• Making progress • A viable plan • Getting something accomplished	• Concerned about global warming • Hopeful for solutions • Reluctant to fund projects that don't change things	• Fearful of global warming • Feel good about doing something to solve the problem
Secondary Readers (Environmental Engineers, Architects, Urban Planners)	• Technical feasibility • Realistic objectives • Attention to detail	• Solid science • Conservation of environment • Aesthetic appeal	• Want to protect the environment • Want to avoid wasting time and money on dead-end projects	• Desire to promote projects that work • Hope for projects that will make lasting changes
Tertiary Readers (Press)	• Raise awareness • Like an interesting story	• Leans toward underdog • Values diversity	• Curious about project • Could become allies in conversion of campus	• Could take up a story as a "cause." • Rooting for people who are doing something positive
Tertiary Readers (Alumni)	• Keep campus the way they remember it • Maintain the reputation of the university	• Desire university to have a positive image • Want to support bettering the university	• Worried that changes to campus will "ruin it" • Like the idea of the university being on the cutting edge	• React negatively to drastic visual changes to campus • Pride in the university
Gatekeepers (President Wilson, Board of Regents)	• Improve university • Lower energy costs • Do something about global warming • Recruit top students and faculty	• A forward-thinking university culture • Changing the university for the better	• Hopeful that the project will succeed • Cautious about stirring up negative feelings among stakeholders	• Positive about the project • Concerned that failure might have long-lasting effects

FIGURE 3.6
Cool Campus Proposal's Context Analysis Worksheet

	Physical	**Economic**	**Ethical**	**Political**
Primary Readers	• Initially, received in the mail, read in their office • Later, proposal might be used on a campus visit	• Want to use funds to the maximum benefit • Want to pay for projects that accomplish specific goals	• Environmental issues are paramount ethical issues	• Use projects as models for action • Good public relations for Tempest Foundation
Industry/ Community	• Issue of global warming changing ecosystems • Raise proposal awareness on a website?	• Money turning from research on global warming to solutions • New advances in technology making renewable energy more affordable	• People waking up to importance of global warming • Social justice issues involved with change	• Desire to make changes to renewable energy • Resistance to changes that cause too much inconvenience
Writers	• Can meet personally with many stakeholders • Can work with other experts to devise good solutions	• Limited means for travel • Have other jobs besides writing this proposal	• Importance of making a lasting change • Using this project as a model for other projects	• Don't want to anger or threaten networks of people on campus • Cannot anger alumni or members of community

interested in a project like this one, but they would question the university's economic and political will to implement the strategic plan.

George said, "We need to show the Tempest Foundation that everyone, from the university president to the students, is interested in transforming this campus into a Cool Campus."

Karen added, "We also should mention that we aren't expecting the Tempest Foundation to pay the whole bill. The funding they give us

would help us develop the strategic plan, but the university would raise the money for implementing these changes."

The physical and ethical issues, fortunately, didn't seem too complex. Physically, the proposal would be used in offices and perhaps on a campus visit. It might be put on a website for easy access. As for ethical issues, the movement toward a sustainable campus seemed to be a plus from an ethical standpoint. However, they would need to be careful to hear diverse viewpoints about any changes to the campus.

George said, "Perhaps we need to plan some campus meetings to solicit feedback. That might help us avoid the ethical pitfalls that can emerge with these kinds of well-intentioned plans."

Anne agreed. "We don't want to trample someone's rights in our eagerness to do the right thing for the environment."

Defining the objectives and the rhetorical situation for their proposal ended up taking them an hour and a half. When they finished, they had developed a much richer sense of the content, purpose, and social/political factors surrounding their proposal. The foundation for writing the proposal had been set.

They were ready to start inventing the Current Situation section of the proposal.

Questions and Exercises

1. Using a proposal or grant from your workplace or one you found on the Internet, write a two-page analysis in which you discuss how the writers handled the proposal's purpose, readers, and context. Can you find any places in the proposal that seem tailored to the specific readers or context? Do you think the proposal achieves its purpose? Are there places in the proposal where the writers stray from their purpose? How might the proposal be improved to fit its rhetorical situation?

2. With a team, choose a problem on campus, at your workplace, or your community that might warrant a proposal. Analyze the rhetorical situation in which that proposal would need to operate. Use a writer-centered worksheet and a reader analysis worksheet to identify the readers and their characteristics. Then, fill out a context analysis worksheet to work through the physical, economic, political, and ethical factors that might influence the readers. Write a memorandum to your instructor in which you summarize the important issues that relate to the proposal's readers and context.

3. In the Cool Campus case study, what are some reader-related issues that will probably require special attention when the group writes the proposal? Look closely at how the writers filled out the reader and context worksheets. What are some issues that jump out at you? What are some issues that the writers will need to keep in mind as they write this complex proposal? Are there any items you might add to these worksheets? What are some of the political and ethical issues that the writers might be neglecting?

4. Writing with a team can be challenging. How might you use the methods and worksheets in this chapter to help you manage a writing team for a proposal? What might you do differently if you were writing a proposal with a team that you might not do if you were writing alone?

5. Study the RFP in Question 6 at the end of Chapter 2. What are the contextual issues (physical, economic, political, and ethical) that might be influencing this rhetorical situation? What political issues would you need to keep in mind as you write a pre-proposal for this RFP? What ethical issues might also be involved?

4 Describing the Current Situation

Overview

This chapter discusses the writing of the Current Situation section in proposals and grants. The chapter will meet the following objectives:

1. Discuss the importance of describing the current situation accurately for the readers.
2. Illustrate how mapping can be used to invent the content of a Current Situation section.
3. Describe the basic parts of a proposal section.
4. Discuss the drafting of a typical Current Situation section.
5. Describe how to write the Current Situation section in a research grant or proposal.

Why Describe the Current Situation?

Having defined the problem, identified your objectives, and analyzed the rhetorical situation, you are now ready to start drafting the proposal itself. In Chapter 1, you learned that proposals tend to follow a pattern, or genre. This genre includes the following areas:

Introduction
    Current Situation
    Project Plan
    Qualifications   ← Four Areas of a Proposal
    Costs and Benefits
Conclusion

The proposal genre is not a formula. Rather, it is a pattern that can be altered and adjusted to fit the needs of any proposal. In fact, clients or funding sources may ask you to conform to organizational patterns that are different from the one shown here. This is especially true of private foundations, which regularly ask for unique arrangements of information. In most proposals and grants, though, you will find that these four areas are addressed one way or another. And, if no pattern is specified by the client or the funding source, then the pattern above is a reliable one to follow.

In this chapter, we are going to discuss how to write the first major section of a proposal, which is usually called the *Current Situation, Background,* or perhaps the *Narrative.* (To keep things simple, we will call it the "Current Situation section" from here on.) The purpose of a Current Situation section is to explain your understanding of the existing problem/opportunity, its causes, and its effects. Depending on the kind of proposal you are writing, this section will include different kinds of information:

- In a business proposal, you need to show the clients that you fully understand their current situation, thus increasing the likelihood that you will offer a reasonable plan to solve their problem or help them take advantage of an opportunity.
- In most grant proposals, you need to educate the readers about the history of the problem you are trying to solve, its causes, and the effects of doing nothing about it.
- In grant proposals for research funding, the Current Situation section is where you should offer a literature review and describe your prior research into the subject.

Put simply, the Current Situation section is where you will provide the readers with the background information they need to understand the project plan that comes later in the proposal. This section sets an important foundation for the whole proposal.

Guidelines for Drafting the Current Situation Section

Your main goal in the Current Situation section is to explain to the readers the *causes* and *effects* of a problem or opportunity. As you draft the Current Situation section, you should keep three guidelines in mind:

Guideline 1: Problems are the effects of causes.

Guideline 2: Ignored problems tend to grow worse.

Guideline 3: Blame change, not people.

Guideline 1: Problems Are the Effects of Causes

This first guideline urges you to seek out the elements of change that are at work behind the current situation. Problems and opportunities do not just happen—they are caused because something in the current situation *changed* to create them. As the writer of the proposal, you need to figure out what caused the problem or opportunity in the first place.

One way to identify the causes of a problem or opportunity is through a technique called *logical mapping,* or just *mapping* for short. Mapping helps you sort out the problem on a piece of paper or computer screen, so you can visualize the logical relationships between the problem and its causes.

To map the current situation, write down the problem in the center of a blank sheet of paper. Put a circle around it. Then identify two to five major causes of

FIGURE 4.1

A Problem–Causes Map

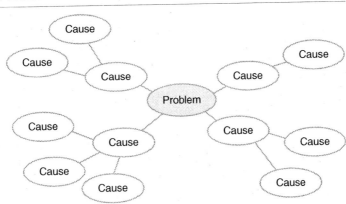

that problem. Write these causes separately around the problem. Circle them and use lines to connect them to the original problem (Figure 4.1).

Then, map out further to identify the minor causes behind the two to five major causes. In other words, treat each major cause as a separate problem and continue mapping further out. In Figure 4.1, for instance, there are four major causes (the ones closest to the problem). By mapping further, we can identify the minor causes that created these major causes.

As you map out the causes of the problem or opportunity, keep asking yourself, "What changed?" As discussed in Chapter 1, proposals are tools for managing change. By paying attention to the evolving elements of the current situation, you will begin to visualize how the problem or opportunity came about.

To illustrate, let us go back to Lisa Miller's proposal for Overture Designs, the Chicago architecture firm experiencing growing pains. When she mapped out Overture's office space problem, she began by writing "lack of office space" in the center of a sheet of paper (Figure 4.2). Then, she identified some of the major causes of that problem:

1. Overture had hired several new architects and staff members over the last year, thereby increasing the amount of people, desks, computers, and equipment taking up space in the office.
2. Overture had experienced a surge in business, forcing the firm to handle several projects at once.
3. She noticed the large amount of computer and printing equipment in the Overture office. When Overture was founded, architects relied on simple drafting tables. Now, computer-aided design (CAD) systems and large format printers were taking up a great amount of space.

Her causes for the problem seemed to be (1) new hiring, (2) surge in business, and (3) an increase in office equipment. Once Lisa identified the major causes of the problem, she treated each of the causes separately as a new "problem" and mapped out further to explore the minor causes.

FIGURE 4.2

A Map of Overture's Problem

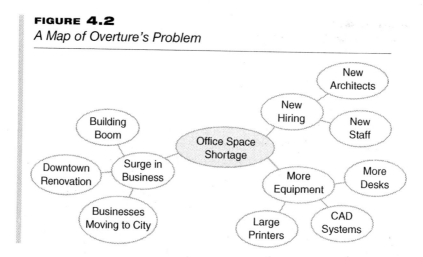

When mapping, you could keep charting the causes indefinitely, teasing out the most obscure reasons for the problem. But, eventually, you will find that you have developed enough detail to fully describe the problem to the readers. At that point, mapping further would not be helpful. That's when you have enough material about the causes of the problem for the Current Situation section.

Guideline 2: Ignored Problems Tend to Grow Worse

When faced with a description of their problem and its causes, your readers will be tempted to ignore the problem or wish it away. The interesting thing about change, though, is that problems tend to grow worse over time, not better. Consequently, if these problems are not addressed, they often evolve into much larger problems. To help your readers understand what is at stake, you should also explore the effects of not addressing the problem or opportunity.

Logical mapping can be used to help you analyze the effects of a problem or missed opportunity. Again, put the problem in the center of a page or screen (Figure 4.3). Then, start mapping out the effects of the problem. This time, though,

FIGURE 4.3

A Problem–Effects Map

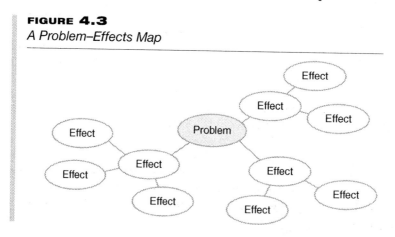

FIGURE 4.4

Mapping Out the Effects of Overture's Problem

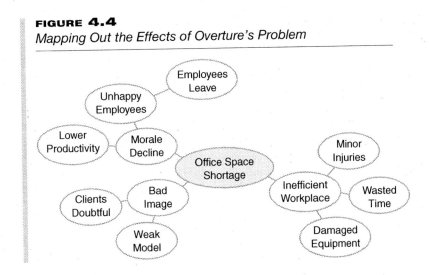

instead of asking what caused this problem, ask yourself, "What are the effects of not addressing this problem?"

As you map out the potential effects of the problem, try to tease out the consequences of not doing something about the problem. Lisa Miller, for example, began mapping the effects of ignoring Overture's office space problem (Figure 4.4):

1. The limited working space would make Overture's operations far less efficient. If employees were required to climb over equipment and other people to do their jobs, a great amount of time would be wasted.
2. Employee morale was almost certain to drop, if it hadn't already. Good employees tend to leave when they feel uncomfortable at work. In the tight labor market for architects and staff, it would be difficult and expensive to replace good employees, especially top-notch architects.
3. Overture's crowded office implied to clients that the company did not practice what it preaches. In their own promotional materials, Overture advertised functional, comfortable workspaces, yet its own office did not meet these goals. When visiting Overture's office, potential clients might become skeptical about whether Overture could create the functional workspaces they promised.

Once she identified the major effects of the problem, Lisa kept mapping out even further to explore some of the minor effects.

When mapping out the effects, there is no need to view the situation in an apocalyptic way. Avoid giving the readers the impression that the whole situation is hopeless and not worth saving. After all, no one wants to put more money into a sinking ship. Nevertheless, mapping the effects of the problem will help you add a sense of urgency to your proposal and prove that the problem should not be ignored.

Guideline 3: Blame Change, Not People

This final guideline reminds us that problems and opportunities come about because reality is always changing around us. As you map out the causes and effects of the problem, it might be tempting to point the finger of blame at someone. But blaming people in a proposal, even your competitors, is almost always a bad idea.

After all, in most cases the readers of a proposal (or people closely associated with them) could be partly deserving of blame, so assigning fault will not gain you any positive points. For instance, imagine the sour taste in the readers' mouths if a proposal stated, "If your chief engineer, Steve Wendell, had chosen to pay for regular servicing of the GH-7000 router, then your company would not be looking to purchase a new machine right now." Even if this statement is true, Steve Wendell is not going to be eager to accept this proposal, and neither will his supervisors. Accepting the proposal would be an admission that Steve and his supervisors had made a serious mistake.

Even when the people to blame could be your competitors, you should avoid pointing the finger at them. Let us say your company was hired to fix a problem that your competitor created. Blaming your competition might score you some short-term points with the readers, but this approach is also risky. For one thing, someone at your client's company was responsible for hiring your competitor in the first place, and he or she is already taking some heat for that choice. Second, your competitor has almost certainly been trashed by the client already. Placing more blame on your competitor might remind the clients to be more cautious, right when they are reading *your* proposal. By blaming your competitor, you are only reminding the clients to keep their guard up—something you want to avoid if you are urging them to say yes to your ideas.

In grant proposals, you should show that the problems you are trying to address came about because of changes in our society, not because somebody messed up. For example, imagine you are looking for funding to fight alcohol abuse by teenagers in your area. Of course, we could blame teenagers, parents, school officials, politicians, advertisers, entertainers, and a whole list of other suspects for this problem. In reality, though, social problems like teenage alcohol abuse are caused by changes in our society. Perhaps these teenagers are reacting to the higher levels of stress placed on them by a culture that has less tolerance for failure or just being average. Perhaps they have less supervision because in your area both parents in a family must work full time to afford food and basic housing. If you look more closely at the problem you are trying to solve, you will usually find that something changed to create it.

In almost all cases, your Current Situation section will be stronger if you *blame change, not people.* Change is ultimately the one aspect of our lives that we can do little about. Roads eventually start to crumble, machines break down, markets shift, companies alter strategies. Change is the culprit behind all these things.

Moreover, change will not be offended if you put the blame on it. By blaming change, you will avoid messy political tensions that will only hurt your proposal. So, in the case of Steve Wendell and the GH-7000 router, you could just blame change by writing that "Over time, the GH-7000 router begins to lose its precision and eventually needs to be replaced. Meanwhile, new advancements in the field require upgraded machines to stay competitive." If you want to mention the importance of paying for regular maintenance, make sure that the issue is mentioned with your project plan later in the proposal, without reference to Mr. Wendell.

Researching the Current Situation

Once you have completed your logical maps of the problem's causes and effects, it is time to do some research. Mapping will point your research in the right direction by highlighting the logical relationships that structure the problem or opportunity to be discussed in the proposal. Mapping helps you identify the if–then, either–or, cause–effect relationships that you can use to reason with your readers. Mapping also tends to bring out examples, similar cases, or anecdotes that can be used to fill out the argument in a Current Situation section.

Now it is time to turn to outside sources to support your claims and modify your ideas where necessary. A good approach to research uses *triangulation* to cross-reference sources. Triangulation involves using three different kinds of sources:

- **Electronic sources**—websites, Internet searches, electronic mailing lists (listservs), television, radio, videos, blogs, CD-ROMs
- **Print sources**—magazines, newspapers, academic journals, books, government publications, reference materials, microfilm/microfiche
- **Empirical sources**—interviews, surveys, experiments, field observations, ethnographies, case studies

To write an accurate Current Situation section, you should draw information from all three of these kinds of sources. Relying exclusively on one kind of source—especially electronic sources—can be risky, because you may only see a narrow view of the problem that you are trying to solve.

To illustrate, let us return to Lisa Miller's mapping of Overture's current situation. Her maps of the causes and effects might seem reasonable, but if she was going to *prove* that her understanding is accurate, she needed to back up her ideas with some solid facts and data. In her causes map, for instance, she claimed that one reason for the lack of office space was a "surge in business." To back up this claim, she could draw growth figures from Overture's annual report or a recent article about Overture she found on the website of the *Chicago Tribune*. In her effects map, meanwhile, Lisa pointed out that a lack of office space would lead to a "decline in morale" among Overture's employees. She might back up this kind of claim by referring to published research that shows how cramped office spaces lead to lower productivity and unhappy employees. To complete her triangulation, she could refer back to her notes taken while she toured Overture's office and spoke with Grant Moser, Overture's office manager.

Solid research is the backbone of any Current Situation section. Mapping may help you highlight logical relationships behind the problem or opportunity, but your follow-up research will provide the support on which those logical arguments stand.

Mapping in Teams

Writing teams probably gain the most from logical mapping, especially on large projects. As you probably know, it is hard for groups of people to write a document together, sentence by sentence. However, team members can easily participate in the mapping process. When you are working with a team, find a whiteboard, chalkboard, or some large sheets of paper. With a marker in hand, you can encourage the team to brainstorm about the causes and effects of the problem. As they explore the logical relationships in the problem, write down their comments and fill the board or paper with their ideas.

The mapping process is a uniquely visual way of bringing out the team's ideas. You will find yourself and team members coming up with ideas you never would have considered if you had been trying to write the document sentence by sentence. Meanwhile, mapping also allows your team members to visualize the overall problem or opportunity that is being addressed in the proposal. It provides them with a global understanding of the changes in the current situation that the proposal is trying to manage.

Once your team is finished mapping out the problem, you can then assign each person on the team a cause or effect to research. Send them to the Internet, the library, company files, or government offices to dig up more data and facts to support the logical relationships your team discovered in the mapping process.

Writing the Current Situation Section

When writing the Current Situation section of a proposal, you will transform your maps and your research into readable sentences and paragraphs. The Current Situation section, like most large sections of a proposal, tends to include three parts: an opening, a body, and a closing (Figure 4.5). In other words, each section of the proposal is like a miniature essay with three parts: an introduction, body, and conclusion. Each part of a section plays a different role. Let us consider each of these three parts separately in more depth.

Opening

The opening paragraph or paragraphs set a context for the body by telling the readers a few important things up front. Directly or indirectly, it will tell the readers the following:

- The subject of the section
- The purpose of the section
- The main point of the section

For example, Lisa Miller might identify the *subject* of her Current Situation section with a heading, like "The Office Space Shortage at Overture." Then, in the opening

FIGURE 4.5

The Basic Organization of a Proposal Section

Typical Section

Opening—identifies the subject, purpose, and main point of the section

Body—provides reasoning and examples to back up the main point of the section

Closing—reinforces the main point of the section and begins transition to next section

paragraph, she might identify the *purpose* of the section by writing, "Before describing our plan, we want to first identify some of the factors that created Overture's office space shortage." And finally, she might state her *main point*, "We believe this shortage is a result of Overture's success and growing influence in the Chicago market. The downside to this growth has been less free space in Overture's office."

Most sections in a proposal require only a one-paragraph opening. The purpose of the opening paragraph or paragraphs is to simply set a framework for the body of the section. Therefore, try to keep the opening of each section as concise as possible.

Body Paragraphs

The body of the section is where you will provide the majority of the details you mapped out in your cause and effect maps. Three approaches to writing the Current Situation section are most effective: the causal approach, the effects approach, and the narrative approach.

Causal Approach

This approach structures the body of the Current Situation section around the causes of the problem (Figure 4.6). When using this approach, each major cause will typically receive one or more paragraphs in the body of the section. For example, the body of Lisa's Current Situation section might include three paragraphs that reflect the three branches in her map of the problem's causes. The first paragraph in the body might discuss the impact of Overture's surge in business. The second paragraph might talk about the new hiring at Overture. And the third body paragraph might discuss the office space demands of more equipment.

Three Approaches to Organizing a Current Situation Section

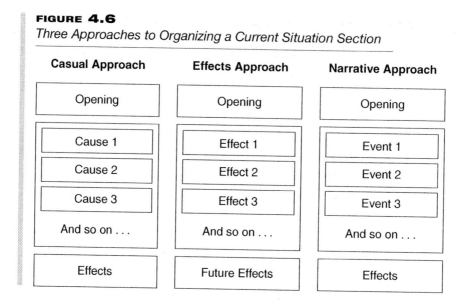

Essentially, the causal approach structures the body of the section around the major causes.

Effects Approach

This approach structures the body around the effects of not taking action (Figure 4.6). Usually, this approach is most effective when you and the readers of the proposal are already fully aware of the causes of the problem. There is little reason to dwell on these causes or prove they exist, because everyone already agrees they exist. In this case, the causes might be concisely mentioned in the opening paragraph or they might be discussed in the first body paragraph of the section. Then the remainder of the section can be devoted to the effects.

When using the effects approach to write the body of the Current Situation section, give each major effect one or more paragraphs in which you discuss consequences of inaction. For example, if Lisa Miller were to use an effects approach in her Current Situation section, she would devote at least a paragraph to each of the major effects in her effects map. Specifically, her Current Situation section would discuss topics like the "decline in employee morale," "inefficient workspace," and "bad impression on clients."

Overall, the effects approach is most successful with readers who know why a problem exists but are reluctant to take action. By devoting most of the Current Situation section to a discussion of the effects of the problem, you urge them to face reality.

Narrative Approach

This approach tells the readers a story about how "change" created the current situation. Each paragraph moves the readers sequentially along a timeline, showing how changes in and around the organization have created the need to take action (Figure 4.6). For example, let us say you are trying to convince a local company that they should hire your accounting firm to handle their taxes. When the clients started the business, their company was small, so they could handle their accounting in-house. Ten years later, however, they are now a multimillion-dollar corporation, and their in-house accounting methods are no longer adequate. With the narrative approach, you would start out at the beginning and then lead them toward the present, showing them how their growth over the years has led to their need for the more sophisticated accounting services that your company provides.

The best approach for organizing the body of the Current Situation section depends on the kind of situation you are trying to describe and the readers to whom you are describing it. The causal approach is most effective if you are educating your readers about the issues that brought about their current problem or opportunity. The effects approach works best if the readers already know the causes of the problem, and you are worried that they might not recognize the importance of doing something. The narrative approach is most effective when you want to show the readers how the problem or opportunity evolved over time. The causal approach and effects approach to organizing the Current Situation section work best when you are describing the situation as it stands now. The narrative approach allows you to describe the historical events that led up to the present.

Closing

The closing of a section can be written a few different ways. The most effective closings are those that summarize the main point of the section while helping make a transition to the next section in the proposal. Above all, the closing should be concise.

The closing for a Current Situation section is a good place to stress the importance of the problem or opportunity. If you used the causal or narrative approach to organize the body of the Current Situation section, you might use the closing to discuss some of the effects of not taking action. The closing thus becomes an opportunity to stress the importance of the problem, giving the readers extra incentive to pay attention to your project plan, which usually appears next in the proposal. If you are using the effects approach to organize the body, you might summarize the major effects of inaction or generally discuss what the readers might "need" to solve the problem. By discussing what is needed, you begin making the transition to your discussion of the project plan.

In some cases, however, proposal writers do not include a closing in their Current Situation section, preferring instead to go straight into their plan. Shorter proposals can certainly do without closings, because closings tend to repeat what was just said in the body of the section. Larger proposals, on the other hand, usually require a closing to round off the section and reinforce main points.

Lisa Miller's Current Situation Section

According to Overture's RFP guidelines, Lisa Miller needed to write a preproposal that would not exceed fifteen pages total, including any graphics or diagrams. The limited available space meant all the sections in the proposal would need to be concise. Lisa also wanted to leave extra space for the Project Plan section, because she believed her plan was going to be the most important part of the proposal. So, she decided the Current Situation section should be as concise as possible. In this section, she would need to show the readers at Overture that she understood their situation, but she did not want to spend too much time telling them what they already knew. Lisa decided to limit the Current Situation section of her proposal to about one or two pages.

Looking over her maps of the causes and effects of the problem, Lisa decided to use the narrative approach to describe the current situation, because she felt the readers already had a rather strong grasp on the causes and effects (Figure 4.7).* The narrative approach would allow her to highlight Overture's growth and success, while stressing that the office space problem exists because of this success. This approach would also help her bring the readers into the story, warming them up for the Project Plan section that would follow.

In her Current Situation section, Lisa had a few goals:

1. She wanted to turn the office space "problem" into a positive by pointing out that the current office space shortage is the result of Overture's success. By reframing the problem in positive terms, she hoped to show that the problem was created by change and that it was not anyone's fault.
2. She wanted to reinforce the award-winning nature of the current office. Her competitors for the contract would almost certainly propose that Overture move out of the current office, something she knew the firm's management was reluctant to do. So, she wanted to remind them of the award-winning history of their current office, using examples to stress the historical importance of the office to their firm.
3. She wanted to reinforce that the current growth in business might just be a short-term "surge" related to the good economy in Chicago. From her discussions with Grant Moser, the POC, she knew the readers were concerned about overextending the firm's expenses. She wanted to use that concern to her advantage by hinting that Overture's growth in business is due to recent trends that may or may not continue.
4. Lisa decided to mention the effects of inaction, but she handled them with a soft touch. She assumed the readers would already be well aware of these effects. Merely mentioning them would be sufficient to motivate the readers to take action.

Overall, Lisa knew that her Current Situation section was telling the readers things they already knew. Nothing in this part of the proposal would come as a surprise to Overture's management. Nevertheless, Lisa was showing them that *she* understood their problem, its causes, and its effects. She also wanted to remind them why they wanted to stay in their current office. By taking this approach, she believed her readers would be most receptive to her proposed plan.

---

*This example and following examples in this book are not intended to be viewed as final drafts. They are unpolished, much like a typical rough draft. If you would like to see a finished draft of this section, please turn to the example proposals in Chapter 12.

FIGURE 4.7
FIGURE 4.7
The Current Situation Section for the Overture Proposal

The Office Space Shortage at Overture

Before describing our plan, we would like to first highlight some of the factors that created the office space shortage at Overture Design. Actually, we believe this shortage is a sign of Overture's success and growing influence in the Chicago market. The downside to this growth has been the loss of free space in Overture's downtown office.

In 1982, Overture moved into its current office on Michigan Avenue. At the time, the firm employed five architects and fifteen staff members. The office seemed roomy, because Susan James designed it with functionality and growth in mind. The five original architects each had a couple of drafting tables and a large desk. Meanwhile, desks for staff members were placed strategically throughout the office to maximize the efficiency of the workspace. The design of Overture's office won accolades and awards as a masterpiece of modernist design. In a 1983 interview with Architectural Review, James explained that the workspace was designed to be both "aesthetic and pragmatic, a balance of form and function." She also wanted it to be a model office that would show clients the advantages of the modernist design.

Almost two decades later, the office is still a modernist masterpiece, but Overture's growth has made the space feel a bit limited. This surge in business began in 1992 when the economy began to rebound from a recession. Soon, downtown businesses began renovating their neoclassical-style offices, adopting the modernist style. By the late 1990s, companies were returning to downtown Chicago from the suburbs. Overture soon found itself one of the firms leading a movement that the Chicago Tribune dubbed the "Downtown Renaissance." Overture's revenues doubled from 1992 to 1999 and then doubled again from 2000 to 2005.

To meet this increased demand, Overture has added ten architects and twenty new staff members. As a result, an office that once seemed roomy was becoming increasingly snug. More architects and staff meant more drafting tables, more desks, and more equipment. Meanwhile, new kinds of equipment not used two decades ago, like CAD systems and large-format copiers, also began using up precious floorspace, further restricting the limited room available.

Left unaddressed, this lack of office space may create some further problems in the near future. According to a Spenser Institute study, a restrictive office tends to undermine employee morale, leading to lower productivity and overall employee discomfort. The workspace will also become increasingly inefficient, wasting employees' time and causing them minor injuries, while also causing damage to equipment. A cramped office also presents a bad image to clients, especially since Overture prides itself on designing functional workspaces that enhance business activities. Clients may come to believe that Overture does not practice what it preaches.

The problems faced by Overture are simply the downside of the firm's success and growing influence in the Chicago market. Now, the challenge faced by Overture is to free up office space without disrupting current projects or jeopardizing future growth. We believe we can help you meet this challenge.

Special Case: Research Grants and Literature Reviews

Research proposals, especially ones written to secure grant funding, require us to think a bit differently about the current situation. In research proposals, the Current Situation section is usually referred to as the Background, Research Problem, or Literature Review. These kinds of sections are designed to meet three specific goals:

- They show where the proposed research adds to or differs from prior research on the subject.
- They discuss the significance of the research and its potential impact.
- They establish the credibility of the study and authors by showing familiarity with the research community's conversation on the research subject.

To meet these three goals, the Current Situation section of a research proposal needs to summarize previous research on the subject, while identifying a gap in the knowledge base or raising questions about prior results (Swales 1984). In most cases, this section of the proposal will include two types of information: (a) a review of the existing literature on the subject, and (b) a summary of the principle investigator's prior research into the subject.

Literature Review

The purpose of a literature review is to familiarize your readers with the subject and the published research that has already been done on the subject. These reviews tend to be written in one of two ways: (a) a summary of the different camps or trends in the field, or (b) a description of how the field has evolved over time:

- When summarizing the different camps or trends in the field, you should start by dividing your field into two, three, or four camps. After a brief opening paragraph in which the camps or trends are labeled, summarize the published work in each. The goal of this kind of literature review is to highlight the knowledge gaps and/or inconsistencies that exist in the published work.
- When describing how the field has evolved, divide the published research into two to five eras. Then, walk the readers era-by-era through the literature, describing how one discovery has led to others. Your goal in this kind of literature review is to show how your research project will add to the existing knowledge base, fill in a knowledge gap, or confirm something believed but not known.

The best literature reviews are ones that tell a story or make an argument. If possible, you want to avoid marching your readers through a lifeless summary of the literature. Instead, your literature review should tell them an exciting story of discovery that has led up to the mystery you want to solve. Or, you should show them that the factions in your field have been engaged in an interesting debate that your research will try to resolve.

Prior Research

In addition to the literature review, you should also describe your prior empirical research into the subject. Describe any experiments or observations you have already completed, showing your results. Your aim is to demonstrate that you are a competent researcher who has already gathered some intriguing data or information. You want the funding agency to see that you are on the right track; but now, you need funding to expand your research or take it to the next level.

One thing to avoid, though, is giving the impression that you have already figured out the answers or solved the problem your research is designed to address. Funding sources generally are most interested in supporting research that discovers something new. So, you need to leave reviewers with the impression that your prior research has been promising but has not yet answered all the questions.

At first glance, it might seem as though Current Situation sections in research proposals are very different from these kinds of sections in other kinds of proposals. But once you look closer, the similarities become apparent. Like other proposals, research proposals suggest ways to solve problems. The problems being solved, however, are gaps or inconsistencies in our current knowledge of the subject.

Like other proposals, you want to show how the field has evolved, creating a problem or opportunity for more research. Perhaps a recently published article exposed a gap in the knowledge base. Or, perhaps a new discovery threw the results of prior studies into doubt. As in other kinds of proposals, you are telling a story of change.

A good way to end the Current Situation section in a research proposal is to stress the importance of your research. Leave any modesty aside and tell the readers how your research, if successful, will impact the field or the lives of others. If possible, quantify how many people will be affected by your research.

Looking Ahead

The Current Situation section is often the most neglected part of a proposal, because many writers mistakenly assume that the readers already understand the current situation. That is not always true.

Readers need a well-written, well-reasoned Current Situation section for two reasons. First, they often do not fully understand the problem or opportunity that they are facing. If they did, why would they be looking to people like you for help? By identifying the causes of the current problem and its potential effects, you might provide them insight that they lack. If they agree with your assessment of their situation, they will be more likely to agree to your project plan.

Second, even if your clients understand the problem, its causes, and its effects, they still want to see that *you* fully understand the situation. Nothing frustrates clients more than the one-size-fits-all, cookie-cutter plans that are forwarded by some large consulting firms. Each individual client is unique, and so are their problems. A well-written Current Situation section shows the readers that you are addressing *their* problem, not fitting their problem to a predetermined solution.

In many cases, a well-written description of the current situation is the difference between success and failure when bidding for a project or seeking funding for research.

CASE STUDY Describing the Current Situation at Durango University

At their previous meeting, Anne, George, Calvin, Karen, and Tim discussed their objectives and defined the rhetorical situation for their grant proposal. They also explored the social and political factors connected to the Cool Campus Project. They now had a much clearer understanding of their proposal's subject, purpose, readers, and the contexts in which it might be used. With the notes from last week's meeting in front of them, the group began developing the Current Situation section of the proposal.

They started by using a problem–causes map to explore the causes of the current problem. The group members had already decided that the problem was that campus infrastructure was designed to only use nonrenewable forms of energy, like coal and gasoline. Placing the problem "reliance on nonrenewable energy" in the middle of a sheet of paper, they began mapping out the causes for that problem.

"One cause that comes to mind is that people haven't really had a choice about their energy use on campus," Calvin said. "I don't want to sound overly negative, but the campus was meant to run on coal and people need to drive their cars to campus. That's the way the campus was designed."

Tim added, "Some of us ride bikes and walk, but there are few bike paths and the streets are busy. You really have to watch for cars. The lack of public transportation, too, is a problem. People who live more than a mile away are almost forced to drive."

"Those aren't easy things to fix," said George. "You're talking about needing to redesign how this campus works."

Anne was filling out the problem-causes map on a whiteboard as they spoke (Figure 4.8). She said, "All right, is there a deeper problem at

work? What has changed to make this problem so important right now?"

"Well," Karen began, "I think we all realize that energy issues will become increasingly important. Global warming is a real problem. Also, it's going to become more and more expensive to use nonrenewable forms of energy."

George agreed. "Plus, the Young Power Plant, which provides heat and electricity to the campus, is going to need to be replaced or overhauled in the next decade. We're going to need to do something, no matter what."

Calvin looked over at Anne's map. "Okay," he said, "it looks like we have two major causes: the reliance of campus on coal-fired heat and electricity and the reliance on cars for transportation. What are the causes of those problems?"

They mapped out those problems further, as shown in Figure 4.8. When they were finished, Anne looked at the map and asked, "All right, what's missing here?"

"Money!" George declared. "Big changes will cost a lot of money. The first question many readers will ask is who is responsible for funding the changes."

Tim added, "Yeah, I think we can all agree that funding is a major issue with something like this. What's interesting, though, is that changes in the campus infrastructure can actually *save* the university money in the long run, through cutting energy costs and such. So, a major part of our proposal might be to explain how spending money to change the campus will actually cut costs in the long-term."

"Good point, Tim. But don't get too far ahead of us!" Anne said with a grin.

Tim smiled and said, "Sorry about that. Okay, so we can agree that a third major cause of the

FIGURE 4.8

Problem–Causes Map for the Cool Campus Project

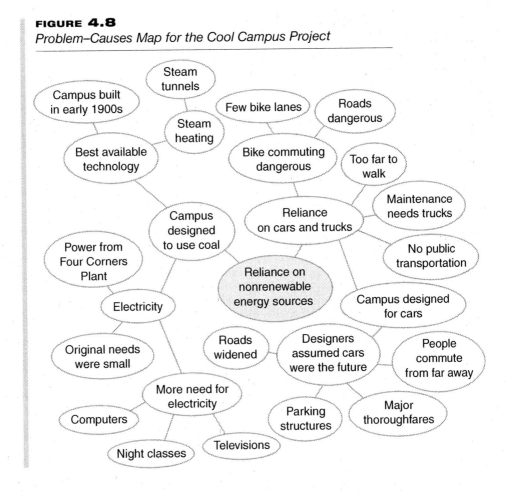

problem is the cost of implementing major changes to the campus infrastructure, as well as the perception that these costs are not worth it."

With the causes of their problem mapped out, the group decided to look at the potential effects of the problem. Moving to a second whiteboard, Anne again wrote the problem, "reliance on nonrenewable energy," in the center of the board. They began using a problem–effects map to find the effects of not taking action.

"The longer we avoid doing something about this problem, the further behind we will be in fixing it," Karen said.

"I agree," Anne added. "There is no question that eventually something will need to be done about energy on campus. The Young Power Plant is not going to last more than ten more years.

It's just a question of when we get started. And the longer we wait, the more we will fall behind."

"And the more money we will spend," George said. "The sooner we figure out a strategy for using renewable energy sources on campus, the more money we will save the university over the long term."

"Absolutely," Calvin agreed. "So, a second effect is that the campus will lose more money over the long term. Then, those costs will be passed along to students."

"I hope this doesn't sound superficial," Tim hesitantly began, "but ignoring environmental concerns could make the university look bad. So many other campuses are looking into what they can do for the environment, and we don't want

FIGURE 4.9

Problem–Effects Map for the Cool Campus Project

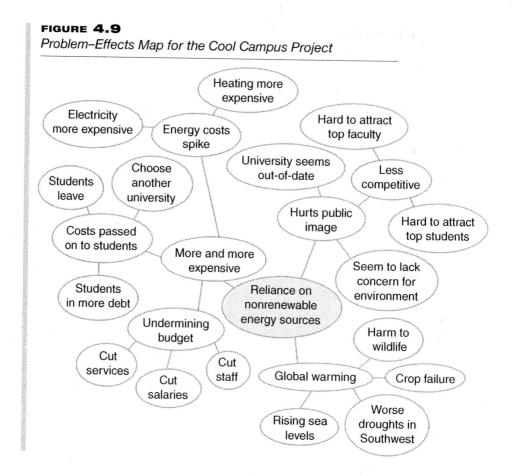

Durango University to appear apathetic toward environmental concerns."

"That doesn't sound superficial at all," Karen said. "It's important that our university keep up and stay tuned into the world around it."

Anne kept scribbling their ideas on the whiteboard. Soon, a full problem–effects map emerged (Figure 4.9).

The two maps they created described the problem's causes and effects. They agreed that each of them should research the causes and effects in more depth at the library and on the Internet.

Their time for the meeting was running out, so Anne took digital pictures of the whiteboards and offered to write a draft of the Current Situation section. She asked them to send her the results of their research by the end of the week. By Friday, the team had sent her a pile of materials to work with.

Anne decided she would use a *causal approach* to organize the Situation section. The causal approach would allow her to educate the readers about the problem, while stressing its causes.

She e-mailed a rough draft of her Current Situation section to the group (Figure 4.10). George replied with an e-mail that offered a few suggestions for improvement. He said, "It seems a bit rough right now. Also, I'm not sure if the financial issues are fully addressed."

Calvin sent a reply, "Yes, but it feels good to have something down on paper. We can always clean it up when we finish writing the rest of the proposal. At least the basic information is all here."

"Let's move on to solving the problem," Anne e-mailed to everyone. "I think we're doing great so far!"

FIGURE 4.10
A Draft of the Cool Campus Situation Section

Energy Issues at Durango University

Durango University began its Green Campus Program in the year 2001 with a grant from the Office of the President. The Green Campus Program has resulted in more environmental awareness on campus, increased recycling, the purchase of renewable energy certificates to offset 3 percent of campus consumption of electricity, and use of compact fluorescent lightbulbs and Energy Star appliances.

The Green Campus Program has been an important step in the right direction, but the long-term energy challenges we face at Durango University are much larger. The university's campus was built in 1914 with the available energy technologies, making it dependent on coal, oil, and petroleum. With the threat of global warming and the increasing costs of energy, our campus is bound to these nonrenewable energy sources, which are not sustainable in the future.

The Legacy of Old Betsy

Our campus's reliance on coal for steam heat is the largest problem we face. In 1914 at its founding, the university had three main buildings, which were heated and supplied with electricity by a small coal-fire plant, nicknamed "Old Betsy," on the eastern edge of campus (where the Student Union is today). The campus's electricity requirements were small, so Old Betsy's boilers mainly kept the campus warm by pushing steam through tunnels running to the buildings. The small amount of electricity required to light the buildings was also generated with steam.

Of course, much has changed since then, but the technologies used to heat and power the campus have not. The campus now has twenty-four buildings, spread over a campus that covers eighty-six acres. Old Betsy was replaced in 1931 by a larger coal-fire plant, and successively larger coal-fire plants were built in 1954 and 1973. But the newer plants only led to an expansion of the infrastructure originally designed for Old Betsy.

Today's plant, the Young Power Plant, still burns coal to make steam, which is pushed through tunnels under the campus to keep buildings warm. The Young Power Plant also generates some electricity, but much of the campus's electricity comes from the Four Corners Power Plant, a massive coal-fire plant that is located west of Farmington, New Mexico. The remainder of our electricity comes from regional power plants that burn natural gas. With the increase in electricity-using devices on campus like televisions and computers, the electricity needs of the campus outstripped the generating capacity of its own power plants in the mid-1970s.

After thirty-five years of service, the Young Power Plant is coming due for replacement or a complete renovation. The boilers in the plant are already expensive to run and maintain, compared to other sources of heat (James 12). Steam is an inefficient way to heat a campus of our size. Moreover, burning coal adds carbon dioxide and other greenhouse gases into the atmosphere, contributing to global warming.

(continued)

FIGURE 4.10
(Continued)

Cars and Campus
Our next largest problem on campus is the over-reliance on cars and trucks for transportation. The campus was originally designed to be pedestrian-friendly. By the 1930s, though, automobiles were already a common way to commute to and around campus. As a result, expansion plans for the campus began to centralize the automobile. Public transportation eventually disappeared. The campus trolley, called the Dinky, stopped operating in 1931, and the campus bus service was discontinued in 1972.

Plans for expanding the campus have routinely called for more parking lots and parking garages to accommodate more and more cars. Streets have been widened and major thoroughfares have been created to accommodate the greater flow of traffic. These changes allowed university employees and students to commute from even farther away, thus causing a cycle of more parking garages, even wider streets, and busier thoroughfares.

Today, the campus is over-reliant on automobiles and trucks for its transportation needs. Complaints about the shortage of parking conceal the much deeper problem that few alternatives are available for commuting to or around campus. The university has encouraged people to walk to campus or ride their bikes, but the design of the campus makes driving a car much more convenient and safe.

Cars have been shown to be the single most important source of greenhouse emissions causing global climate change (Union of Concerned Scientists). Our campus's over-reliance on gasoline-powered cars is part of that problem. But there are few alternatives to driving, forcing even environmentally conscious people to rely on their automobiles.

Effects of Inaction
Doing nothing really isn't an option for Durango University. The Young Power Plant will need to be completely overhauled or replaced within the next decade. The burning of coal and gasoline will only continue to cause global warming. Meanwhile, the costs of energy are driving up costs all around campus. If we do nothing, more and more of the university's budget will be used to pay for heating, electricity, and gasoline. These additional costs will either be passed along to students or they will lead to cuts in salaries, services, and staff across campus. We also recognize that our own reputation is at stake as other universities take the lead in the move to renewable and sustainable energy sources.

Durango University's Green Campus Program has been effective so far on a smaller scale, but we are ready to make the kinds of large-scale changes that will be needed for a sustainable future.

Questions and Exercises

1. Find a problem on your campus, in your workplace, or in your community that you believe needs to be addressed, such as commuting, health, or safety. Using the mapping techniques discussed in this chapter, map out the causes of that problem. Then, map out the effects of not taking action.

2. For the problem you mapped out in Exercise 1, outline three Current Situation sections that follow the three approaches discussed in this chapter (causal, effects, narrative). Which approach would be most effective for the readers of this Current Situation section? How does your choice of approach influence how the readers will respond to your subject and purpose?

3. Following your work in Exercises 1 and 2, write a two-page Current Situation section in which you describe the problem, its causes, and its effects.

4. Locate a proposal on the Internet that includes a substantial Current Situation section. What are some ways the writers use logical reasoning or examples to support their arguments? Identify specific examples where the writers use reasoning (if–then, cause–effect, either–or). Identify different kinds of examples used in the document. Can you find places where the writers need to use better reasoning to support their points? Where might some examples help illustrate their claims?

5. Using the proposal from Exercise 4, recreate the problem–cause and problem–effects maps that may have been used to write these sections. In other words, place the problem in the middle of a sheet of paper. Then, map out the causes you see in the Current Situation section of the proposal. Map out the effects that the proposal identifies.

6. Look at the food choices available on your campus or at your workplace. Write a one-page Current Situation section in which you describe the current status of the food (healthy or not) where you learn and work. What is the problem with the current food choices? What are some of the causes and effects of that problem? Remember to blame change, not people, in your description of the current situation.

7. The Current Situation sections for the Cool Campus proposal is still rather rough. How would you change the section to make it stronger or more persuasive? Are the writers missing anything you would add? Write a memo/e-mail to the Cool Campus writing team in which you suggest improvements to their Current Situation section.

Overview

This chapter discusses how to write project plans in proposals and grants. The chapter will meet the following objectives:

1. Discuss the purpose and importance of the Project Plan section.

2. Illustrate how to set a top rank objective and secondary objectives.

3. Show how to answer the "how question" by mapping a solution.

4. Show how to invent and organize the plan.

5. Discuss the importance of answering the "why questions" in the plan.

6. Illustrate the writing of the Project Plan section.

7. Comment on how to describe a research methodology.

The Importance of the Project Plan Section

A thorough description of the project plan is the heart of any successful proposal, including grant proposals. A proposal's Project Plan section—sometimes called the *Approach, Methodology, Project Plan, Research Program,* and *Solution,* among other titles—typically offers a detailed step-by-step process you will follow to solve the problem or take advantage of the opportunity. When describing your plan, you are going to tell the readers *how* the problem should be solved and *why* the problem should be solved that way. You will also identify the *deliverables,* the tangible results of your proposed plan.

When writing the Project Plan section, the hardest task you face is the creation of something new. In other words, the project you are proposing does not currently exist, so you need to look into the future and use your imagination to see your plan in action. In some cases, writing the Project Plan section might mean simply adapting a previous plan to the new situation. In other cases, writing this section will require the invention of a whole new product, organization, or approach from the ground up. That is why writing the Project Plan section can be exciting and challenging—and also frustrating. In this chapter, you will learn how to avoid some of that frustration by setting objectives, answering the *how* and *why* questions, and writing a well-organized plan that will attract your readers.

Refining Objectives for the Project Plan Section

In Chapter 3, you learned how to set objectives for your proposal or grant, including a *top rank objective*. Now that you are working on the Project Plan section for your proposal, you should revisit and refine your understanding of these objectives.

Earlier, you were primarily concerned about *your* objectives. Now you should look closely at your readers' objectives to determine the key places where your needs and their needs line up. You need to sharpen your top rank objective and then establish a list of two to five *secondary objectives* that you and your readers' can agree upon.

Start by listing out the client's or funding source's objectives. You can find their objectives in a couple different places:

- **The Request for Proposals**—Clients and funding sources will often spell out their objectives in the RFP. Look for key words, like *goal, aims, targets, ends, intentions, purpose,* and of course *objectives.*
- **The Point of Contact**—When communicating with the POC, listen carefully for any objectives that are priorities or didn't appear in the RFP. For example, the POC might say something like "Above all, here are the three things we need accomplished." These kinds of verbal objectives may or may not be listed in the RFP.

Now, merge together your original list of objectives with your readers' objectives to create one set of objectives for the project. In almost all cases, it is wise to use the readers' words where possible to phrase to your plan's objectives. By using their words, you will demonstrate to them that they are getting what they asked for.

When you have merged your objectives with your readers' objectives, you will have written down a top rank objective and a list of two to five secondary objectives. Now, you can use these objectives to help you design the project. Then, these objectives will be inserted directly into your Project Plan section, usually early in the section. These stated objectives are the goals that your project will be designed to achieve.

Refining Objectives for the Overture Designs Project

Formally and informally, Overture Designs had already furnished Lisa Miller with a list of objectives that her plan would need to meet. The original RFP provided a clear idea of the plan's top rank objective when it stated that the plan should "manage the physical growth of [Overture's] architectural design operations." This top rank objective, Lisa noted, was the antithesis of the problem— lack of office space—that she had already discussed in the Current Situation section.

FIGURE 5.1
Objectives Worksheet

Objectives for the Proposal's Plan
Our top rank objective objective is to manage the physical growth of Overture's architectural design operation. While meeting this primary objective, we should also strive to meet the following secondary objectives:

- Minimize disruption to Overture's current operations.
- Minimize costs, so the firm will preserve financial flexibility.
- Retain Overture's current office on Michigan Avenue.
- Foster a dynamic workplace that will be appealing to Overture's architects and staff.

A couple secondary objectives also stood out in the RFP. For one thing, the RFP mentioned that the plan should "cause the least disruption to our current operations." The RFP also mentioned cost, giving Lisa the impression that a less expensive solution would strongly appeal to the decision makers at Overture.

Looking over her notes from her meeting with Grant Moser, Lisa further identified a few other secondary objectives:

- She sensed that the clients wanted to find a way to retain Overture's award-winning Michigan Avenue office, even though they had reluctantly conceded that their office space shortage might require them to relocate.
- Another unstated secondary objective Lisa picked up from Mr. Moser was the client's wish to avoid overextending the firm's revenues. Mr. Moser seemed to suggest that the Chicago architectural market would not always be this strong, so the firm did not want to chain itself to an expensive office that would be a burden when the market weakened.
- A final secondary objective, Lisa noted, was the desire to maintain high employee morale at Overture. In her Current Situation section, she had pointed out that employee morale would suffer if Overture did not address the office space problem. On the other hand, the employees also seemed resistant to relocating the office to the suburbs. Maintaining morale would be an important objective, Lisa felt, even though the RFP and Mr. Moser had not mentioned it directly.

On a worksheet, Lisa wrote down her top rank objective and secondary objectives (Figure 5.1). Where possible, she tried to rephrase these objectives in positive terms that implied action and progress.

As you will notice, Lisa's objectives are all somewhat abstract. They are not solutions to the problem. Rather, they are milestones that any successful plan would be able to meet. This simple act of identifying objectives creates some boundaries for a potential solution while providing a method for determining which plans are suitable and which are not.

Answering the *How* Question

With the objectives set, we are faced with a question that has followed us since we started the proposal writing process: *How* are we going to solve the problem or take advantage of the opportunity? *How* are we going to achieve the top rank objective and secondary objectives? One way to answer the *how* question is to begin mapping out a solution on your computer screen or a sheet of paper. In the last chapter, you learned how to map out the current situation for the readers. We can use this same mapping technique to invent a plan for solving the problem.

To begin, it is important to recognize that objectives are met when people take specific steps to reach them. A plan is like a roadmap of steps that will take us from the current situation to a preferable situation in the future. So, when mapping out the solution to a problem, you want to identify all the steps, some larger and some smaller, that will allow you to meet the goals you have set for yourself.

Step 1: Identify a Possible Solution to the Problem

To begin the mapping process, you first need to identify a solution that might achieve the top rank objective and secondary objectives you have identified. Fortunately, while writing the Current Situation section, you more than likely will identify one or two possible solutions that might work.

On the first try, you do not need to identify the right solution. You might even list a few possible solutions. Then, you can map them out separately, seeing which one best meets your top rank objective and secondary objectives.

Step 2: Map Out a Possible Solution

As we discussed in the last chapter, mapping allows you and a team of others to highlight the logic behind your ideas. In this case, we can use mapping as a logical method to construct the steps in a plan:

1. Place your most promising solution in the center of your computer screen or a piece of paper. Circle it. (When working with a team, you'll find that a whiteboard is an especially useful tool.)
2. Ask yourself and your team, "What are the two to five major steps needed to make this solution a reality?"
3. Write down those major steps around the solution, circle them, and connect them to the solution (Figure 5.2).
4. Map each major step separately. Ask yourself or your team what minor steps are needed to make each major step a reality.

As you map further out, each level of the plan should be supported by levels of smaller steps. For example, let us say one of your major steps is to "collect information." Some smaller steps connected to this major step might be "survey client's customers," "interview client," and "study client's marketing plan."

FIGURE 5.2

Mapping the Solution

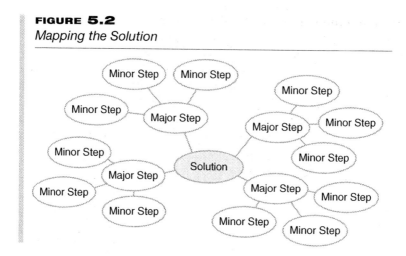

Each of these smaller steps might have further substeps attached to them. The step "survey client's customers" might branch out with even smaller steps like "create survey," "secure a mailing list," and "administer user-test survey."

Of course, you and your team could probably keep mapping out indefinitely, identifying even the minutest steps that might be required. However, there comes a point in the mapping process when you begin generating too much detail. When you begin identifying steps that probably will not be mentioned in the proposal, it is time to stop.

During the mapping process, you will often find yourself and your team coming up with steps that might never have occurred to you otherwise. This added creativity is the advantage of the mapping process. Because you are working visually and spatially, not linearly, your mind can more freely develop new ideas.

A rule of thumb, again, is to try to limit your plan to five or fewer major steps. A plan that includes too many major steps will become unmanageable for the readers, because it will force them to wade through a seemingly never-ending list of tasks. When you are finished mapping, if your map of the solution includes more than five major steps, consider whether some of the less-significant major steps could be consolidated with one of the other major steps. If consolidation will not work, then you should sort the major steps into two or three larger *phases* that bundle larger steps together.

The Importance of an Evaluation Step

One step that should appear in almost all proposals is an *outcomes assessment* or *evaluation phase,* in which the results of the project are assessed after completion. The purpose of an evaluation step (i.e., customer satisfaction surveys, product testing, or impartial evaluators) is to reassure the clients or a funding source that your work met the objectives listed in the proposal. The strongest outcomes assessment tools yield quantifiable ways of measuring whether the project was a success. In most cases, the evaluation step is the last step in the plan.

In grant proposals, usually the evaluation step includes the names of two or more impartial outside reviewers who will look over the project when it is completed. These reviewers typically write a report back to the funding source, and they usually receive an honorarium, which is paid for out of the grant budget.

Step 3: Review Your Top Rank Objective and Secondary Objectives

When you are finished mapping, look back at the objectives you identified earlier. Does your mapped solution meet those objectives? Are there any objectives, especially secondary objectives, that are not being met? When reviewing your objectives, you may find yourself adding some new major and minor steps to your map. In some cases, you may cross out major or minor steps because they go beyond the needs specified by the objectives. You may even find that your map does not meet your objectives at all. In these cases, try mapping out another solution to see if another plan will achieve them.

In the end, mapping will allow you to answer the *how* question. Your map of the solution illustrates roughly how you are going to achieve the top rank objective and secondary objectives you identified, thus solving the problem or taking advantage of the opportunity.

Mapping a Project Plan for the Overture Proposal

Lisa Miller knew that there were several possible solutions to Overture's office space problem. However, her company, Insight Systems, could only offer Overture one particular type of solution, a local area network (LAN) and intranet that would allow Overture's employees to telecommute from home.

To help her rough out a solution, Lisa called a planning meeting that included other engineers at her company. She gave each of them a copy of her proposal's Current Situation section, which they read and discussed. Then, on a whiteboard, she wrote "Telecommuting" and circled it. With a marker in hand, she asked the engineers to help her identify the major steps needed to develop a telecommuting system at a company like Overture.

As the group brainstormed, Lisa wrote on the whiteboard some of the major steps needed to achieve that solution. Around the solution, she wrote, "Build computer network," "Study telecommuting needs," "Train Overture employees," and "Conduct outcomes assessment." She was already beginning to visualize the plan through the map developed with her team (Figure 5.3).

Once they had roughed out the major steps, Lisa and the other engineers began mapping further to identify the minor steps required to achieve each major step. For instance, under "Train employees," they wrote smaller steps like "Offer workshops," "Develop training materials," and "Create a help desk for new telecommuters." Their map began to fill the sheet of paper.

After mapping the plan with her team of engineers, Lisa looked back at the top rank objective and secondary objectives she listed out before (Figure 5.1). For the most part, she felt their mapped plan was meeting those objectives. Even in its

FIGURE 5.3

A Map of the Telecommuting Solution

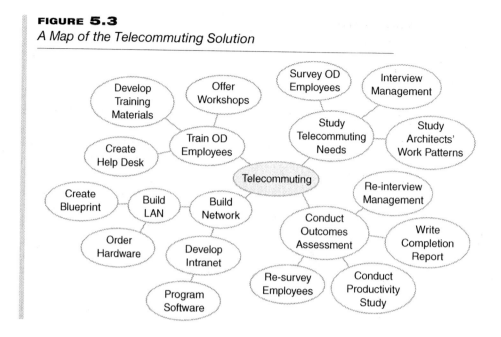

rough form, their plan seemed to show how Overture could manage its office growth while minimizing disruption, reducing costs, and fostering a dynamic workplace. Best of all, their plan would allow Overture to keep its Michigan Avenue office—an unstated objective that she thought would be appealing to the readers. Lisa was ready to begin organizing and drafting her Project Plan section.

Organizing the Project Plan Section

After mapping out the logic of your plan, you need to arrange the major and minor steps into a pattern that the readers will understand. Sometimes, it is helpful to think of the Project Plan section as a recipe for solving the problem. For instance, baking a cherry pie requires four major steps: (1) make the cherry pie filling, (2) prepare the crust, (3) pour the filling into the crust, and (4) bake the pie. Once you have partitioned the process into larger steps, you can describe the minor steps under each of these major steps. Instructions for making the pie filling would require some smaller steps like (a) combine cherries, sugar, and cornstarch, (b) heat mixture until thickened and bubbly, (c) cook for one more minute, and (d) remove from heat and allow to cool.

Organizing your proposal's Project Plan section is a similar process. List the major steps in the order they will be followed. Then, fill in the minor steps under each of these major steps. You should begin to see an outline of your Project Plan section emerge out of the logical map you created earlier.

For example, Lisa Miller might outline her plan as shown in Figure 5.4. In this outline she organizes the major steps into the order in which they will be taken. Of course, like any outline, Lisa's description of the plan is still rather crude and skeletal.

FIGURE 5.4
Outline of Office Space Solution for Overture

Our Plan: Telecommuting

In order to provide suitable working space for Overture's employees, we propose a program that allows some employees to telecommute from home. Implementation of this program would require a procedure that includes the following four steps: studying telecommuting options, building a telecommuting local area network (LAN), training employees in telecommuting strategies, and assessing the telecommuting program.

Step One: **Study telecommuting options.**
- Survey employees to determine work patterns.
- Interview management to determine most suitable telecommuting system.
- Research architects' work patterns.

Step Two: **Build telecommuting network.**
- Develop blueprint for hardware.
- Build hardware structure for LAN system.
- Code intranet software.

Step Three: **Train employees in telecommuting strategies.**
- Offer telecommuting workshops.
- Create a help desk for telecommuting employees.
- Develop training materials.

Step Four: **Conduct outcomes assessment.**
- Survey employees and management.
- Study employee productivity.
- Write completion report offering recommendations for improvements to telecommuting system.

Nevertheless, turning the logical map into an outline allowed her to see the basic structure of the plan. Now Lisa could begin putting some muscle on that skeleton.

Answering the *Why* Questions

When studying a proposal, the readers' overriding question is always *why*? *Why* should we do it this way? *Why* is this step necessary? *Why* not try doing it a different way? As the proposal writer, your job is to answer these *why* questions as you explain the various steps in your plan. Answers to the *why* questions are the

FIGURE 5.5
A Why Table

Major Step:	Why?
Minor Steps • 1. 2. 3. 4.	**Why?** 1. 2. 3. 4.
Deliverables?	

muscles that hold the plan together. One way of developing answers to the readers' *why* questions is to chart them out in a Why table like the one in Figure 5.5.

In this table, write down one of your major steps on the top line and offer a short answer to the *why* question. Then, write down the minor steps that support this major step and provide answers to the *why* questions next to each smaller step. Finally, looking over the contents of the table, ask yourself whether there are any deliverables that will result from these steps.

Deliverables are the tangible results of each major step. They are what you will "deliver" to the readers as your project progresses and after it is completed. In some cases deliverables are finished products of some kind (e.g., a machine, a building, a software package, or some noticeable physical change). In other cases, a deliverable might be some form of communication to the readers (e.g., a completion report, a progress report, or even just a regular summary at a meeting). Whenever possible, though, you should try to come up with some kind of deliverable for each major step. After all, your clients should be able to observe the tangible results of your work as you finish each step. They should feel as though they are receiving something they could see or touch in return for their investment in your project.

In grant proposals, clearly identifying deliverables is one of the tricks of a professional grant writer's trade. Grant writers know that funding sources don't like to fund projects that evaporate when the money runs out. By showing the reviewers that each major step in the project leads to a tangible deliverable of some kind, you will show them that their money will be used to create something that lasts beyond the grant itself.

When you are finished with the *why* tables, you will have created the basis for a well-reasoned argument. When you turn these *why* tables into paragraphs in your Project Plan section, you will be answering both of the readers' main questions (i.e., *how* and *why*). Also, you will have specified the tangible results of your work. To illustrate, Figure 5.6 shows how Lisa Miller might fill out one of these *why* tables.

The advantage of a *why* table is that it helps you invent answers to the *how* and the *why* questions that the readers will be asking of your plan. Essentially, each of the *why* tables tells the readers *how* you are going to achieve a particular part of the plan, *why* you are taking particular steps, and *what* deliverables will

FIGURE 5.6
A Why Table for Overture

Major Step: Study telecommuting options	**Why?** To identify specific workplace needs of employees and management
Minor Steps	**Why?**
1. Survey employees	To determine which employees might be eligible for telecommuting and why
2. Interview management	To understand management's strategies to adapt telecommuting system to management's needs
3. Research architects' work patterns	To determine what telecommuting system would best suit the needs of the principal employees of the firm

Deliverables? A report that summarizes the results of our research and describes the best telecommuting system for Overture's needs

result. Of course, you still need to track down sources, statistics, or facts that support your answers to the *why* questions. But when you have finished filling out the why tables, you are ready to start writing your plan into its final form.

Writing the Project Plan Section

In Chapter 4, you learned that each body section in a proposal typically has three parts: an opening, a body, and a closing. All three of these parts are found in a good Project Plan section. An *opening* is needed to tell the readers the purpose and main point of your Project Plan section. The *body* of the Project Plan section will describe the steps in your plan. And the *closing* will round off the Project Plan section by summarizing some of the deliverables you are promising the readers.

The Opening of the Project Plan Section

Like the opening of any larger section in a document, the opening of the Project Plan section is designed to set a framework for the information in the body of the section. But the opening of the Project Plan section is especially important, because here is where your readers need to make the critical transition from your description of the *situation* to your description of the *plan*.

This transition is difficult, because the Current Situation section sometimes sets a negative tone. After all, in your Current Situation section, you just told the readers that they have a problem and that some rather unpleasant consequences will occur if they avoid taking action. Even in a Current Situation section that describes a golden opportunity, you will probably close your discussion by mentioning some of the negative effects of not taking advantage of the opportunity. The Project Plan section, on the other hand, needs to be as optimistic as possible. From this point forward in the proposal, you will leave the problem and its consequences behind, concentrating instead on the advantages and benefits of solving the problem a particular way.

Essentially, your opening paragraph in the Project Plan section needs to shift the readers from a negative viewpoint to an optimistic one. To negotiate this tricky transition, the opening of the Project Plan section should make most, if not all, of the following important moves:

- **Transition**—signals to the readers that you are starting your discussion of the plan
- **Statement of the Purpose of the Section**—tells the readers that the purpose of this section is to provide a detailed step-by-step plan
- **Statement of the Plan's Objectives**—lists the objectives that any successful plan would be able to meet
- **Naming of the Overall Solution**—in a sentence or phrase, identifies your overall strategy for solving the problem
- **Forecast of the Plan**—briefly lists the major steps of your plan

Of course, these moves need not be made in this order, and some of them might not be made at all. However, if the opening paragraph or paragraphs of your Project Plan section accounts for these moves, you will have established a clear framework for the detailed plan that follows.

To illustrate, let us return to Lisa Miller's proposal for Overture Designs. As she drafts the opening of her Project Plan section, she tries to address each of the opening moves separately. For her transition, she writes, "Let us now turn to our strategy for managing Overture's limited office space." It's a crude transition, but it will work for now. She then writes, "The purpose of this section is to describe a plan for providing suitable working space for Overture." Then, she states her main point: "We propose that Overture implement a telecommuting program that allows employees to work at home, thus freeing up space in the current office." And finally, she forecasts her plan: "We will follow a four-part process that studies Overture's telecommuting options, develops a computer network to facilitate telecommuting, trains employees to be effective telecommuters, and assesses the outcomes of the telecommuting program." Putting all these sentences together, she writes the text shown in Figure 5.7.

In Lisa's opening to the Project Plan section, all of the *opening moves* are accounted for. The heading "Our Plan: Maintaining Flexibility through Telecommuting" signals the transition into the discussion of the plan. In the first paragraph of the Project Plan section, she tackles these issues:

- She identifies the subject of the section (the plan).
- She states the purpose of the section (to offer a plan for managing Overture's limited office space).
- She expresses the section's main point (telecommuting is the solution).
- She forecasts the structure of the plan (four steps).

In addition to these moves, the opening also states the objectives that any successful plan should be able to meet, establishing a set of criteria that the readers can use to measure the success of the plan that will follow.

FIGURE 5.7

An Example Opening of a Project Plan Section

Our Plan: Maintaining Flexibility through Telecommuting

Management of Overture's limited office space requires a plan that allows the company to grow while maintaining financial flexibility in the quickly evolving Chicago market. Therefore, we believe a successful solution must meet the following objectives:

- Minimize disruption to Overture's current operations
- Minimize costs, preserving Overture's financial flexibility
- Retain Overture's current office on Michigan Avenue
- Foster a dynamic workplace that will be appealing to Overture's architects and staff

To meet these objectives, we propose to collaborate with Overture toward developing a telecommunication network that allows selected employees to work at home a few days a week. The primary advantage of telecommuting is that it frees up office space for employees who need to be in the office for the day; yet, it avoids overextending Overture's financial resources during a period of significant growth.

Our plan will be implemented in four major phases. First, we will study Overture's telecommuting options. Second, we will develop a computer network that will allow selected employees to telecommute from a home office. Third, we will train Overture's employees to be effective telecommuters. And finally, we will assess the outcomes of the telecommuting program. With this program in place, Overture will enjoy a more flexible workplace with even more room to grow.

The Body of the Project Plan Section

The body of the Project Plan section is where you are going to describe your plan and tell the readers why you believe the problem should be solved a particular way. The Project Plan section's body will be built around the major steps you identified earlier. For example, if you have four steps in your plan, the body of your Project Plan section will likely have four major parts. Each part will describe one of the steps in detail.

Writing each of these parts should not be difficult at this point. Start by looking over the why table that describes the first step in your plan. State the major action up front and then support that major action with a discussion of the minor steps needed to achieve it. As you describe these major and minor steps for the readers, flesh out the discussion by answering those *why* questions that the readers will be asking at this point. Finally, at the end of the discussion of each step, you might discuss some of the deliverables that will be the end results of this part of the plan.

To illustrate, Figure 5.8 shows how one of Lisa's why tables (shown in Figure 5.6) can be developed into part of her plan. This description of the plan's first step is

FIGURE 5.8
Example Description of a Step

Phase One: Analyze Overture's Telecommuting Needs

Before moving forward, we believe it is important to analyze the specific workplace needs of Overture's employees and management. This analysis would allow us to work closely with Overture's management to develop a telecommuting program that fits the unique demands that a dynamic architecture firm like yours would put on such a system.

In this phase, our objective would be to collect as much information and data as possible, so the transition to telecommunication would be smooth and hassle-free.

- First, we would conduct thorough surveys of your employees to determine which people might be willing and able to telecommute. These surveys will tell us about their work habits and the way in which a telecommuting system might be adapted to their needs.

- Second, we would interview Overture's management. These interviews will help us tailor the telecommuting system to your corporate culture and your managers' specific needs.

- Third, we will conduct empirical studies to identify and understand the office dynamics at Overture. These empirical studies will help us replicate those office dynamics in a virtual environment.

We estimate this phase will require thirty days. At the end of that time period, we will submit a report to you in which we analyze and discuss the findings of our surveys, interviews, and empirical studies. In this report, we will also describe the various telecommuting options available and recommend the option we believe best suits the needs of Overture.

---

rather concise. Lisa could expand it considerably by describing in greater detail how her company will conduct and analyze the surveys, interviews, and empirical studies. Or, she might spend more time answering the clients' *why* questions in greater depth.

In the end, though, the length of any part of the plan—and the plan altogether—depends on the amount of information your clients will require to say yes to your ideas. If your clients are unfamiliar with you, your techniques, or your field of expertise, you may need to spend more time explaining your methods and the reasoning behind your plan. If your clients are familiar with you and your methods, the description of the plan can be more concise and to the point. In Lisa's case, she decided to keep the discussion of each step concise because the RFP imposed a fifteen-page limit on the pre-proposal. Also, she needed to save room for the other sections of the proposal.

The text in Figure 5.8 also demonstrates how answers to the clients' *why* questions can be interwoven with the steps in the plan. As you compose your plan, you should imagine your readers asking you "why?" as you describe each aspect of the plan. If you can answer these questions while you describe the steps, you will help the readers understand the rationale for your plan. Meanwhile, you will immediately address any potential objections the readers might have toward your methods.

Finally, Lisa also mentioned a deliverable (a report) that would be provided to Overture when this step is completed. Not all steps need to include deliverables, but if possible, you should try to come up with ways to deliver something tangible to the readers at the end of each major phase. They will feel they are receiving something concrete for their money. Clients want updates and information. They want to feel like they are part of the plan, not just the recipient. By identifying deliverables clearly, Lisa hoped to bring the clients into the process as active participants.

The Closing of the Project Plan Section

In the closing of the Project Plan section, you should not offer any new information to the readers. You should summarize the section's major points and stress the importance of your plan. You might also summarize some of the major deliverables you promised your clients in the body of the plan. Your aim in the closing is to concisely round off the discussion, giving the readers an overall view of your plan and the tangible results that will come about if they say yes to the proposal. Some proposal writers use the Project Plan section's closing to show that their plan satisfies the objectives mentioned in the opening of the section.

The closing of the Project Plan section is not the proposal's conclusion, so this is not the place to pour on the persuasion. The closing merely puts an endpoint on your description of the plan and prepares the readers to make a transition into a discussion of your company's or organization's qualifications.

Developing a Project Timeline

Your proposal's Project Plan section should describe a clear project timeline. To create a timeline, each major step should include the date when that step will be completed. A timeline provides your clients or a funding source with milestones to track your progress.

To develop a timeline, start at the project's completion date and work backward toward its starting date. Assign a specific date to each major step in the project plan. Specialists in time management call this "backward planning." Scheduling backward will help you scale the project's timeline to fit the completion date. By working backward from the completion date, you will avoid the temptation to be unrealistic about the time requirements of the later steps (and often the most important steps) in your project plan.

Even if you aren't exactly sure about dates, you should include them. Real dates will make your project seem more realistic, and they will give the readers a clear sense of when you expect the project to start and be completed. If, for some reason, you are unable to start the project on time, the dates on the timeline can be adjusted accordingly. In these situations, you will need to discuss the new dates with your clients or the funding source.

Larger proposals and grants often use graphics to illustrate the project timeline. You might include a list of dates and events or a chart that shows important dates and the major steps that will be completed by those dates. Gantt charts, like the one shown in Chapter 10, are especially popular in proposals, because project management software programs can draw them automatically.

A Comment on Research Methodologies

If you are writing a research proposal, especially one aimed at securing grant funding, the process described in this chapter might not seem exactly suitable to your needs. But when you recognize that a Methodology section is really just a description of a plan, you will see that this process actually works quite well.

A Methodology section in a research proposal describes how and why a subject will be studied in a particular way. This part of your proposal needs to do more than simply describe the procedure of your study; it should also tell the readers *why* your approach is the most appropriate for this subject (Penrose and Katz 1998, p. 45). After all, the reviewers of your proposal will scrutinize your methods closely to determine whether they will yield useful results. If you are using a methodology adapted from other studies, you should carefully describe and cite it. When inventing a new methodology, you need to justify your decision to blaze a new path.

In a research proposal, the methods section often begins with a list of objectives that the study will strive to achieve. In most research proposals, this list of objectives is specific about the kinds of quantifiable results that would mark whether the research project was a success. Indeed, much like a business proposal, the objectives of a scientific methodology establish the aims of the study and the benchmarks for success.

A Methodology section should define the subject that will be studied and the conditions under which it will be observed. If the subjects are animals, insects, places, or people, the Methodology section should be clear about their characteristics and the environments and circumstances (e.g., time, temperature) in which the subjects will be studied.

After defining the subject, a Methodology section usually offers a step-by-step description of the process that will be used to study the subject. The description should be exact and complete, mentioning any materials, tools, formulas, and calculations that will be used during the study. Essentially, the description should be exact enough that other researchers could replicate the study and calculations to test its results.

Methodology sections often close with a discussion of the analysis tools that will be used to study the data generated by the experiment or observation. Any statistical procedures or software packages that will be used to process the data should be mentioned here. Some researchers even mention the types of computers that will be used to analyze the results of the study. That way, other researchers can exactly replicate the analysis of the results.

In most cases, Methodology sections in research proposals are written in passive voice, because who did what is often not important. For example, the passive sentence "The herons will be observed for 30 days from April 10 to May 10" would work just fine, because it is probably not necessary to say "Mandy Jervis will observe the herons from April 10 to May 10." Nevertheless, methodologies are increasingly being written in active voice, especially from a "first person" perspective (e.g., "We will measure the PCB level of the lake every two days at 8:00 A.M."). Active voice reinserts the researchers into the study, reminding the readers that the researchers were part of the experiment and may have influenced the results.

Researchers should always remember that the Methodology section is the most scrutinized part of any funding proposal, because it establishes the validity of any results that will be generated by the research. If the proposal's reviewers have any doubts about the methodology of a study, they will more than likely choose not to fund the project. After all, a questionable methodology will invariably lead to questionable results. Consequently, it is crucial that the Methodology section answer all of the reviewers' *how* and *why* questions in exact detail.

Looking Ahead

The Project Plan section is the heart of your proposal. It explains *how* the problem should be solved and *why* it should be solved a particular way. Most proposal writers see the Project Plan section as the most challenging part of the proposal-writing process. From here, they usually find, the writing is a bit easier. In the next chapter, we will discuss the writing of the Qualifications section. There is definitely a sense of relief that comes when the plan is finished; however, a good plan is only as strong as the people who will put it into action.

CASE STUDY Developing the Project Plan for the Cool Campus Project

Describing the current situation at Durango University was hard work for the Cool Campus team. As they began to better understand the problem, though, they grew increasingly eager to come up with a solution that would solve it. So, when they turned to developing the Project Plan section, they were energized. "Now it's time to start figuring out what we need to do," Tim said as the group began brainstorming solutions.

George picked up the marker and stood at the whiteboard. "OK, let's go back over our objectives.

What would we like our plan to achieve? What goals would any successful plan need to meet?"

Anne said, "Earlier, we said our top rank objective was to develop a comprehensive strategic plan for converting the campus to sustainable forms of energy."

George wrote that down.

Karen spoke up, "It also seems important that we get people talking about energy issues on campus and global warming. Right now, it seems like a lot of people simply aren't talking about it."

"I agree," George said, and wrote "Begin conversations about energy and global warming" on the whiteboard.

After a pause, Calvin added, "I would add to Karen's point by stressing that people in the local community need to be involved. Speaking as a member of the community, I can honestly say that working with this group is the first time I've ever talked about environmental issues with someone from the university."

"Good point," said George, as he kept scribbling. "We definitely need to begin a dialogue between the university and the community."

Anne added, "One of my major concerns is that our plan will get tossed out after a couple of years. We need to think about the future and create a plan that will guide future decisions. We need something that will last, or people will simply lose interest in it or forget about it."

"Umm-hmm," George agreed as he wrote. "We certainly need a plan that will be realistic and useful in the long run, or all of our efforts will be wasted."

"I know we want to emphasize our own campus," Tim said, "but it would be cool if we came up with something that could help other campuses figure out what to do about converting to renewable energy as well."

"That's a good point, Tim," Anne responded. "Plus, if we could figure out how our project can be used beyond our campus, that would make it much more attractive to the Tempest Foundation."

"OK, this list of objectives looks pretty good so far," said George, as he finished adding, "Create plan that will help other campuses" to his list. "Now comes the hard part. What kind of project would allow us to achieve all these objectives?"

Calvin spoke. "I've been giving that a great amount of thought. Last year, I participated in something called a 'charrette' that was used to do urban planning to renovate a neighborhood in Albuquerque. We could probably do something like that here."

Karen looked puzzled. "A charrette? I've never heard of that before."

"Yeah," Calvin replied. "It's an urban planning tool that brings all the stakeholders into the planning process. Everyone is invited, like people from the community, administrators, customers, business owners, and politicians. They get together for a night or a weekend and work in design teams to develop their own plans for a neighborhood. That way, everyone gets input into the process. In Albuquerque, I was amazed at some of the creative ideas that came out of the charrette."

Anne said, "Something like that would really encourage people to buy into the process. Here on campus, we usually meet resistance when we just make decisions without input from the community. Something like a charrette would allow us to get people involved at the grassroots level."

Karen was still skeptical. "But how are a bunch of regular people going to do urban planning, especially when they don't know much about how to do it?"

"In Albuquerque," replied Calvin, "urban planners were hired to facilitate the meeting. They gave us all the information we needed and explained the process. Then, we worked all afternoon on our plans. That evening, they had us present our design plans to the whole room. There were about a hundred people there. We all discussed and debated the best ideas. Then, we voted on the best plans. It was very exciting to see all those people decide together how they wanted to change their own neighborhood. People got really excited."

Tim asked, "But what happened then? Who followed up? Who wrote the final plan?"

"That's the cool part," said Calvin. "The urban planning firm took all those plans and comments back to their office. In a month, they called a meeting to present a draft of their strategic plan for rebuilding the neighborhood. I thought it was amazing how they took the ideas of amateurs

FIGURE 5.9

Mapping the Cool Campus Project Plan

and turned them into professional drawings and schematics."

Anne said, "I think this charrette idea sounds great. I really like how it gets people involved from the community."

Karen added, "OK, I was skeptical, but it sounds like this charrette idea might work."

George wrote in the center of the board, "Use charrette to develop the Cool Campus Strategic Plan." He circled it and said, "All right, what are the two to five major steps we need to take to achieve this objective?"

The group began brainstorming by mapping out their project plan on the whiteboard (Figure 5.9). Some of the larger steps included, "Gather information for charrette," "Host charrette," "Hire an urban planning firm," and "Present the strategic plan." They also agreed that a steering committee would need to be formed to oversee the whole process. The Steering Committee would also be in charge of hiring the urban planning firm.

They were amazed at how quickly their plan grew in depth and detail. Their map of the Project Plan showed their answers to the *how* questions and explained how their plan would work.

They then turned to answering the *why* questions by filling out why tables for each major step of their Project Plan. George drew the why tables on the whiteboard, and they filled them in. They wrote down deliverables for each major step. Figure 5.10 shows a why table for one of the major steps, "Host charrette."

An hour went by quickly, and a few of them needed to leave, so George and Calvin agreed to draft the Project Plan section for the grant proposal. They worked on it for a couple weeks and

FIGURE 5.10

A Why Table for a Major Step

Major Step: Host charrette to allow members of the community to participate in developing Cool Campus Strategic Plan	**Why?** To involve people collectively in planning process and gather the best ideas available
Minor Steps	**Why?**
1. Reserve ballroom in Student Union	We need plenty of room to work and big tables
2. Order food for participants	To encourage people to commit to project
3. Form diverse design teams	To bring out a wide variety of ideas and experiences
4. Present plans to audience	To give people a chance to comment and pull the best ideas from a variety of plans

Deliverables? Design will be placed on the Cool Campus website for public viewing. A podcast will be placed on the website. A progress report will be sent to the Tempest Foundation that shows the charrette in action (lots of pictures needed).

then e-mailed the team a draft, which is shown in Figure 5.11 (pages 95–97).

"Wow," Tim wrote back. "This is amazing. We just pulled this stuff out of thin air. It looks great!"

Anne replied, "That's what proposals are all about. They give us a chance to be creative and come up with something new. We are definitely finished with the hard part."

Questions and Exercises

1. Find a proposal or grant on the Internet, and analyze its Project Plan section. Do the writers of the proposal provide a step-by-step process for achieving some stated (or unstated) objectives? Do they answer the *how* questions and the *why* questions in each part of their plan? Do they identify some deliverables at the end of each step or the end of the plan? Write a memo to your instructor in which you evaluate the effectiveness of this Project Plan section. Offer recommendations for improvement.

2. Using the proposal you found for Exercise 1, reconstruct the map the writers may have used to invent this section. Put the solution in the middle of a sheet of paper. Then, map out the major and minor steps that make up their plan. Looking over this map, does their solution seem logical and reasonable? Are there any gaps in content or organization you would like to see filled? Would you write the section differently?

3. Look closely at an RFP in your area of interest. With a team, identify the top rank objective and secondary objectives that the readers would like submitted

FIGURE 5.11

A Draft of the Cool Campus Project Plan

Our Plan: A Cool Campus Charrette

Converting a college campus to renewable energy will take careful planning and time. Therefore, our primary aim is to develop a comprehensive Cool Campus Strategic Plan that will guide our campus's transformation into a net-zero carbon emission campus. To create this plan, we will host a charrette that would invite the whole community into the planning process.

A charrette is a weekend retreat, facilitated by professional urban planners, that puts citizens and stakeholders into design teams. These teams develop separate plans, drawing from their collective wisdom and their knowledge of the community. Then the urban planners use the ideas generated by these teams to create professional designs, and they present them back to the community. The advantage of a charrette is that it works from the grassroots up, drawing on the knowledge, desires, and experiences of the community, while encouraging all stakeholders to participate and buy into the project.

Our objectives in the Cool Campus Charrette would be the following:

- Develop a comprehensive Strategic Plan that would guide Durango University's efforts toward energy conservation while shaping future decisions about renovation and construction.

- Create and foster a community dialogue about renewable energy that extends beyond the campus.

- Develop a new model of campus planning that shows how other campuses can use this kind of planning to work toward converting to renewable energy sources.

Step One: Create the Cool Campus Steering Committee, May 2008
To achieve these objectives, our first action would be to create a Cool Campus Steering Committee that would be responsible for making initial decisions about the charrette.

The members of the Steering Committee would hire an urban planning firm that has experience with issues of renewable energy and facilitating charrettes. Specifically, we would look for a firm that has experience meeting LEED standards (Leadership in Energy and Environmental Design) developed by the U.S. Green Building Council.

The purpose of the Steering Committee would be to lay a solid foundation for the charrette. The members of the Steering Committee would include a range of people, including executive-level university administrators, faculty and staff, student leaders, and local citizens. We envision a planning committee of about twelve people that would meet weekly for two months until the charrette was planned and scheduled.

When the charrette is scheduled, the Steering Committee will write a report to the Tempest Foundation and the university president that describes its actions and decisions. The Steering Committee would welcome any feedback from the Tempest Foundation regarding the report.

Step Two: Create a Charrette Library and Website, July 2008
Once the urban planning firm has been hired, its first action will be to work with the Steering Committee to assemble information about the campus and identify options for renewable energy, conservation, and public transportation.

Working with librarians from Durango University, the urban planning firm will help create a library that brings together any information that might be useful during the charrette. That way, people participating in the charrette would have the necessary information already at hand. The library would include documents, books, information from websites, archival materials, and any other documents that people participating in the charrette might need. Durango University's librarians would set aside a separate room for these materials and organize them into an accessible system that is cross-referenced and electronically searchable.

With the charrette library in place, the urban planning firm will then work with Durango University's webmaster to create a website that would offer information and updates on the Cool Campus Project, as well as provide opportunities for the public to participate through weblogs and electronic bulletin boards.

FIGURE 5.11
(Continued)

Documents from the Cool Campus library would be made available through this project website. The website will be accessible through a link on Durango University's homepage.

When this step is concluded, we will have developed a library of materials that can be accessed by anyone through the Internet. We will also have created the Cool Campus website, which will serve as a forum for the public as well as an information clearinghouse.

Step Three: Host the Charrette at the Student Union, September 2008
In the Fall of 2008, we will host a weekend charrette that will bring together stakeholders and any others who might be interested in the project. We expect about a hundred people to attend, and we will reserve the Student Union's Chandler Ballroom and breakout rooms for the weekend. We will also order lunches and refreshments, so participants in the charrette can stay focused on the planning process.

At the Friday evening kickoff meeting, we will introduce the urban planning firm that will lead the charrette. Facilitators will explain the Cool Campus project, discuss how the charrette will work, and make the Cool Campus library available to participants. We will then divide into design teams of six people and let members of the teams introduce themselves to each other.

On Saturday, each design team will develop its own plan for converting the campus to renewable energy sources. Experts from the urban planning firm and the Environmental Engineering Department will work with teams to explain technological abilities and limitations, while answering any questions that might arise. The experts, however, will only serve as resources for the teams, not leaders. Our aim is to maximize the creativity of the design teams by offering guidance while not limiting their ability to be innovative.

On Sunday afternoon, each team will have two hours to finish its plan and create a PowerPoint presentation. Then each team will be asked to present its plan to the assembly. Members of the audience will be allowed to ask questions, identify the strengths of each plan, and probe any weaknesses. This Sunday meeting will be videotaped, and the urban planning team will take close notes on the proceedings. At the end of this meeting, all of the plans will be submitted to the urban planning firm.

Our expectation is that the design teams will develop plans that incorporate a variety of renewable energy sources, like wind, solar, and geothermal power, as well as offer ideas for conserving energy and improving public transportation. We will ask the design teams to develop plans that have both long-range and short-term features: (1) a long-range plan that eliminates or offsets all greenhouse gases produced on campus, and (2) a short-term plan that allows us to make immediate changes to campus that will help us conserve energy and reduce our emissions of greenhouse gases.

Ultimately, the aim of the charrette will be to draw on the collective creativity of the participants. Charrettes used for urban planning have been shown to bring out more creativity and knowledge than would be gathered by an urban planning firm alone. Moreover, charrettes like this one bring more stakeholders into the planning process, encouraging more buy-in and less resistance to change. The community participates in the planning process.

When this step is completed, we will put copies of the designs and a podcast of the Sunday meeting on our website. We will also write a progress report to the Tempest Foundation that highlights the events of the weekend.

Step Four: Presentation of the Strategic Plan, October 2008
Using the plans from the charrette, the urban planning firm will develop a comprehensive Cool Campus Strategic Plan for converting the campus to renewable forms of energy. They will also identify any limitations that might keep us from achieving the goals discussed in the charrette.

At a Saturday meeting one month after the charrette, the urban planning firm will present the draft of their Cool Campus Strategic Plan to the participants of the charrette. They will explain their version of the plan and solicit feedback from the audience. These proceedings will be videotaped, and all comments will be recorded by the university and the urban planning firm.

FIGURE 5.11

(Continued)

Our goal for this meeting will be to reach consensus among stakeholders. If the charrette process is successful, people will rally around the plan because they helped make it. When this meeting is over, we will put a copy of the design on the Cool Campus website, as well as a podcast of the meeting. We will write a progress report to the Tempest Foundation that shows and discusses the plan developed by the urban planning firm.

Step Five: Finalizing the Plan, December 2008
Using the comments from the meeting, the urban planning firm will then develop a final version of the Cool Campus Strategic Plan. The full version will be due within two months. The final plan will be submitted by President Wilson to the university's Board of Regents for consideration.

The purpose of the Cool Campus Strategic Plan will be to provide a blueprint for converting the campus to renewable energy sources while minimizing the campus's emissions of pollution and greenhouse gases. Upon approval by the Board of Regents, the Cool Campus Strategic Plan will be used to guide all future decisions about building and renovating the campus. All campus budgeting, construction, and renovation decisions will be required to satisfy the guidelines described in the Cool Campus Strategic Plan.

We will present the Cool Campus Strategic Plan to the Tempest Foundation at its January 2009 meeting. At that point, we can answer any questions and discuss our plans for implementing the plan.

Dissemination
One of our goals is to blaze a path that other universities can follow. For this reason, we will disseminate our plan through the Cool Campus website, at national conferences, and in a variety of publications. The website will make the Strategic Plan available to anyone who requests it. That way, other universities can use it to help them develop their own charrettes and strategic plans. Meanwhile, at conferences, our administrators and faculty will present the results of the charrette. These conference presentations will lead to publications in academic journals and magazines.

The Tempest Foundation will be prominently mentioned on our website and in any printed materials related to this project. At conferences and in articles, the Tempest Foundation will be warmly thanked for its support of this project.

Assessment
To assess the program, we will retain two outside evaluators who are experts in urban planning and renewable energy. We will submit their credentials for consideration and approval by the Tempest Foundation. Funds from the grant will be used to pay their expenses and an honorarium of $500 each.

The evaluators will observe all aspects of the Cool Campus Project and have full access to any participants, meetings, and materials. When the project is completed, the evaluators will write a report to the Tempest Foundation that discusses their impressions and their appraisal of our efforts.

---

proposals to achieve. Can you think of any unstated secondary objectives that are not mentioned in the RFP but might be important to the readers? After you have identified the top rank objective and secondary objectives, write a memo to your instructor in which you identify your objectives. Tell your instructor why these objectives are the ones "any reasonable plan would be able to achieve."

4. Working with a team, find a problem on your campus, at your workplace, or in your community that needs a solution. Identify some objectives that a successful solution would need to meet. Then, map out a plan to solve the problem. Carefully look over your map to determine whether your plan would be able to meet all the objectives you identified.

5. Follow up on Exercise 2 by writing a two- to three-page Project Plan section in which you answer the *how* questions and the *why* questions and identify some deliverables.

6. The Cool Campus proposal's Project Plan section still has some gaps in it. What are some major and minor steps that might still be missing? Do you think all the current steps in their map and Project Plan section are necessary? What would you do differently? Write a memo to the Cool Campus team in which you identify the strengths in their Project Plan section and make suggestions for improving it.

7. You have been asked to develop a mentoring program at your college or workplace. The current problem is that new students or employees often feel overwhelmed by the immediate onslaught of work. As a result, they often drop out or quit within a couple of months. Your task is to set some objectives, map out a solution, and write up a two-page description of your mentoring plan. Your plan should answer the *how* and *why* questions while providing some tangible deliverables.

6 | Describing Qualifications

Overview

This chapter discusses how to write the Qualifications section in a proposal or grant. The chapter will meet the following objectives:

1. Explain why Qualifications sections should be written as arguments.
2. Define the four types of Qualifications sections.
3. Show how "what makes you different makes you attractive."
4. Discuss the contents of a Qualifications section.
5. Show how to organize and compose a Qualifications section.
6. Illustrate how mapping can be used to create a persona.

The Importance of Trust

The Qualifications section occupies a sensitive place in the structure of a proposal. Your plan just energized the readers by showing them how their problem will be solved or how they are going to take advantage of an opportunity. If you are writing a grant proposal, you just finished showing them an interesting project that will make a difference in the lives of others.

Now, you want the Qualifications section to preserve that momentum as you make the transition from your description of the project plan to a discussion of the costs and benefits of that plan. A well-written Qualifications section can maintain or even build the readers' interest by showing them your strengths and capabilities. On the other hand, a poorly written Qualifications section is sure to take some of the shine off your proposal at this crucial point.

The purpose of the Qualifications section is to certify to the readers that your team, company, or organization has the personnel, experience, expertise, and facilities to carry out the plan proposed in the Project Plan section. Going a step further, the Qualifications section should also prove to the readers that you are *uniquely* qualified to take on the job. You need to show them the special qualities that set your team, company, or organization above the competition.

When writing the Qualifications section, you should remember that proposals and grants do more than offer plans and costs. They create relationships between people. By saying yes to your proposal, the readers are essentially putting faith in you. They are agreeing to trust you. Indeed, the best plan is not worth a dime if the readers do not trust your company or organization. The Qualifications section is the place in the proposal where you can best build your readers' sense of faith in you and your abilities.

Readers of proposals put great emphasis on the contents of the Qualifications section. As the writer, you should take advantage of their interest at this crucial moment in the proposal by persuading them you are the right people for the job. In this chapter, you will learn to go beyond standardized descriptions of qualifications. You will learn how to shape the Qualifications section into a dynamic component of the proposal that keeps the positive momentum going.

Types of Qualifications Sections

The Qualifications section is the place where issues involving character tend to take the lead. In proposals, character is built on the shared motives, values, and attitudes that your company or organization has in common with the readers.

As you begin developing the Qualifications section, you should first identify the type of relationship that exists between your proposal's readers and your team, company, or organization. For example, internal proposals tend to stress the credentials of the people who will work on the project, because presumably the readers, as managers in the company, are already aware of the facilities and equipment available. On the other hand, external proposals, especially when the readers are not familiar with the bidder or nonprofit organization, require a much more thorough discussion of personnel, facilities, and experience. In these kinds of proposals, you need to describe your company's or organization's credentials by showing the readers your capabilities and values.

Depending on your relationship to the readers, there are four types of Qualifications sections you might write in a proposal:

Business to Business, or Organization to Funding Source

Business-to-business sections describe your company or nonprofit organization, demonstrating why your company or organization is uniquely qualified to handle the project. These Qualifications sections introduce the client or funding source to your company or organization, showing them who will be working on the project and what kinds of resources will be devoted to it.

Team to Management

Team-to-management sections are often written for proposals that suggest changes or pitch new ideas at your own company. The Qualifications section would show management why your team is capable of carrying out the plan. In some cases, you might find yourself using a team-to-management Qualifications section to nominate a group of individuals for a team, drawing various experts at your company to your project.

Recommendation

Recommendation sections propose a specific outside contractor, consultant, or company to carry out the plan. In an internal proposal, this kind of Qualifications section recommends a company that the management should hire to carry out the project. Often, consultants use these kinds of Qualifications sections to refer a client to the best company for putting the consultant's plan into action.

No Qualifications Section

Not all proposals need a stand-alone Qualifications section. In some cases, especially with short proposals, you can work the discussion of qualifications into other sections of the proposal. For instance, some proposal writers like to handle qualifications in their description of the plan, because any answers to the *why* questions in the Project Plan section rely heavily on who is handling the project and what facilities and equipment are needed. Therefore, a separate discussion of qualifications would unnecessarily repeat what was said earlier in the proposal.

These different types of Qualifications sections have different purposes. Nevertheless, they all are designed to show the readers *who* should do the project, *why* they are uniquely qualified for the project, and *what* kinds of resources will be used. More importantly, though, they highlight the relationship between the readers and the people who are proposing the project.

What Makes You Different Makes You Attractive

In a Qualifications section, it is not enough to merely list your company's personnel, experiences, facilities, and so on. Rather, you should strive to prove to the readers that your team, company, or organization is uniquely qualified for the project. You need to prove to them that your differences from the competition make you especially qualified to handle the work. Of course, something you should always remember is that all companies and organizations have their strengths and weaknesses—there is no perfect team for any project. By paying attention to what makes your company or organization different, you can often persuade the readers that your team has the common sense, commitment to excellence, and attitude to best meet their needs.

Never let your differences be seen as weaknesses. For example, proposal writers at small companies will sometimes complain, "Our competitors are the big sharks in this field. It's hard to compete with their huge facilities and armies of consultants." Ironically, proposal writers at the large companies (feeling more like whales than sharks) complain that they are competing against all those aggressive smaller companies that are more flexible and can avoid the massive overhead costs of a large corporation.

The lesson to be learned is that *what makes you different makes you attractive*. If you work for the smaller company in the industry, you should look for ways to show that your company's size allows it to be flexible and innovative—unlike your larger competitors, who will waste gobs of money on overhead and try to sell the "same old pre-packaged solution." And if you work for the larger company or organization, you should stress experience, facilities, and the ability to find the right people within your organization to handle this unique project. A successful Qualifications section capitalizes on your company's or organization's unique qualities, showing the readers why you stand out among your competitors.

FIGURE 6.1
Strengths and Weaknesses Worksheet

My Company	Competitor 1	Competitor 2	Competitor 3	Competitor 4
Strengths	Strengths	Strengths	Strengths	Strengths
Weaknesses	Weaknesses	Weaknesses	Weaknesses	Weaknesses

How do you figure out what makes you different? One good way is to list your top competitors on a sheet of paper, assuming they too are probably pursuing this same opportunity (Figure 6.1). Then, write down each of your competitors' strengths and weaknesses. Consider issues such as size, experience, personnel, facilities, and previous history with the client or funding source. When you are finished, write down your company's or organization's strengths and weaknesses. Be honest with yourself at this point—you are trying to develop a candid assessment of where your company or organization fits among its competitors. For yourself, you want to be clear about the weaknesses of your company or organization, because you might need to address or avoid them when you write the Qualifications section.

When you are finished sorting out your competitors' strengths and weaknesses and your own, note the places where your company or organization is different from the others. On your worksheet, circle any of your company's or organization's strengths that your competitors lack. Then, turn any of your competitors' weaknesses into your strengths, and write them down in your Strengths column.

For example, perhaps your competitors lack an R&D department, which is a unique strength of your company. You might point out in your Qualifications section that your company's ability to commit researchers to the project full time gives your company an innovative advantage. Merely mentioning this fact in your Qualifications section will draw attention to the absence of R&D departments at your competitors.

In grant writing, too, identifying strengths and weaknesses of competitors can be helpful. Whether we want to admit it or not, nonprofits and researchers compete with each other for funding. By identifying your organization's strengths (and other organization's weaknesses), you can show that you are better able to use a funding source's money effectively.

Finally, look for ways in which you can turn your company's or organization's weaknesses into strengths. For instance, if your company is new to the client's area—though you have a long history of success in other areas—you could use this "weakness" to your advantage by pointing out that you are going to bring fresh ideas and new strategies to the client. Or, perhaps a "weakness" is that your company lacks the top-dollar research scientists employed by your competitors. In this case, you might point out that your company hires experts on a per-project basis, keeping overhead low and ensuring that the most knowledgeable people are involved in each project.

In the Qualifications section, you should concentrate on your strengths and avoid directly mentioning or your competitors' weaknesses or your own. If your company or organization has a weakness that cannot be turned into a strength, then you should probably avoid mentioning it in the Qualifications section altogether. It is better to discuss your weaknesses with reviewers in person—if you must—after they have received the proposal.

You should also not directly mention your competitors' weaknesses. A hatchet statement like, "Our main competitor, Gopher Technologies, lacks the kind of experience you are looking for in this project," leaves a bad taste in everyone's mouths. You are better off throwing a barb at your competitors by turning their weakness into your strength.

When you are finished weighing your strengths and weaknesses, identify the *main strength* that sets your team, company, or organization apart from the competition. You will use this strength as the basis for your Qualifications section. You can weave the other strengths you have identified into the rest of the section where appropriate. We will use this main strength in a moment.

Developing the Content of the Qualifications Section

If you were a reviewer considering a proposal or grant, what would you want to see in the Qualifications section? Readers typically want to know whether your company or organization has a history of success with similar projects. They want to know whether your management and workforce have the education and training to handle the complexities of the project. And, they will look closely to see if your company or organization has the necessary facilities and equipment to carry out the project. The aim of the Qualifications section is to describe these qualities to the readers.

To address the readers' needs, a typical Qualifications section tends to break down into three areas:

Description of Personnel—biographies of management, demographics of labor force, special training of employees, security clearances

Description of Company/Organization—corporate/organizational history, mission statement, business or research philosophy, facilities, equipment, patents or proprietary procedures, security and privacy procedures, quality-control procedures

Experience of Company/Organization—past successful projects, experience of personnel in the industry or field, successful similar cases to the proposed project

Description of Personnel

The most critical part of the Qualifications section—and perhaps the whole proposal—is the description of the personnel who will be involved in the project. Clients and funding sources want to do more than check whether you and your employees can do the job. They want to see if there is a foundation for building a positive working relationship. Therefore, your descriptions of personnel should not simply list their credentials; you should also offer a strong sense of the human qualities these people will bring to the project.

Descriptions of the personnel are typically divided into three areas:

Management—includes project leaders, supervisors, and key employees who will occupy specific leadership roles on the project

Labor—includes members of the workforce who will provide the service, do the lab work, or manufacture the product

Support Staff—includes assistants, bookkeepers, secretaries, repair technicians, and other employees who will support management and labor

Your description of the management team should offer concise biographies of the managers who will devote significant time to the project. Start by describing the project leader's qualifications and qualities. Then, describe each of the remaining managers, supervisors, and key employees according to their importance in the project. Each leader's biography should run about one or two paragraphs. Mention the project leader's experience, education, and capabilities and tell the readers why each specific executive is an important member of the management team.

Your biographies of the management should offer enough detail to familiarize the readers with your project leaders; however, avoid overwhelming the readers with each manager's life history. In most cases, the project leaders' resume's will be included in an appendix, so you want to provide just enough biographical information to demonstrate that your management team is experienced, educated, and able to succeed. Also, in each biography, you might want to mention a personal attribute that offers some insight into each project leader's personality. For example, use phrases like, "Jane's consensus-building management style . . ." or even, "A careful listener, Dr. Perkins has always prided herself on responding personally to her customer's needs." Never go too far with personal attributes. One small comment per biography is usually enough to give the readers a sense of the personality of each person on the team.

The description of your labor and support staff should provide demographic information on your company's or organization's employees. Tell the readers how many laborers and staff members would be working on the project. Also, identify their roles in the project. You might further identify their general level of education and any special training they have received.

You should not discuss each laborer or staff member; rather, you want to give the readers an overall feel for the kinds of employees that your company or organization tends to hire. For instance, let's say your company's manufacturing plant is in Ames, Iowa, a small university town just north of Des Moines. When describing your labor force and staff, you might mention the various levels at which employees work and their different responsibilities in the company. You might also highlight your employees' high level of education and their strong work ethic. Meanwhile, you might specify that the local university and community college help you train and retrain your employees for new projects. Essentially, your description of your company's labor and staff uses demographic information to give the readers a general feel for the kinds of people who work at your company or organization.

Overall, the description of your management, labor, and support staff should demonstrate that the members of your team or the employees at your company or organization are qualified to take on the proposed project. It should also give the readers a sense of the people with whom they will be working.

The Dreaded Organizational Chart

One eternal question faced by proposal writers is whether to include the requisite organizational chart, or *org-chart* for short, that identifies the management hierarchy for the project (Figure 6.2). Organizational charts take up a great amount of space in a proposal, so they should be used with care and only when needed.

Organizational charts are needed when the project is complex and there are numerous levels of managers involved. In these complex Qualifications sections,

FIGURE 6.2

An Organizational Chart That Is Not Helpful

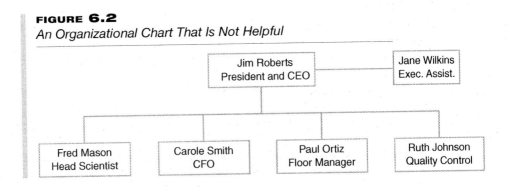

the organizational chart should be designed to help the readers figure out who answers to whom in the management structure.

Organizational charts should not be used in smaller projects where the management structure is apparent. After all, the readers have limited time and patience. If an organizational chart is simply being used to show the obvious connections between managers at your company, then it is wasting the readers' time while unnecessarily adding to the length of your proposal. That limited time and patience would be better used in the rest of the proposal.

Description of the Company/Organization

Of course, as the writer of the proposal, you are familiar with your company or organization, but your readers are likely unfamiliar with much of its history, mission, or operations. Even when two companies have long-standing business relationships, a thorough description of your company in the Qualifications section is often needed because relationships change over time. In other words, the two companies that began doing business together two decades ago no longer have the same managers and employees. Often, the companies' missions have changed, and their facilities are somewhat different.

In your description of the company or organization, you want to offer the readers an overview of your operations. The following elements are often included in a description of the company:

Corporate or Organizational History—describes when the company or organization was founded, by whom, and for what purpose. A history often describes the evolution of the company or organization into its present form

Mission Statement—identifies the goals and principles of operation of your company or organization

Corporate Philosophy—explains the company's or organization's approach, its management style, and the standards by which it does business

Facilities and Equipment—describes resources, manufacturing capabilities, and machinery

Quality-control Measures—highlights compliance with specific quality-control guidelines or international standards like ISO-9000

Your description of the company or organization should use details, preferably quantifiable details, about its operations. Using numbers where possible, tell the readers the size and output of your facilities. Tell them what kind of equipment you will devote to the project—by name, if possible. Be specific about dates in your company's or organization's history. These data points will add a strong sense of realism to your Qualifications section.

Experience of the Company/Organization

Proposal writers often prefer to round out the Qualifications section by stressing their company's or organization's experience and highlighting successful past projects.

When discussing the experience of your team, company, or organization, you want to show a track record of success with similar projects. At the very least, you want to show that your personnel have experience in this particular industry or area. In some cases, a Qualifications section might list similar projects completed in the past. In other cases, you may just list the companies or funding sources with whom your team, company, or organization has done business in the past.

Again, details are important in a description of experience. Where possible, you should name people, projects, and any other concrete facts to support your claims about experience. These details will add a sense of realism.

Writing the Qualifications Section

Earlier, you identified a main strength about your team, company, or organization. This main strength will now become the claim around which you are going to draft the Qualifications section for your proposal. It will show why your team, company, or organization is uniquely qualified to handle the needs of the client or funding source.

Opening

Like the other major sections in the proposal, the content of the Qualifications section should be organized into an opening, body, and closing. The opening of the Qualifications section, usually a short paragraph or two, will identify the purpose of the section and state a *main claim* (i.e., your main strength) about the qualifications of your company or organization. Specifically, in the opening you want to claim in some fashion that your team, company, or organization is "uniquely qualified" or "most qualified" for the project, because you possess a particular strength that sets you apart or above the competition. Of course, you do not need to use words like *uniquely* or *most,* but your main point for the section should be some kind of provable claim about the qualifications of your team, company, or organization. This kind of statement is not only the heart of the opening paragraph; it is the basis for the entire section.

For example, in her proposal to Overture Designs, the opening of Lisa Miller's Qualification section is rather short (Figure 6.3). Her heading "Background and Qualifications" identifies the subject of the section. Her first paragraph then mentions her purpose and main point, using her company's main strength to focus the Qualifications section.

Body

The body of the Qualifications section needs to back up the main claim you made in the opening. For instance, the opening of Lisa's Qualifications section claims that Insight Systems is "uniquely qualified to handle this project, because we provide flexible, low-cost communication networks that help growing companies stay

FIGURE 6.3

Insight Systems' Qualifications Section

Background and Qualifications

At Insight Systems, we know this moment is a pivotal one for Overture Designs. To preserve and expand its market share, Overture needs to grow as a company, but it cannot risk overextending itself financially. For these reasons, Insight Systems is uniquely qualified to handle this project, because we provide flexible, low-cost communication networks that help growing companies stay responsive to shifts in their industry.

Management and Labor

With more than fifty combined years in the industry, our management team offers the insight and responsiveness you will need to handle your complex needs.

Hanna Gibbons, our CEO, has been working in the telecommuting industry for more than twenty years. After she graduated from MIT with a Ph.D. in computer science, she worked at Krayson International as a systems designer. Ten years later, she had worked her way up to vice president in charge of Krayson's Telecommuting Division. In 1993, Dr. Gibbons took over as CEO of Insight Systems from its founder John Temple. Since then, Dr. Gibbons has grown Insight Systems into a major industry leader with gross sales of $15 million a year. Excited about the new innovations in telecommuting, Dr. Gibbons believes we are seeing a whole new kind of workplace evolve in front of our eyes.

Frank Roberts, chief engineer at Insight Systems, has thirty years of experience in the networked computer field. He began his career at Brindle Labs, where he worked on artificial intelligence experiments with analog computer networks. In 1985, he joined Insight Systems, bringing his unique understanding of networking to our team. Frank is very detail-oriented, often working long hours to ensure that each LAN exactly meets the client's specifications and needs.

Lisa Miller, Insight Systems' senior computer engineer, has successfully led the implementation of thirty-three telecommuting systems in companies throughout the United States. Earning her computer science degree at Iowa State, Lisa has won numerous awards for her innovative approach to computer networking. She believes that clear communication is the best way to meet her clients' needs.

The resume's of our management team are included in Appendix B.

(continued on page 109)

---

responsive to shifts in their industry." Then, Lisa used the body of the Qualifications section to back up this claim. The body of the Qualifications section begins with biographies of Insight Systems' management. To support her claim in the opening paragraph, Lisa used the biographies of Insight Systems' managers to stress the company's flexibility and innovativeness. Meanwhile, her description of Insight Systems' workforce highlights the experience and education of Insight Systems' engineers and technicians, thereby showing how Insight Systems preserves flexibility and innovation in the industry.

FIGURE 6.3
(Continued)

Our management team is supported by a progressive corps of high-technology employees. Insight Systems employs twenty of the brightest engineers and technicians in the telecommunications industry. We have aggressively recruited our employees from the most advanced universities in the United States, including Stanford, MIT, Illinois, Iowa State, New Mexico, and Syracuse. Several of our engineers have been with Insight Systems since it was founded. To keep our technicians on the industry's cutting edge, we maintain an ongoing training relationship with Simmons Technical Institute.

Corporate History and Facilities

Insight Systems has been a pioneer in the telecommuting industry from the beginning, and it has stayed at the forefront of the field by continuously looking for innovative ways to improve its products and services. The company was founded in 1975 by John Temple, who believed that workplaces in the post-computer age would require more flexible communication options.

Since then, Insight Systems has become one of the "100 Companies to Watch" according to *Business Outlook Magazine* (May 2006). The company has worked with large and small companies, from Vedder Aerospace to the Cedar Rapids Museum of Fine Arts, to create telecommuting options for companies that want to maintain flexibility while keeping costs down and productivity high.

Insight Systems' Naperville office has been called a "prototype Information Age workspace" (*Gibson's Computer Weekly*, May 2005). A model of workspace efficiency, Insight Systems' office handles the needs of fifty employees in a 9,000-square-foot office.

Experience You Can Trust

As members of a dynamic growing business ourselves, we at Insight Systems understand the challenges that face Overture Designs. The key to success is innovation, flexibility, and efficiency. Insight Systems will allow you to maintain these qualities as you continue to grow your business.

In her description of the history and facilities of Insight Systems, Lisa's Qualification section continues to stress flexibility and innovativeness. She pointed out that the company's founder emphasized flexible workspaces from the start. Also, she reinforced Insight Systems' reputation as an innovator by citing an article from a prominent business magazine and naming some prominent projects that they have already completed. Finally, Lisa pointed out that Insight Systems' office in Naperville is a model of the modern office. She decided not to go into detail about Insight Systems' facilities, because they were not relevant to the project being proposed. However, if your Qualifications section needs to describe a manufacturing plant or important equipment, you should add in a detailed description of your facilities and machinery.

Closing

A closing paragraph, especially in smaller proposals, is often not needed in a Qualifications section. If the body seems to taper off into a logical ending point, then you can move on to writing the next section. But, if it looks like the body is still rather open-ended, you might want to include a concise closing paragraph to round out the discussion of the qualifications.

As with the closing of any section of the proposal, you should not introduce new information at this point. If you still have new information to add, make it part of the body of the section. The closing should simply reinforce and restate the main claim you made in the opening paragraph of the section. Essentially, the aim of the closing paragraph is to show the readers that your main claim has been proven in the body of the section.

In Lisa's proposal, for example, the closing is very short. It simply reinforces the claim she made in the opening paragraph of the section. She may not have needed the paragraph at all, but she felt it helped her make a smoother transition into the next section of the proposal.

Creating a Persona

An important part of building character in a proposal or grant is the development of a persona. In ancient Greece, the word *persona* meant "mask." Your persona is the public face that you show the world around you. For a speaker or writer, persona is the image that he or she wants the audience to have of him or her.

When writing a proposal, especially the Qualifications section, you should be conscious of the persona, or image, that you want the proposal to project. In many cases, you can simply turn to your own public relations materials. What is the slogan or key word that your materials project to the public? What is the recurring theme that seems to be reinforced in all your company's or organization's public correspondence?

If your company or organization does not have a defined image or persona, mapping can help you create one for your proposal. Look at your analysis of *what makes us different makes us attractive*. What is the key word that you think characterizes your company or organization? Is it *aggressive* or *conservative*? Is it *technologically advanced* or *experienced*? When you have settled on a key word, write it down on a sheet of paper and create a map around it. For example, let's say the persona you want to create is that of a "progressive" company. Putting progressive in the center of a sheet of paper, start coming up with synonyms and phrases that reflect this quality. Words like *advanced, cutting edge, new,* and *innovative* come to mind (Figure 6.4). Mapping further, you can find more words and phrases that reflect the persona of your company or organization.

When you are finished mapping out the persona you have in mind, you will have created a whole vocabulary of words that you can now carefully blend into your proposal's Qualifications section. As you repeatedly use these key words in the Qualifications section, you will create a persona by developing what

FIGURE 6.4
Mapping Out a Persona

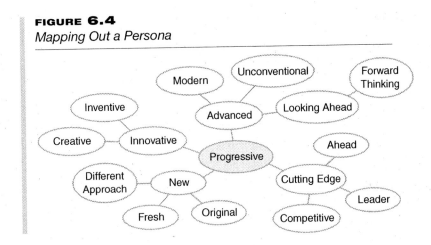

rhetoricians call a *theme* in your writing. The best part about creating a persona in the Qualifications section is that the effects on the readers are subtle if not subliminal. After repeatedly seeing key words that bring up images of a "progressive" company, the readers will come to believe that your company is indeed innovative and advanced. This use of key words works effectively with grants, too.

Creating a persona, however, is like adding spices to food. In moderation, using key words will tastefully bring out a particular persona in your Qualifications section. In excess, however, just like excess spices in food, the use of too many key words will overcome the real persona you are trying to enhance. Of course, a persona is always strongest when the key words are backed up by actions that reflect that persona. In other words, if your company is a rather stodgy firm, your attempts to build the "progressive" persona into your proposal will ultimately fail. After all, image eventually needs to measure up to reality. In the end, it is always best to assess the real persona of your company or organization and then reflect that persona consciously in the Qualifications section of your proposal.

To Boilerplate or Not to Boilerplate

Before long, you will run into the word *boilerplate* when talking about proposals and grants. Boilerplates are generic descriptions of the company or organizatoin, which are often pasted into proposals instead of project-specific Qualifications sections. In the rush to push the proposal out the door, some writers simply slap in their company's or organization's boilerplate rather than write an original description customized for the project and client.

The problem with boilerplates is that these generic files are often a hodgepodge of text fragments, sewn together from past proposals. They regularly contain information that is outdated or irrelevant to the project being proposed. And, all too often, the boilerplate has ballooned into a multipage monstrosity, because it has served as a catchall for clips about the company or organization.

Moreover, boilerplate Qualifications sections tend to use an impersonal, antiseptic tone that does not match the tone in the rest of the proposal. This antiseptic tone often undermines the attempts of the proposal to maintain the readers' enthusiasm for your plan.

How do you avoid using the same old boilerplate? Professional proposal writers and grant writers usually collect assorted files of qualifications-related information, such as short biographies of key personnel, a mission statement, a description of facilities, and so on. It is fine to use these preexisting files to help you invent the Qualifications section. What you need to do, however, is fashion these disparate parts into a cohesive argument that is specific to the project you are proposing. Essentially, you need to *persuade* the readers that your team, company, or organization has the right people, facilities, equipment, and experience to handle their specific needs.

When deadlines approach, it is tempting to use the old boilerplate with minimal adjustments. Try to avoid that temptation. The few hours spent customizing the Qualifications section to the project and client/funding source will be rewarded with a leaner, more focused section that stresses your company's or organization's unique strengths and qualities. Moreover, it will help you build trust with the client or funding source.

Looking Ahead

One of the most common mistakes made by writers of proposals and grants is underestimating the importance of the Qualifications section to the readers. You should always remember that proposals do more than simply offer plans and budgets. They also build relationships between people. So, it is important to recognize that the readers are not merely agreeing to a plan, they are agreeing to trust you. In the end, people hire people, not plans or budgets, so it is critical that you show the readers of your proposal why you are experienced, reliable, and responsive to their needs—essentially building your character in the eyes of the readers. The Qualifications section gives you the opportunity to do just that.

CASE STUDY Who Is Qualified to Do the Work?

The members of the Cool Campus grant-writing team felt good about what they had accomplished so far. They had identified and described the problem faced by Durango University, and they had developed a plan that took positive steps toward solving that problem.

Now they needed to write a Qualifications section for the grant proposal. The university had plenty of administrators who could lead the project. Plus, a number of faculty members were available who specialized in environmental issues and alternative energy research. One of the members of their team, George Tillman, was a professor of environmental engineering who specialized in renewable energy.

The grant-writing team decided to let Anne and George write this part of the grant, because they were in the best position to find people who could lead the project. The two met in Anne's office.

"George, I think we need someone like you to be our project leader," said Anne. "You have experience in these kinds of issues."

"I have some experience," George replied, "but I don't know anything about urban planning. The first time I ever heard the word 'charrette' was when Calvin said it a couple weeks ago."

Anne said, "I've thought about that already, so I started looking around for someone who specializes in urban planning, who also understands environmental issues. We don't have anyone on the faculty or staff that does that kind of work. Usually, we bid out that kind of project to planning and design firms."

"Did Calvin remember the name of that urban planning firm that ran the charrette in Albuquerque?"

"You and I are on the same page," said Anne. "Calvin sent me the address for their website, and I gave them a call. The firm that ran the charrette was Summers & Mondragon, and they are located in Santa Fe, New Mexico."

"At least they're close to us," said George. "That's only a four-hour drive from here."

"I talked with one of their partners, Diane Smith. She specializes in environmental urban planning. But she has never worked on designs for a university campus before. She acknowledged that her firm would need to do some research about the needs of our campus, but she felt they could at least run a charrette for us."

"Do we need to bid out this kind of project?" asked George.

"Not this part of the project. Running the charrette and developing the first set of designs won't be too costly, so we can hire a firm without putting out the contract for bid. But, when we move beyond that point, we are going to need to bid out the project."

"So, you're saying that we should propose hiring Summers & Mondragon to facilitate the charrette?"

"Yes," answered Anne, "and I want to put you and me down as the co-project leaders who will lead the planning process."

"Who else needs to be named as leaders of the project?" asked George.

"I think we need to put in one of our librarians, because setting up the charrette library and website will be a big part of the project."

George thought for a moment and then said, "I know Gina Sanders over there. She has worked with the Environmental Engineering department to gather information on a variety of issues. She's really knowledgeable about environmental issues."

"Good," replied Anne. "We'll ask her if she's interested."

"Now comes the hard part," said George. "Why is Durango University worthy of the funding for a project like this one? Surely, we're not the only university who is thinking about converting its campus to renewable energy sources. Other universities may even be asking the Tempest Foundation for a grant. So, why us?"

Anne thought about this question for a moment. "That's a good question. Certainly, there are more prominent universities out there looking for this kind of funding. We need to figure out what makes us different."

"Well, our location is one difference. We get lots of sun here, the wind's usually blowing, and we can tap geothermal energy from the mountains," said George. "That gives us lots of options for renewable energy."

Anne added, "Another thing that makes us different is the size of our campus. We're not too big, so we can offer a good test site for this kind of project. If the conversion to renewable energy works here, others could use our experiences to guide conversions at larger campuses."

"We also have a solid Environmental Engineering department—it was one of the first of its kind in the Southwest. We've received grants from the National Science Foundation to do research in geothermal energy and other kinds of alternative energy."

"Good. We can put that in the Qualifications section."

"Most of all," said George, "I think we have a commitment to making this transformation happen. From the university president to the students, we want to make this work. It's not just an intellectual exercise. We actually want to do it. That sets us apart."

For the rest of the hour, George and Anne roughed out a draft of the Qualifications section for the grant proposal (Figure 6.5). They wrote bios for themselves and left a space for Diane Smith from Summers & Mondragon. They also left a space for Gina Sanders, the librarian at the

FIGURE 6.5

A Draft of the Cool Campus Proposal's Qualifications Section

Qualifications of the Cool Campus Team

Durango University would be an ideal setting to undertake this kind of campus transformation to renewable energy. Located in southwestern Colorado, our campus has access to a variety of alternative forms of renewable energy, including solar, wind, and geothermal energy. We also have a forward-thinking administration that is committed to converting the campus to renewable energy. We want to be a positive role model for the nation.

Biographies of Key Personnel

The project leaders for the Cool Campus Project will be Professor George Tillman and Vice President Ann Hinton.

- Professor George Tillman, Ph.D., is the John Connell Chair of Environmental Engineering. He has worked on geothermal energy issues for twenty-two years. He has authored or co-authored fifty-four articles on renewable energy and has worked with several small towns in Colorado to incorporate renewable energy into their energy grids. In 2003, Dr. Tillman was awarded the Environmental Engineer of the Year Award by the Colorado Environmental Protection Agency. He has been a principal investigator on $6.2 million of grants in renewable energy research.

- Dr. Alice Hinton is the vice president for Physical Facilities at Durango University. Before taking on this position, she was dean of the College of Management. She is a specialist in international management and entrepreneurship. Her most recent book is *Managing Diversity: A Guide to Entrepreneurship*, which was published in 2005. She is a leading expert in fostering creativity in diverse teams of people.

- Diane Smith is a partner with Summers & Mondragon, an urban planning firm located in Santa Fe, New Mexico. Ms. Smith has facilitated twenty-three urban planning charrettes and has worked with numerous cities on urban renewal, including Albuquerque, Chicago, Toledo, Santa Fe, and Santa Barbara. Summers & Mondragon has been a leading firm in using "New Urbanism" to reconceptualize commerce and transportation to make cities more pedestrian-friendly and less congested.

- Gina Sanders is a senior research librarian at the Laura Vasquez Library on the Durango University campus. She has worked with many departments and local groups to gather information on technology issues. Her specialty is assembling information into electronically accessible formats. Her work with the Durango University e-Library won a Top Innovator Award from the National Librarians Council.

Curriculum vitae for the project leaders are included with this grant application.

Other faculty and staff members will also be assigned to this project. Durango University is the home of one of the leading environmental engineering departments in the nation. Our five faculty members and their graduate students will serve as resources for the community and the charrette. Meanwhile, staff members will be involved in developing the website for the charrette and assembling the library.

Background on Durango University

Another strength is Durango University itself. Since its founding in 1912, the university has had a long history of environmental leadership in the region. We were one of the first

(continued)

FIGURE 6.5
(Continued)

---

universities in the Southwest to develop an environmental engineering program. The program began in our Mining Engineering Department in 1958, drawing leaders in environmental engineering to its faculty. In 1970, the department was renamed Environmental Engineering to reflect environmental conservation as its primary mission.

Past Grants at Durango University
The university has received a variety of grants from government sources and foundations. Recently, the National Science Foundation awarded the Environmental Engineering department a $1.2 million grant to research opportunities for using geothermal energy in remote mountain communities. A $2.3 million Department of Energy grant was awarded to the Electrical Engineering department for research into solar energy. The U.S. Department of Education also awarded Durango University a $780,000 grant to develop a program on global warming that could be used in high schools throughout the United States. We have received funding from private foundations for our efforts to address world poverty in mountainous areas throughout the world. The Geneva Foundation provided a $630,000 grant to one of our research teams to help improve access to electricity for people living in the Himalayas.

Durango University has a track record of success in environmental issues. To learn more about the university and its successful grant-funded projects, please visit www.DurangoU.edu and www.DurangoU.edu/research.

---

university. Then they pulled some information from the university website to fill out the subsections that described the university and its accomplishments.

That afternoon, Anne called Diane Smith to see if her firm would be interested in working on the project, if it were funded. Diane said they would. Meanwhile, George wrote an e-mail to Gina Sanders that described the project and asked her if she would want to work with them. She said yes.

Anne and George asked Diane and Gina to send them brief biographies that they could put in the grant.

George finished up the Qualifications section later that week and sent it to the rest of the grant-writing team for comments. Figure 6.5 shows the initial draft of this part of the grant proposal.

Questions and Exercises

1. Find a business proposal on the Internet that includes a stand-alone Qualifications section. Does the section prove that the bidding company is "uniquely qualified" for the job? Does the section have a clear opening, body, and closing? What topics did the authors choose to include in their Qualifications section? What information did they leave out? Why? Write a two-page memo to your instructor in which you analyze the content and organization of this Qualifications section. In your analysis, point out any strengths and suggest improvements.

2. On the Internet, locate the websites of three competing companies in an area with which you are familiar. For example, you might study bookstores, record shops, restaurants, computer manufacturers, and so on. In a table like the one shown in Figure 6.1, identify each of these companies' strengths and weaknesses. What is each company's main strength? What makes each company different from its competitors? Can you turn any weaknesses into strengths?

3. With a team, write a one-page Qualifications section for your company or university. Identify what makes your company or university unique or different from its competitors. What are some topics (e.g., mission, history, experience, management, employees, or facilities) that you believe need to be mentioned? What are some topics you would not mention? Why? Also, can you turn any of your company's or university's weaknesses into strengths?

4. Map out a persona for your company or university. If you had one positive word to describe your company or organization, what would it be? Put this word in the middle of a sheet of paper and map out the persona associated with this word. Then, try to weave this persona into the Qualifications section you wrote for Exercise 2.

5. In your class, interview one of your classmates or colleagues. Write a one-paragraph biography of this person in which you discuss his/her education, experience, and special abilities. Also, add a statement that personalizes the biography.

6. In this chapter, you learned how to turn your company's weaknesses into strengths. At what point should concerns about honesty overcome the urge to make your company look more qualified? Where is the point at which trying to turn weaknesses into strengths becomes unethical? What are some ways you can determine when ethics are being infringed?

7. Study the Qualifications section from a real proposal. What persona, if any, is woven into this section? Underline some of the key words used in the Qualifications section. Do they show a common persona that the writers are trying to reinforce? If not, use mapping to develop a persona for this Qualifications section and seed the text with some key words that reflect that persona.

7 Introductions, Costs, and Benefits

Overview

This chapter discusses how to write introductions and conclusions for proposals and grants. The chapter will meet the following objectives:

1. Show how introductions and conclusions frame, or set a context, for the body of the proposal.
2. Discuss the purpose of an introduction and how to develop its content.
3. Describe the "six moves" that make up the content of an introduction.
4. Show how a conclusion can be used to "amplify" the benefits of the proposal's plan.
5. Describe the "five moves" that make up the content of a conclusion.

Framing the Body of the Proposal

In many ways, introductions and conclusions are reflections of each other in proposals and grants. An effective introduction defines the proposal's subject, purpose, and main point while stressing the importance of the subject. Then, at the end of the proposal, the conclusion restates the main point and discusses the costs and benefits of the plan. The conclusion should bring the readers back around to the beginning, restating the overall argument while stressing the advantages of taking action.

A good way to understand the different roles of the introduction, body, and conclusion is to remember the old speechmakers' adage: "Tell them what you're going to tell them. Tell them. And, tell them what you told them." In other words, a good introduction first lays out the argument in brief for the readers. Then, the body supports that argument with facts, reasoning, and examples. And finally, the conclusion restates the argument concisely, demonstrating that the main point of the argument has been proven.

The introduction and conclusion can also be seen as framing devices for the body of the proposal or grant. The aim of the introduction is to create a cognitive framework for the readers, so they can conceptualize the whole argument at once. The body of the proposal fills in that framework with facts, reasoning, and examples. Then, the conclusion reframes the argument for the readers, again helping them comprehend the whole argument at once.

Because introductions and conclusions are similar, they will be discussed together in this chapter. First, you will learn how to write powerful introductions that invite the readers to sit up and pay attention to your ideas. Then, you will learn how to amplify your conclusion, stressing the importance of your proposal and driving your ideas home for the readers.

Setting the Stage: The Purpose of an Introduction

To be effective, the introduction for your proposal or grant needs to lay a foundation for the rest of the document. After reading your introduction, the readers should know exactly what the proposal is trying to achieve. Your proposal's introduction is especially important, because the beginning is where your readers are most attentive. Here is the best place to tell them what the proposal is about, what is being proposed, and why they should take notice.

You should never underestimate the importance of the introduction, because it often makes or breaks a proposal. In so many ways, your introduction makes your first impression on the readers. If you make a positive first impression, the chances are good that your readers will see you and your proposal as credible and trustworthy. A bad first impression, though, could negatively taint the rest of the document.

Developing the Introduction

Fortunately, you have already done most of the preparation work necessary to write the introduction. When you defined the rhetorical situation in Chapter 3, you answered two key questions that will form the basis of the introduction. Specifically, on your rhetorical situation worksheet you addressed these issues:

- What is the *subject* of my proposal?
- What is the *purpose* of my proposal?

Now that you have written the body of the proposal, it might seem like a long time since you initially defined your subject and purpose. At that time, you probably had a vague idea of what you were writing about and what you wanted the proposal to achieve. But now that you have written the body of the proposal, you possess a much clearer idea of the subject and the purpose. The subject and purpose are the core elements of your introduction.

A typical introduction will include up to six moves:

Move 1: State the *subject* of the proposal.

Move 2: Identify the *purpose* of the proposal.

Move 3: State the *main point* that will be proven in the proposal.

Move 4: Stress the *importance* of the subject to the readers.

Move 5: Provide some *background information* on the subject.

Move 6: *Forecast* the organization of the proposal.

It is not always necessary to include all six moves in an introduction. At a minimum, you should include statements defining the subject, purpose, and main point in the introduction of a proposal. You can decide whether you will include statements that identify the importance of the subject, provide background information, and forecast the structure of the proposal.

Of course, these six moves are not necessarily made in this order, nor are they always made in separate sentences. Rather, *they should be accounted for* somewhere in the introduction. The moves themselves can be handled in a variety of different ways. Let us look at these moves in more depth.

Move 1: State the Subject of the Proposal

The *subject* of the proposal or grant is what you are writing about. In your introduction, you should clearly define the subject and what is included in the subject.

A common mistake, especially among grant writers, is to assume that the readers know about the subject (e.g., "Everyone knows about teenage drug abuse in rural areas, right?"). In reality, though, you probably know vastly more about your proposal's subject than your readers, so you need to define the boundaries of the subject for them. Be specific about the issue you are addressing in the proposal.

Move 2: Identify the Purpose of the Proposal

Your *purpose statement* tells the readers what your proposal is supposed to accomplish. In one sentence, complete the phrase, "The purpose of this proposal is to. . . ." If you cannot boil down your purpose statement to one sentence, the purpose of your proposal may not be clear to you or the readers. Earlier, you wrote a statement of purpose on your rhetorical situation worksheet. Right now might be a good time to see if your purpose changed as you wrote the Current Situation, Project Plan, and Qualifications sections.

The actual purpose statement in the introduction may or may not include a phrase like "The purpose of this proposal is to. . . ." Nevertheless, a sentence should specifically tell the readers what the proposal will accomplish.

Move 3: State the Main Point That Will Be Proven in the Proposal

The *main point* is the one idea above all that you would like the readers to take away from the proposal. In most proposals, you should just tell the readers your solution to the problem or how you will help them take advantage of an opportunity. In a research proposal, you might phrase your main point as your *research question* or *hypothesis*.

By stating your main point up front, you provide the readers with a primary claim or question that will focus their attention as they read the rest of the proposal. Once the readers know your main point, they can then study the details of your proposal through the focal point created by this statement. You are essentially saying, "Here's what we want to do." The rest of the proposal leads the readers through the thought process that brought you to that main point.

Move 4: Stress the Importance of the Subject to the Readers

In the introduction, proposals need to hook the readers and capture their full attention. Therefore, somewhere in the introduction, you should tell the readers why the subject is (or should be) *important* to them—why they need to take action. You need to give your readers a good reason to pay attention.

The importance of the subject can be expressed in a positive or negative way. The positive approach stresses the opportunity available to the readers (e.g., "This new state-of-the-art facility will allow us to increase our share of the market by 15 percent."). Briefly, it shows them the advantages of taking action at this particular moment. The negative approach puts the readers on alert (e.g., "If we don't build a new facility now, we will likely lose significant market share."). Of course, alarming the readers is a sure way to stress the importance of the subject, but you risk making the readers defensive or resistant to change. Therefore, you should be careful when using negative statements in the introduction.

Move 5: Provide Some Background Information on the Subject

Typically, *background information* is made up of information that the readers already know or won't find overly controversial. This information is designed to start the readers on familiar ground so they feel comfortable as they begin reading some of the new ideas you have to offer. Specifically, you might mention some basic facts or historical information about the subject of the proposal or grant. Background information allows the writer to show that the problem is due to change. The inclusion of background information also hints that the writers have done their homework as they prepared to write the proposal, thus increasing their credibility.

Other forms of background information are available. Perhaps you might talk about the current state of the industry. Or, you might simply say something like, "At our meeting on January 30, we discussed some of your options for improving. . . ." The most effective background information simply tells the readers something they already know, so they have a comfortable reference point from which to start considering new or different ideas.

Move 6: Forecast the Organization of the Proposal

Forecasting describes the body of the proposal by identifying the larger topics that the document will cover. By describing the content up front, forecasting helps the readers build a cognitive framework to understand the whole structure of the proposal.

Effective public speakers often use forecasting to lay out the topics they are going to cover in their speech. In their introduction, they tell the audience, "Today, I am going to talk about three important topics. First, I want to talk about . . . . Second, I will explain why. . . . And finally, I will discuss. . . ." The effect of this kind of forecasting on the audience is that they can now visualize the structure of the speech and follow the progress of the speaker as he or she works through the

FIGURE 7.1
The Six Moves as Questions

Elements of the Introduction

What is the subject of this proposal? What is *not* the subject of this proposal?

What is the purpose of this proposal, in only one sentence?

What main point is this proposal trying to make to the readers?

Why is this subject important to the readers?

What background information should the readers know before reading the proposal?

How will the body of the proposal be organized?

---

topics. As the speaker reaches transition points from one topic to the next, the audience can shift focus with the speaker, concentrating separately on each new topic.

In a proposal, forecasting has much the same effect on the readers. If your introduction briefly describes the structure of the proposal, the readers will be better prepared to consider each topic separately. The forecasting will provide them with a map of your proposal, so they have an overall idea of how you are going to lead them from the current situation, through your plan, through your qualifications, to the costs and benefits. As a result, the readers will know in advance how the argument will progress.

Working Out the Six Moves on a Worksheet

As you invent the content for the introduction, it is helpful to begin by writing down a sentence or two for each of these moves. The worksheet in Figure 7.1 shows how you can phrase these moves as questions. Once you have written down answers to these questions, you should find yourself ready to write the introduction.

Writing the Introduction

The six introductory moves can be made in almost any order. Usually, proposals start out with some background information or a statement that stresses the importance of the subject to the readers. But there are other ways to begin a proposal.

Many proposals start out with a statement of purpose. For example, the first sentence might state boldly, "Our intent in this proposal is to. . . ." This first sentence is not going to shake the rafters, but it tells the readers up front what you are going to do.

The statements of your purpose and main point are the most important features of the introduction—and perhaps of the whole proposal. Before reading the body of your proposal, the readers must have a clear idea of what you are trying to do (purpose) and what you are trying to prove (main point), so you should not bury these statements somewhere in the middle of a paragraph in the introduction. They should appear at the beginning or end of a paragraph, where the readers are paying the most attention. If you are not sure whether your purpose and main point are clear, you should make them painfully obvious. In these cases, use a sentence like, "The purpose of this proposal is to. . . ." And, if you want to make your main point absolutely clear, say something like, "Our aim is to prove to you that. . . ." It is better to be too blunt than too subtle about your purpose and main point.

Finally, your introduction should be concise. When readers begin reviewing a proposal, a mental timer starts in their heads. With their timer running, they immediately start asking questions like, "What is this proposal about? Why are these people writing to me? What is the point? Why should I care?" If you take too long to answer these questions, the readers will become frustrated or bored. To avoid frustrating the readers in the introduction, simply address the six moves, and then move the readers into the body of the proposal.

A good rule of thumb is to limit the length of introductions to the first page of a single-spaced proposal. The number of paragraphs used in an introduction is not important, but typically a writer can only put about two or three paragraphs on a given sheet of paper. Of course, there are always exceptions, but if your proposal has a three- or five-page introduction, there is a good chance that the readers will lose their patience. Moreover, it is likely that all the extra content in your introduction will muddy your attempts to clearly state your subject, purpose, and main point.

Without a doubt, the introduction can be the hardest part of the proposal to write, but two strategies will make it much easier to write. First, write the introduction after you have written the body of the proposal. Doing so will save you hours of writer's block, because you will know exactly what needs to be said in the introduction. Second, write out the six moves before writing the introduction, addressing each move separately. If you do these two things, writing your proposal's introduction will be simple.

The Introduction to the Overture Designs Proposal

Figure 7.2 shows the introduction of Lisa Miller's proposal to Overture Designs. Lisa wanted her introduction to grab the readers, because she knew her introduction would essentially make or break the proposal. Lisa's solution for the Overture's office space shortage was likely different from her readers' expectations,

FIGURE 7.2

Proposal Introduction for Overture Designs

Proposal to Overture Designs:

Telecommuting, Growth, and Flexibility

Founded in 1979, Overture Designs is one of those classic entrepreneurial success stories in the architectural industry. With one thousand dollars of capital, Susan James and Thomas Weber began designing functional buildings for the Wrigleyville business community. Three years later, the company cleared its first million dollars in revenue. Today, Overture is one of the leading architectural firms in the Chicago market with more than $50 million in annual revenue. The *Chicago Business Journal* has consistently rated Overture one of the top–five architectural firms in the city, citing the company's continued innovation and growth in the industry.

With growth, however, comes growing pains. Overture now faces an important decision about how it will manage its growth in the near future. The right decision could lead to more market share, increased sales, and even more prominence in the architectural market. However, Overture also needs to safeguard itself against overextension should the Chicago construction market unexpectedly begin to recede.

To help Overture make the right decision, this proposal suggests an innovative strategy that will support the company's growth while maintaining its flexibility. Specifically, we propose that Overture implement a telecommuting system that allows selected employees to work a few days each week at home. Telecommuting will provide Overture with the office space it needs to continue growing; yet, it will avoid the large investment in new facilities or disruption to the company's current operations.

In this proposal, we will first discuss the results of our research into Overture's office space needs. Second, we will offer a plan for using a telecommuting network to free up more space at Overture's current office. Third, we will review our qualifications at Insight Systems to assist Overture with its move into telecommuting. And finally, we will go over some of the costs and advantages of our plan. Our aim is to show you that telecommuting is a way for Overture to continue growing while maintaining the innovative spirit that launched this firm so many years ago.

---

so she assumed her plan would never be considered if her introduction made a bad first impression.

In the first paragraph of her proposal's introduction, Lisa provided some background information. The readers at Overture were almost certainly familiar with all the details in this paragraph. Nevertheless, Lisa used these details to warm up the readers by telling them things they already knew. Moreover, this background information gave Lisa an opportunity to stroke the egos of the readers a bit—making them feel good about their company.

In the second paragraph, Lisa identified the subject of the proposal—that is, managing Overture's growth as a firm. She then stressed the importance of this subject to the readers. Specifically, she pointed out that the right decision would lead to further growth and influence, while the wrong decision might leave the firm vulnerable in a receding market. In this way, Lisa stressed the opportunity for growth while lightly hinting to the readers that inaction or wrong action could lead to negative consequences.

In the third paragraph, Lisa stated the purpose and the main point of the proposal. For her purpose, Lisa wrote ". . . this proposal suggests an innovative strategy that will support the company's growth while maintaining its flexibility." Then, for her main point, she wrote ". . . we propose that Overture implement a telecommuting network that allows selected employees to work a few days each week at home." Lisa was not subtle about her purpose and main point, because she believed the readers would want to know them before reading further. With her purpose and main point stated up front, the readers could keep them in mind as they studied the details in the body of the proposal.

Finally, the last paragraph in the introduction forecasts the structure of the proposal. By outlining the body of the proposal for the readers, Lisa created a framework that the readers could use to visualize the rest of the proposal. They would know the topics covered and the logical progression of the text.

Overall, Lisa's introduction concisely lays out her argument for the readers. It prepares them for the body by making the introductory six moves while saving the content of the proposal for the body. Lisa did not need to make all six moves. For example, she could cut out the background information in the first paragraph or the forecasting in the last paragraph, but she felt these paragraphs helped set a context for the body of the proposal. Thus, she decided to make these moves in the introduction.

Costs and Benefits: Concluding the Proposal

As mentioned earlier in this chapter, the conclusion is, in many ways, a reflection of the introduction. The conclusion is where you should bring the readers back to your main point while emphasizing the benefits of accepting your ideas.

The best way to conclude a proposal or grant is to stress the benefits of your plan. The conclusion is where you are going to finally persuade your readers to say yes to your plan. Nothing new really happens in the conclusion of a proposal, except perhaps a brief discussion of the costs. After all, when the readers reach this point in the proposal, they have already heard and considered your description of the current situation. They have already studied your plan and considered your qualifications. So, they know almost all the information they need to make a decision. At this point, it is your goal to *sell* them your plan by stressing its advantages. In the conclusion, you need to amplify your proposal by showing them the positive things that will happen if they say yes.

The only new information in the conclusion should be a brief discussion of the costs of the project. As you might guess, for many readers the costs are a major focal point of any proposal, perhaps *the* focal point. In some cases, the costs can be bitter medicine for the readers, because you are essentially telling them that they need to trade something valuable, usually money, for your plan and expertise. Fortunately, the costs can be strategically positioned in the conclusion, thereby sweetening the bitter medicine by stressing the benefits of accepting your ideas. That way, the readers will be able to weigh the costs against the benefits that your plan will bring.

Writing the Conclusion

Usually, the conclusion is much shorter than the other sections of a proposal. Nevertheless they are crucial toward finally persuading the readers to say yes to your ideas. Proposal writers often use a gymnastics phrase, "stick the landing," to remind themselves that no matter how complicated the body of the proposal, the conclusion needs to land on both feet—with a smile.

The conclusion should be positive and forward-looking. It should never rehash the clients' problems, and it should never try to scare the readers into saying yes. Bringing up problems at this point just puts readers in a bad mood—so attempts to scare them at this point usually backfire. After all, no one likes to be browbeaten into agreeing with a plan (e.g., "Accept our plan or bad things will happen to you."). They want to feel as though accepting the proposal will make their lives better. With few exceptions, then, the proposal's conclusion should be positive in content and tone.

Like the introduction, the conclusion of the proposal can be built around specific moves. These moves are intended to stress the benefits of the plan while specifying its costs.

Move 1: *Transition* from the body of the proposal.

Move 2: State the *costs* of the plan.

Move 3: Highlight the *benefits* of the plan.

Move 4: Look to the *future*.

Move 5: Identify the *next step*.

Of course, all these moves do not need to be made in the conclusion. A combination of some or all of them will round out the proposal in a strong way. Let us look at these moves more closely.

Move 1: Transition from the Body of the Proposal

Transition points are found throughout proposals, but there is one particular transition that merits special attention—the transition from the body of the proposal to the conclusion. Think of the public speeches you have heard over the years. When the speaker says, "In conclusion," or something to that effect, everyone in the audience perks up and starts listening. This kind of transition to the conclusion is a signal that the speaker is going to summarize the main points—that is, the important stuff.

In written documents, the purpose of a concluding transition is the same as one in a speech. As soon as you write "To sum up" or use a concluding heading like "Final Points," the readers will start paying closer attention to what you are writing because they know you are going to summarize the main points of the document.

The transition from the body to the conclusion should be obvious to the readers, because you want the readers to start paying close attention again. After reading the body of the proposal and wading through the Qualifications section, your readers are tired when they reach the conclusion. The proposal has already given them numerous details to sort out and mull over. The transition, then, needs to wake them up.

There are three ways to make an obvious transition into the conclusion:

- Use an active heading that signals the conclusion and gently cues the readers that you are going to bring the proposal to a close. A heading like "Concluding Remarks," "Our Recommendations," or "What Are the Advantages of our Plan?" will usually prompt the readers to start paying closer attention.
- Start the first sentence of the conclusion with a transitional phrase, such as "In summary. . ." "To conclude. . .," or "To wrap up. . . ." Even these small phrases will bring the readers' attention back to your proposal, preparing them to consider your overall points.
- State or restate your proposal's main point. For example, a proposal's main point might be, "We believe a modernized manufacturing plant will give Hanson Industries the flexibility and capacity to become the leader in the controls industry." Stated up front in the conclusion, this sentence will signal that you are bringing the proposal to a close.

The transition into the conclusion is a critical point in any proposal or grant, so it should be handled with care. Once the conclusion has been signaled, you probably have a few paragraphs, at most a page or two, to make your final points. Public speakers often make the crucial mistake of saying "In conclusion. . ." or "In sum. . ." and then ramble on for ten more minutes. By the end of that ten minutes, the people in the audience are ready to fall out of their chairs. Once a speaker signals the conclusion he or she probably has a minute or two to make his or her main points.

Likewise, in a proposal, when you use a transition to signal the conclusion, you probably have about a minute or two of the readers' heightened attention. If you go longer, they will become frustrated, restless, and annoyed.

Move 2: State the Costs of the Plan

Obviously, the costs are the bottom line of any proposal or grant. And yet, finding out how much a project will cost is typically not a high point for the readers— unless you are asking for less money than they expected. So, you need to find a way to present the costs in a positive light.

Presenting the Costs

Various strategies are available for presenting the costs. In smaller proposals, costs can be concisely itemized in a short table, accompanied by a few explanatory comments in the body of the proposal. The table in Figure 7.3, for example, shows how major budget items can be summarized for the readers in a concise manner.

FIGURE 7.3
A Small Table of Costs

The costs of the project are the following figures:	
Development of a prototype	$ 15,390
Retooling manufacturing line	89,600
New promotional campaign	32,200
Retraining of labor and staff	11,100
Contingency	10,000
TOTAL	$ 158,290

In larger proposals, writers will sometimes include a separate Budget section sandwiched between the Qualifications section and the proposal's conclusion. In these stand-alone Budget sections, the readers typically find an itemized table of costs and a detailed rationale for major and minor expenses. These large Budget sections can often run on for several pages.

The problem with placing a full budget, tables and all, inside the body or conclusion of your proposal is that it kills the momentum of your argument, almost completely disrupting the story you are trying to tell. After all, by the time the readers sift through pages and pages of budgetary items, dollar figures, and justifications for various lines in the budget, they will more than likely forget your descriptions of the current situation, your plan, and your qualifications. As a result, when they reach the proposal's conclusion, all they will remember is how much money your project is going to cost them. In most cases, you do not want your readers thinking solely about the price tag when you are trying to persuade them to say yes to your ideas.

Offering a Synopsis of Costs

There is a better way to handle the costs in a proposal. If possible, it is best to include only a brief synopsis of the project's overall costs in the conclusion of the proposal. Then, provide an itemized budget and a detailed rationale in an appendix. For example, a simple statement in the conclusion like, "As shown in our budget in Appendix B, we estimate the Goodman Restoration Project will cost $40,560,300," is sufficient for even the largest projects. This kind of simple sentence provides the readers with a bottom-line figure while directing them to a place where they can analyze the figures in greater depth.

The advantage of this approach is that the readers avoid slogging through a detailed discussion of costs at this crucial point. If the readers want that detailed discussion, they can turn to the appendix where the figures are handled in depth. (In Chapter 8, we will discuss how to write stand-alone budgets for an appendix or a Budget section.)

If you think your proposal's conclusion needs more than one sentence about costs, then you might include a small table that breaks down the budget into its larger parts, much like the table shown in Figure 7.3. This kind of budget table sketches out the basic elements of the budget without breaking down the figures into itemized bits and pieces. You can then refer the readers to an itemized budget in the appendix that fills in the specific details behind these costs and offers a rationale for each expense.

How to State the Costs

State the costs of your project in a straightforward, matter-of-fact way. Some proposal writers and grant writers feel a strange urge to become apologetic or defensive when they mention how much the project will cost. They say, "We're sorry, but the cost of your new manufacturing plant will probably sound very expensive, but it's really not. We estimate it will cost. . . ." Or, they defensively state, "We have tried everything in our power to keep expenses to a minimum, but it looks like the project is going to cost. . . ." Even worse, they sometimes use a phony-sounding sales pitch: "And for the very, very low cost of $1,983,000, you can have the best manufacturing plant on the planet!"

These attempts to soften, defend, or put a positive spin on costs usually only end up backfiring, because they highlight your company's or organization's insecurities about the budget while needlessly drawing attention to the price of the project. Instead, when you mention how much the project will cost, just tell the readers the figure in a straightforward way. Apologizing, defending, or putting a phony-sounding sales spin on the costs will only have a negative effect on the readers.

Proposals as Contracts

One final note on costs: Something to keep in mind is that a proposal is a *de facto* contract until it is replaced by a formal agreement or actual contract of some kind. Once the proposal is accepted, it is a binding contract in most cases. In some cases, especially when the proposal is signed by the bidder and the client, the proposal *is* the contract for the project. So, if you promise that you can complete the project for a specific amount of money and the client accepts, then you are more than likely obligated to charge only that amount. Therefore, costs in a formal proposal should be as exact as possible, and they need to be defensible in a court of law, if necessary.

Move 3: Highlight the Benefits of the Plan

In proposals as well as life, the best way to persuade people is to stress the benefits of your ideas to them. In a proposal or grant, you need to show them the specific advantages of saying yes to your plan. The primary aim of a proposal's conclusion, therefore, is to stress the importance of your plan by summarizing and amplifying the benefits of your plan, urging the readers to accept your ideas.

In proposals, benefits tend to take three forms:

- **Hard Benefits**—deliverables, outcomes, and results
- **Soft Benefits**—quality, service, and satisfaction
- **Value Benefits**—common ideals and standards shared by client and bidder

Hard Benefits

Hard benefits are the quantifiable outcomes of the project that the readers can see, touch, or measure. These benefits can be found in your Project Plan section, when you discussed the deliverables of your project. The deliverables are the "hard" (i.e., seeable, touchable, measurable) results of your efforts. You will notice that hard benefits work on two levels:

1. The clients receive *direct benefits* associated with possessing the deliverables highlighted in the Project Plan section (a building, PR campaign, a report).
2. *Consequent benefits* accompany these deliverables (more efficient employees, better relations with the community, understanding and insight).

For example, the direct benefits resulting from an implementation proposal might be tangible things like a new building, a new product, or a public relations campaign. These items are quantifiable objects that the readers can see, touch, or measure. These direct benefits also bring other consequent benefits to the client. A new building might make employees more efficient or allow the client's company to expand its services. A new product might mean more market share. A public relations campaign might result in a higher corporate profile or better ties to the community.

To identify the direct and consequent hard benefits, look back at your plan and list all the deliverables you promised the readers. Write those deliverables on the left-hand side of a benefits chart like the one shown in Figure 7.4. Then, in the

FIGURE 7.4
Benefits Chart

Hard Benefits		Soft Benefits	
Deliverables (Direct Benefit)	*Added Benefits* (Consequent Benefit)	*Strengths*	*Added Benefits*
Value Benefits			

right-hand column of the Hard Benefits section, write down all the additional advantages to the readers of possessing each deliverable. Write down anything that comes to mind, placing yourself in the position of the readers. Ask yourself how each deliverable would make the readers' situation better than it was before.

Soft Benefits

Soft benefits are the intangible advantages of working with your company or organization. These benefits include nonquantifiable qualities like trust, efficiency, satisfaction, and confidence. Overall, soft benefits cannot be held, seen, or even measured. Nevertheless, they are important benefits that your company or organization will bring to the readers. To find these soft benefits, look back at the Qualifications section at the strengths you wrote down for your company or organization. Pay special attention to your answer to the *what makes you different makes you attractive* question. Then, list these intangible benefits in the left-hand column of the benefits worksheet (Figure 7.4). In the right-hand column, write down the advantages of these soft benefits for the readers.

Of course, you can make any claims you want about things like quality or satisfaction, but the best soft benefits are ones that highlight special qualities unique to your company or organization. For example, if your company has a reputation for high-quality work, then stressing quality in the conclusion would be a good idea. However, if your company has had some notable quality failures, then your attempts to sell the readers on quality will sound a little hollow. For this reason, when you are discussing the soft benefits in the conclusion, you should concentrate on what makes your company or organization special or different from the competition.

Value Benefits

Value benefits refer to the common values held by the readers and your team or company. Look back at the reader analysis worksheet you developed in Figure 3.2 of Chapter 3. In that worksheet, you wrote down the primary readers' motives, values, attitudes, and emotions concerning the project. Under the *values* part of the worksheet, you identified some qualities that the readers value in themselves; therefore, it is pretty safe to assume they will value these qualities in the people they hire to complete a project.

For example, let us say you are bidding for a contract with Grandview Manufacturing. After reading through their literature and talking with the Point of Contact, you find that the CEO of the company values on-time production above all else. In the past, Grandview has been burned by suppliers who were not able to meet deadlines. As a result of these missed deadlines, their just-in-time manufacturing methods were completely undermined. Now, the CEO of the Grandview Manufacturing is adamant that all contractors will meet strict deadlines, even if timeliness costs his company more money up front. So, in your conclusion, you might stress your company's commitment to prompt, on-time service.

The bulk of the conclusion will be taken up with a discussion of the hard, soft, and value benefits that your proposal or grant is offering. In one way or another, you have already mentioned all these benefits in the body of the proposal, so there is no new information here. Rather, in the conclusion you are summarizing the benefits for the readers. By putting all these benefits together at this point, you will amplify the ending of the proposal—inviting the readers to say yes to your ideas.

Move 4: Look to the Future

Whether you are solving a problem or taking advantage of an opportunity, the bottom-line promise you are making to the readers is that the future will be better if they agree to your proposal or grant. For this reason, many writers will include a "Look to the Future" paragraph that illustrates for the readers the long-term advantages of the proposal's plan. For example, if you are proposing a new building, you can describe the company's employees working efficiently in its new state-of-the-art facility. If your grant is proposing a new summer jazz festival for your town, briefly describe people enjoying themselves on that summer day.

If you include a "Look to the Future" feature, you should keep it short—at most one paragraph. Its aim is to simply show the readers that your plan leads to long-term results, not a short-term fix.

Move 5: Identify the Next Step

A good way to put the final touches on a proposal is to thank the readers, ask them to contact you with any questions, and tell them the next step. The next step is what you want the readers to do immediately when they are finished looking over your proposal. Should they call you? Should they set up a meeting with you? Will you be calling them or scheduling a visit? The readers should finish your proposal with a clear idea of what action is needed to put the proposal into action.

Why is a next-step statement a good way to end the proposal? It is very common for readers to look over a proposal with approval, even excitement. Then, they file it away in some "good idea" stack or folder, because they do not know what needs to be done right now. The next-step statement is a trigger for the proposal. It tells the readers the small step they need to take right now to put the project into motion. Even million-dollar proposals need a starting place. Sometimes that starting place is a simple phone call to set up a meeting.

Concluding the Overture Designs Proposal

Lisa Miller's proposal to Overture Designs was starting to take shape. She felt good about her description of the current situation and her plan for developing a telecommuting system to manage Overture's limited office space. But she knew her conclusion would need to end the proposal on a strong note.

Figure 7.5 shows a rough draft of the conclusion she wrote for her proposal. In the first paragraph, Lisa decided to make two concluding moves. First, she

· FIGURE **7.5**

A Conclusion for the Overture Proposal

The Benefits of Telecommuting and Project Expenses

To conclude, let us summarize the advantages of our plan and discuss the costs. Our preliminary research shows us that Overture Designs will continue to be a leader in the Chicago market. The strong economy, coupled with Overture's award-winning designs, has bolstered the demand for its services. We believe the best way to manage growth, while maintaining Overture's financial flexibility, is to develop a LAN that will allow some of the company's employees to telecommute from home or from their worksite.

Cost is the most significant advantage of our plan. As illustrated in Appendix A, implementation of our plan would cost $177,611. We believe this investment in Overture's infrastructure will preserve the company's financial flexibility to react to the market's crests and valleys.

But the advantages of our plan go beyond simple costs. First, a telecommuting system will allow Overture's current operations to continue without disruption. When the telecommuting system is ready to go online, its employees will simply need to attend an afternoon of training sessions on using the LAN and intranet. At these training sessions, we will also teach them time-tested strategies for successful telecommuting from home. Overture's management team can then gradually convert selected employees into telecommuters.

Second, employee morale will benefit from our telecommuting plan. With fewer employees at the office, there will be more space available for the employees who need to be in the office each day. Studies have shown that telecommuting employees report more job satisfaction, and they increase their productivity. We believe this improved employee morale is especially important in the field of architecture, because architects often feel more comfortable working in less formal environments. The flexibility of telecommuting will allow Overture to recruit and retain some of the best people in the industry.

When the telecommuting system is in place, Overture will be positioned for continued growth and leadership in the Chicago architectural market. The key to Overture's success has always been its flexibility and innovativeness in an industry that seems to change overnight. Telecommuting will open up space at the current downtown office while maintaining the morale and productivity of the employees as its business continues to grow.

Thank you for giving Insight Systems the opportunity to work with you on this project. We are looking forward to the opportunity to submit a full proposal that describes our plan in greater depth. Our CEO, Dr. Hanna Gibbons, will contact you on May 15 to discuss the proposal with you and, if possible, set up a meeting.

If you have any suggestions for improving our plan or you would like to ask questions, please call Lisa Miller, our senior computer engineer, at 1-800-555-3864. Or, you can e-mail her at lmiller@insight_systems.com.

signaled the transition into the conclusion with phrases like "To conclude" and "let us summarize." With these obvious concluding sentences, Lisa intended to recapture the readers' interest and urge them to pay closer attention. Second, at the end of this opening, Lisa restated her main point for the proposal paragraph: "We believe the best way to manage growth, while maintaining Overture's financial flexibility, is to develop a LAN that will allow some of the company's employees to telecommute from home or from their worksite." Lisa hoped her repetition of the main point would create closure for the readers, driving home the most significant idea she wanted the readers to remember.

In the second paragraph, Lisa handled the costs. Because she was convinced her plan would cost less than the competitors' plans, she decided to phrase the costs as a benefit. Nevertheless, she stated the figure in a simple way, directing the readers to the appendix should they want to study the costs of the proposal in greater depth.

In the third and fourth paragraphs, she continued to stress the benefits of the telecommuting plan. She mentioned hard benefits like the minimal disruption to Overture's operations, increased morale, more office space, and increased productivity. These benefits were all quantifiable differences that would result from implementing the telecommuting system. She also mentioned some soft benefits, such as employee job satisfaction and comfort. These benefits would not be measurable, but they would be important quality-of-life issues for the readers. And finally, she worked in a few value benefits by stressing words like *success, flexibility, growth, innovativeness*, and *award-winning*. Lisa believed these words would highlight some of the common values that Overture and Insight Systems shared.

In the fifth paragraph, Lisa offered a look to the future. She tried to show the readers at Overture how the telecommuting system would create a better situation than their current one. She wanted to give them the impression that telecommuting would be a long-term solution in line with progressive thinking about the modern office.

Finally, in the last two paragraphs, Lisa told the readers the next step that would put the proposal into motion. She told the readers that Insight Systems' CEO, Hanna Gibbons, would be contacting them to discuss the proposal and set up a meeting. Then, she ended the proposal with contact information in case the readers would have questions.

Overall, Lisa's conclusion makes the five concluding moves mentioned in this chapter. But, most importantly, her conclusion stresses the main point (her plan) and its importance (the benefits). In her proposal's conclusion, Lisa did not include any new information, except a brief mention of the costs. Instead, she amplified her main points, driving home her argument for the readers.

Looking Ahead

Introductions and conclusions are partners in a proposal or grant. The role of an introduction is to create a framework, or context, for the body of the proposal. It identifies the proposal's subject, purpose, and main point while stressing the importance of the subject. The role of the conclusion is to bring the readers back to the proposal's main point while again stressing the importance of the subject. An effective conclusion reframes the discussion, amplifying the benefits of saying yes to the plan.

Even when the conclusion is finished, the proposal writing process is not over. In the next chapter, we will discuss how to write budgets. In the remaining chapters, we will discuss the style and visual presentation of a proposal. When you are finished with the conclusion, however, you should feel some satisfaction. After all, you are on the home stretch in the proposal-writing process.

CASE STUDY Beginnings and Endings

The Cool Campus Project was starting to look doable. Certainly, the grant proposal to the Tempest Foundation was making a persuasive argument. With the body of the proposal drafted, the group thought it was time to write the introduction and conclusion.

It seemed long ago that they wrote their original notes about the rhetorical situation. As they reviewed these notes, they were surprised at how much their ideas had evolved and matured while they drafted the body of the grant proposal. Originally, they had made some comments about things like recycling that were no longer part of the proposal. Also, when they started on the grant, they hadn't considered a charrette as a planning tool.

George said, "Our ideas have evolved quite a bit. To write the introduction and conclusion, we are going to need to refine some of our statements about the subject, purpose, and main point of the Cool Campus Project."

Tim went up to the whiteboard with a marker. "OK, what's different?"

Together, they revised their understanding of the rhetorical situation and then wrote down the grant's six introductory moves (Figure 7.6). They wrote a sentence for each move.

Defining the subject, purpose, and main point was not too difficult, but deciding how to stress the importance of the subject caused some debate.

"I think we need to say something scary," said Karen. "We need to stress the importance of global warming and doing something about it."

Anne was a little leery about that approach. "I think we need to remember that the Tempest Foundation has already acknowledged the importance of global warming. That's why they are willing to put money into these kinds of projects. We don't need to scare them."

"But we need to show them that we think the problem is a very important one," said Karen. "They need to see that we are taking this issue very seriously."

Calvin looked for middle ground. "Is there a way we can show the reviewers that we see global warming as a threat but also stress the advantages of doing something about it?"

Karen thought for a moment and said, "How does this sound: Global warming often seems like something that we can't do anything about, but at Durango University we believe we can do something by transforming our campus into a carbon-neutral site."

Anne said, "It still seems a bit too negative, but I like how you are contrasting the crisis with doing something about it. I think we should emphasize solving the problem more than describing the global warming crisis. Let's write Karen's sentence down for now."

To help them come up with background information, Tim had brought in the summary of the report from the Intergovernmental Panel on Climate Change (IPCC), which had been released in 2007. It offered some specific numbers about the effects of global warming.

"This looks great," said George. "These facts from the IPCC will tell the Tempest Foundation something they probably already know, but they will give us a common place to begin discussing the issue with the reviewers."

Finally, they wrote some forecasting statements that described the body of the proposal.

FIGURE 7.6

Sketching Out the Six Introductory Moves

Introduction	
Subject	The Cool Campus Project
Purpose	The purpose of this project is to develop a comprehensive strategic plan that will guide Durango University's conversion to renewable and sustainable forms of energy.
Main Point	We believe we can do something about global warming, and we are asking the Tempest Foundation to support our efforts to convert our campus to renewable and sustainable forms of energy.
Importance of Subject	Global warming poses a serious threat to our world, as described in the 2007 IPCC report, which shows significant rises in global temperature, rises in sea levels, increases in heat waves and droughts in the United States, heavier rainfall elsewhere, and meltoffs of the polar icecaps.
Background Information on Subject	Global warming is a significant problem that will have dire consequences unless we start taking action now. People feel helpless to do anything about it, but we all need to start doing our parts.
Forecasting	This proposal will (a) describe Durango University's current energy problem, (b) describe how we would use an urban planning charrette to write a strategic plan, (c) discuss our qualifications, and (d) describe the costs and summarize the benefits of our project.

Taking the notes from the group, Tim and Calvin began working on drafting the introduction. With the six introductory moves on the whiteboard, writing the introduction was not difficult at all. At times, they were tempted to put in too much content that was already in the body of the proposal. So, Calvin took it upon himself to delete any unnecessary content that was already handled in the body of the grant proposal.

While Tim and Calvin worked on the introduction, shown in Figure 7.7, the others began working on the conclusion.

Anne said, "All right. Let's go through the Project Plan section and Qualifications section to find any benefits and deliverables that we are promising. We need to summarize the most important benefits at the end of the proposal, so we can show the Tempest Foundation what they are receiving for their money."

While Anne and Karen were underlining the benefits in the Project Plan section, George pulled out a piece of paper and drew a benefits chart with four columns. The three of them began to fill out the chart. They also talked about *added benefits* and *value benefits* from the project. Figure 7.8 shows how they filled out the chart.

Soon afterward, Tim and Calvin were finishing up with the introduction. They read their rough draft out loud to the others, making notes for improvement. Then the team decided to draft the conclusion together.

FIGURE 7.7
A Draft of the Cool Campus Proposal's Introduction

The Cool Campus Project at Durango University: A Grant Request to the Tempest Foundation

The crisis of global warming can often seem overwhelming. How do we respond to a report like the one from the Intergovernmental Panel on Climate Change (IPCC), which describes some of the dire consequences of global warming:

- Global temperatures will rise from 2 to 11 degrees Fahrenheit this century.

- Sea levels will rise 7 to 23 inches, causing significant flooding of lowland areas.

- Heat waves and droughts will be more frequent and severe in the United States.

- Many parts of the world will experience much heavier rainfall.

- The polar icecaps will experience dramatic meltoffs, sending large ice shelves and icebergs into the ocean.

The report from the IPCC calls the evidence for global warming "unequivocal" and warns that unless humans dramatically cut emissions of greenhouse gases, the impact of global warming on this planet will be significant and perhaps catastrophic. These dire facts might lead people to conclude that we cannot do anything about this complex global problem.

At Durango University, we believe we *can* do something. In this proposal, we are asking the Tempest Foundation to support the Cool Campus Project at Durango University. The Cool Campus Project would convert our campus to alternative sources of energy, resulting in a carbon-neutral status. We would also create a model of energy independence that other universities can follow.

The campus has already made significant strides toward conserving energy, but a conversion to alternative energy sources requires much more thought and planning. Thus, we are turning to the Tempest Foundation for a grant to help us develop a Cool Campus Strategic Plan that will guide the conversion of our campus to renewable and sustainable energy sources. With a long-term strategic plan in place, we believe the Durango University campus could eliminate or offset its emissions of greenhouse gases by 2025. Meanwhile, as we work toward converting our campus to renewable energy sources, we would help other universities around the world follow our lead.

In this grant proposal, we will discuss Durango University's current energy usage and describe how we would use an urban planning charrette to develop and write the Cool Campus Strategic Plan. We will discuss our qualifications and the costs and benefits of the project. The funding provided by the Tempest Foundation would allow us to develop the Cool Campus Strategic Plan. With this plan in place, we can then devote our own resources toward making the Cool Campus Strategic Plan a reality.

Writing the conclusion was a little harder than the introduction, but it wasn't too difficult. As shown in Figure 7.9, they wrote down an obvious transition (i.e., "Let us conclude. . .") and then restated the purpose and main point of the project. The purpose became, "We are requesting $ XXX,000 from the Tempest Foundation to help us develop a Cool Campus Strategic Plan." The main point was, "With this strategic plan in place, we can start taking positive steps toward addressing the causes of global warming."

FIGURE 7.8
Benefits Chart for Cool Campus Proposal

Hard Benefits		Soft Benefits	
Deliverables	*Added Benefits*	*Strengths*	*Added Benefits*
• Cool Campus Strategic Plan	• Comprehensive local solution to global warming	• Community-centered	• Bring us together as a community
• Urban planning charrette	• Community involvement in process	• Variety of local alternative sources of energy	• Options and flexibility in solutions
• Create on-going dialogue about energy conservation and sustainable lifestyles	• Get buy-in from community and awareness	• Campus is not too large	• We can make significant changes without getting bogged down
• A steering committee that will guide the beginning of the Cool Campus Project	• A flexible, focused group that will be responsible	• Environmental Engineering program	• Experts available on campus for advice and insight
• Cool Campus library and website	• Local and worldwide access to information	• History of successful grants on environmental issues	• Confidence that project will be completed
• Model that other universities can follow	• Others could use our experiences		
• Regular progress reports to Tempest Foundation	• Keep foundation informed and involved		

Value Benefits
Independence to solve our own energy problems
Leadership in environmental issues
Better future for everyone
Knowledge and wisdom of the community

They then used a bulleted list to itemize the major benefits of their project. They couldn't mention all the deliverables and benefits they listed on the worksheet, so they concentrated on the most compelling ones.

They then wrote a "Look to the Future" paragraph that painted a positive image of a sustainable future fueled by renewable energy.

In the final paragraph, they thanked the reviewers and provided Anne's name, phone

FIGURE 7.9

FIGURE 7.9
The Conclusion of the Cool Campus Proposal

Conclusion: The Benefits of the Cool Campus Project

Let us conclude with a discussion of the costs and benefits of the Cool Campus Project. We are requesting $XXX,000 from the Tempest Foundation to help us develop the Cool Campus Strategic Plan. With this strategic plan in place, we can start taking positive steps toward addressing the causes of global warming on our campus. Our itemized budget is enclosed, and we believe that cost sharing with the Tempest Foundation is an important part of our contribution toward the project.

The benefits of the Tempest Foundation's support for the Cool Campus Project will be well worth the investment:

• The Cool Campus charrette will allow us to begin converting our campus to renewable energy from the grassroots up. The charrette will draw from the knowledge, wisdom, desires, and experiences of the community, while encouraging people to participate in and commit to the transformation process.

• The project will generate and cultivate an ongoing dialogue about energy conservation and sustainable lifestyles, which will have a direct impact on lives in our community and other communities.

• The Cool Campus Project will provide a model that other universities can follow to convert their campuses to renewable energy and a carbon-neutral status.

• The library we will develop will be accessible worldwide through the Durango University website, offering a comprehensive resource on issues related to global warming.

• The Cool Campus Project will be supported by our Environmental Engineering program, which has a track record of success in energy-related projects.

Perhaps the most significant benefit of the Tempest Foundation's investment is the development of a comprehensive strategic plan that will guide the conversion of our campus to a carbon-neutral status. We can then centralize the Cool Campus Project in our campus planning and take bold steps toward doing something about global warming.

We believe the Cool Campus Project at Durango University will give us a way forward into the future—a future that we can all look forward to. When the Cool Campus Project is completed, Durango University will have demonstrated that energy independence and sustainability are not only possible but highly advantageous. Today, our society no longer has the luxury to wait for others to take the lead on issues of global warming. At Durango University, we believe we can take steps right now that will help all of us to solve the global warming problem.

Thank you for your time and consideration. We look forward to hearing back from you about this request for a grant. If you have any questions, comments, or suggestions for improvement, please feel free to contact Anne Hinton, vice president for Physical Facilities at Durango University. Her phone number is (970) 555-1924. She can also be reached at anne.hinton@durangou.edu. We appreciate your willingness to consider our request.

---

number, and e-mail address as a point of contact. That seemed to end the grant proposal on a positive and professional note.

When they were finished drafting, Karen offered to revise the introduction and conclusion into a final form. She would e-mail it to them the next day for comments.

Tim spoke up, "Hey, it looks great, but there's an obvious problem here. We don't have an estimate for how much this project will cost."

"Yeah, that's always a tough thing to figure out," said George. "We still need to work out the budget. If you folks don't mind, I will sketch out the budget and schedule a meeting with the development officer for the College of Engineering. His name is Bill Vonn, and he is always very helpful."

"While you're doing the budget, I'll start editing the grant proposal to make the language smoother," said Anne. She turned to Calvin. "Calvin can you do some page design to make this thing more readable and attractive?"

Calvin said yes. Then, Tim said, "I'll come up with some graphics and images to add to the proposal. We can't just send them a bunch of words. We need to show as well as tell."

At this point, they were tired of working on the grant, but they were also excited about having a draft completed. There was still a good amount of work to be done, but they were getting closer all the time. They agreed to meet a week later with their parts of the project completed.

Questions and Exercises

1. Look at a proposal or grant you found on the Internet or at your workplace. In the introduction of the proposal, do the writers effectively frame the body of the proposal by clearly telling the readers the subject, purpose, and main point of the text? Does the introduction also stress the importance of the subject, offer background on the subject, and forecast the remainder of the proposal? Mark specific sentences where the writers make some or all of the six moves that are made in the introduction of a proposal. If some of these moves are missing, do you think the writers of the proposal had good reasons for leaving them out?

2. Now look at this proposal's conclusion. Does the proposal make a clear transition from the body to the conclusion? Where and how are the costs handled in the proposal? Were the authors hesitant or reluctant when they expressed the price of the project? Does the conclusion highlight hard, soft, and value benefits? Does it offer a look into the future for the readers? And finally, does it identify the next step, or trigger, that will put the proposal into motion? Mark specific sentences where the writers made some or all of the five moves common in a proposal's conclusion. If some of these concluding moves are missing, do you think the writers of the proposal had good reasons for leaving them out?

3. A common problem in most workplaces and campuses is obsolete computer facilities. Using a benefits worksheet like the one shown in Figure 7.4, list the hard, soft, and value benefits that would be gained if your university or workplace upgraded its computer hardware or software. Compare the benefits you listed with those listed by others in your class.

4. For a practice or real proposal of your own, fill out a six moves worksheet like the one shown in Figure 7.1. Then, write an introduction for your proposal in which you try to address only these moves.

5. Then, write a conclusion for your practice or real proposal in which you address only the five moves described in this chapter. Pay special attention to the benefits described in the body of your proposal. Summarize those benefits in your conclusion.

6. Compare the introduction you wrote for Exercise 4 with the conclusion you wrote for Exercise 5. Does the introduction "tell them what you're going to tell them" and does the conclusion "tell them what you told them"? In other words, do the introduction and conclusion reflect each other in ways that frame the body of the proposal?

8 | Developing Budgets

Overview

This chapter will discuss the basic elements of a budget and show you how to write stand-alone budget rationales for proposals and grants. The chapter will meet the following objectives:

1. Discuss the importance of a budget in a proposal or grant.
2. Provide a vocabulary for talking about budgets.
3. Discuss the different elements of a budget.
4. Show how to write a budget rationale.
5. Discuss additional strategies for creating budgets for grants.

Budgets: The Bottom Line

Like it or not, budgets are often one of the most important parts of any proposal or grant. After all, the bottom line *is* the bottom line. Clients and funding sources will scrutinize your project's budget with the eyes of a hawk. They will challenge the weak points in the budget, and they will try to cut away what they perceive to be fat. The more your readers cut out of your budget, the less flexibility you will have to complete the project. So, you want to be certain that your proposal's budget is sound and defensible.

Why are budgets so important? Put simply, proposals and grants are really about money. So, if the budget has problems, the whole proposal has problems. An unsound budget is one of the primary reasons why a proposal or grant is rejected. Worse yet, if the budget does not anticipate all the costs for the project, your company or organization will usually need to pay for the cost overruns. That is never a pleasant experience.

One way to safeguard against unsound budgets is to find a good accountant or bookkeeper to help you handle the money issues in a proposal. Let's be honest. Most people have trouble keeping their checkbooks straight. A budget for a project is vastly more complicated. To avoid these complications, a good accountant can help you anticipate some of the pitfalls of budget development. He or she can also flag costs that you may have overlooked or forgotten to include. You should visit an accountant soon after you have written a rough draft of your proposal so you can start identifying costs.

This chapter is not designed to be a substitute for a good accountant. Instead, it will discuss some of the basics of budgeting a proposal or grant. That way, you can sketch out a rough budget before visiting your accountant. In some cases, especially where the project is small, the concepts in this chapter will help you create a budget without an accountant.

Budget Basics

Like any profession, accountants have their own vocabulary. Let us start by going over some of the basics of budget development.

Itemized and Nonitemized Budgets

Budgets can either be *itemized* or *nonitemized*.

Itemized Budgets

Itemized budgets break down the proposal's expenses to their smallest elements (within reason). It shows the readers exactly how much money is going to be spent on each part of the project. In an itemized budget, there is little or no gray area or fungible places. You need to account for every dollar in the project. Itemized budgets often run several pages in a proposal.

Nonitemized Budgets

Nonitemized budgets, on the other hand, tend to be less exact. They are used when the readers do not need to know exactly where each dollar will be spent. Instead, the readers receive a rough breakdown of expenses to show them how you came up with the figures in the budget. Nonitemized budgets are shorter than itemized budgets because they tend to consolidate smaller costs into larger categories. In business proposals, the budget given to the client is often nonitemized, because the calculation of costs is considered proprietary information. For smaller grants, a few government foundations, like the National Science Foundation (NSF) and National Institutes of Health (NIH), allow brief nonitemized budgets called *modular budgets*.

For the following reasons, it is best to develop an itemized budget whether you intend to include one in the proposal or not:

- *An itemized budget helps you control your own costs.* This more detailed account of costs will help you keep track of where the money is being spent, even if your clients are satisfied with a nonitemized budget in the proposal. As the saying goes, the devil is in the details, especially when it comes to budgets. Itemization will help you find any hidden costs that will bleed money from your budget.
- *Clients and funding sources will often ask you how parts of the budget were calculated.* For example, if your budget lists a hundred-page training packet that

costs ninety dollars, the readers may want to know exactly how you came up with that figure. (After all, it would only cost them five dollars for each packet if they ran it off on their own copier.) If you create an itemized budget, you can point out in exact amounts how much hidden expenses, such as labor and overhead, add to the production of the packet.

You can always convert an itemized budget into a nonitemized budget, so it is best to create the itemized budget first.

Fixed and Flexible Budgets

Budgets can also be *fixed* or *flexible*.

Fixed Budgets

Fixed budgets promise to provide the readers a particular product or service for a set price. In fixed budgets, that bottom-line price does not change, even if production costs rise or fall during the project. For example, when using a fixed budget, if the costs of the materials used to make a product suddenly rise, you cannot go back to the client or funding source and expect them to increase your budget to cover those additional expenses. On the other hand, if the price of your materials drop, thus decreasing your costs, then you can usually keep that windfall. A fixed budget means the total price of the project will not increase or decrease.

Flexible Budgets

Flexible budgets tend to be used in proposals that describe ongoing projects, especially internal company projects. A flexible budget is adjusted monthly, quarterly, or yearly to reflect changes in project costs. At the end of each reporting period, the projected costs in the budget are compared to actual costs, and adjustments are made for the next reporting period (see Donnelly 1984, p. 42). A flexible budget allows a company to regulate the costs of a project, modifying the budget to suit changes in objectives or the economy. With external proposals, flexible budgets tend to work only when there is a close relationship between a supplier and client. In these cases, the proposal and its budget are rewritten periodically to suit changes in costs.

If you are uncertain, you should talk to your readers and your accountant about whether a fixed or flexible budget is appropriate for your proposal.

Fixed, Variable, and Semivariable Costs

An accountant will often begin a budget discussion by helping you identify the fixed, variable, and semivariable costs that will be involved in the project. Even with a fixed budget, some of your costs will fluctuate during the project. By identifying which costs are fixed, variable, and semivariable, the accountant can anticipate the behavior of these costs and estimate the appropriate figures for the budget (see Ramsey and Ramsey 1985, pp. 26–30). To save time (and money), you should try to break down your costs into these fixed, variable, and semivariable categories before you meet with an accountant.

Fixed Costs

Fixed costs are those expenses that will remain constant over the duration of a project. These costs might include the rent for facilities or equipment, yearly depreciation of facilities or equipment, and management's salaries and benefits. Fixed costs tend not to change with increases or decreases in production. In other words, even if your company increases production by 15 percent, the fixed costs will generally remain the same.

Variable Costs

Variable costs are expenses that change proportionally with increases or decreases in production. For example, if your company needs to increase production 5 percent, then variable costs like labor, materials, and energy costs will also increase by about 5 percent. An increase in production, after all, means you will need to buy more materials, hire more labor, and pay more energy costs.

Semivariable Costs

Semivariable costs are those expenses that fluctuate with production but not in direct proportion to production. For example, if you need to temporarily increase production by 5 percent to complete a project, you may need to pay your current hourly employees overtime at 1.5 times their normal rate. Also, if production increases 5 percent, the costs to repair your equipment may increase 15 percent. On the other hand, higher volume often means lower prices on materials, causing these costs to be lower. The difference between variable and semivariable costs is how they fluctuate with production. Variable costs rise and fall in step with production, while semivariable costs rise and fall in ways that are not in step with production.

For the most part, do not lose any sleep over this three-part division of costs. The division into fixed, variable, and semivariable costs is really only a convenient way for accountants to anticipate fluctuations that may occur as you take on a new project. Of course, the lines between these three categories are blurred. Mostly, the categories provide a starting point from which to identify which kinds of costs can be predicted safely and which need to be estimated.

Budgeting in Teams

Budgeting a project with a management team can be a real headache. The best way to talk over the budget with a team is to decide whether your proposal needs a fixed or flexible budget. If the project has a clear conclusion date, your team will most likely need a fixed budget. If the proposal describes an ongoing program or operation, then your team may decide to develop a flexible budget with specific dates that identify when the budget will be reevaluated and adjusted.

Once you have decided what kind of budget you are creating, ask the team to list expenses. Then, sort these expenses into fixed, variable, and semivariable categories. For the variable and semivariable items, ask each team member to write notes describing how these costs fluctuate with production. Where possible, have team members provide examples describing how costs rise and fall with production. For instance, a team member might write, "Our suppliers charge us thirty dollars per chip for 100 microchips. For each additional 100 chips, we receive a dollar per chip price reduction, up to 500 chips. Therefore, if we buy 500 chips, they will each cost us twenty-six dollars per chip."

Pulling together all these costs is a complicated process. Once all team members have submitted their projected costs, you can create a master file of costs that you will bring to your accountant. The explanations and notes provided by the team members will help you and the accountant devise an overall budget.

Developing a Budget

Some clients, especially the federal government, will tell you exactly how they want you to break down project costs. In these cases, you should follow the guidelines they provide. If the clients or funding sources do not provide any guidelines on the budget, you can start the budgeting process by dividing your costs into the following categories:

- Management, principal investigators, and salaried labor
- Direct labor or staff
- Indirect labor
- Facilities and equipment
- Direct materials
- Indirect materials
- Travel
- Communication
- Profit (business proposals only)
- Facilities and administrative (F&A) (grant proposals only)
- Cost sharing (grant proposals only)

Depending on whether you will include an itemized or nonitemized budget in your proposal, all of these categories may or may not be represented in the budget you submit with the proposal. Nevertheless, all costs for a project should be assigned to a category in your itemized budget. Let us look at these categories individually.

Management, Principal Investigators, and Salaried Labor

As a fixed cost, the rates for management, principal investigators, and salaried labor are calculated according to the percentage of their time that they will devote to the proposed project (Figure 8.1). For example, let us say the project leader, who makes $120,000 per year, is going to spend 100 percent of his time on the project for six months. In the budget, you would identify him by name, write down his total yearly salary, and then multiply by .5 because he is spending half his time that year on the project. So, you would write down $60,000 for this manager on the budget sheet. Another manager who makes $120,000 is only going to

FIGURE 8.1

A Basic Budget Worksheet

			Total Cost
1. Management	Salary	Time Devoted to Project	
a. Project Manager (listed by name)			
Benefits			
b. Principal Managers and Supervisors (listed by name)			
Benefits			
c. Other Managers (indirect labor)			
d. Consultants			
e. Additional Management Training			
Total Management Costs			
2. Labor	Hours on Project	Cost per Hour	
a. Direct labor			
Level One			
Level Two			
Level Three			
b. Indirect labor			
Level One			
Level Two			
Level Three			
c. Hiring			
d. Training			
e. Labor Overhead			
Fringe Benefits Insurance Vacation Sick Leave Retirement			
Total Labor Costs			
3. Facilities and Equiptment			Total Cost
Facilities			
a. Building Lease			

FIGURE 8.1
(Continued)

			Total Cost
b. Retooling Costs			
c. Depreciation of Facilities			
d. Insurance			
Equipment			
a. Computer Hardware and Software			
b. Tools			
c. Tables, Chairs, Desks			
d. Depreciation of Equipment			
Total Facilities and Equipment Costs			
4. Materials			
a. Direct Materials			
b. Indirect Materials			
c. Documentation (e.g., user manuals)			
Total Materials Costs			
5. Travel			
a. Air Travel (itemized by trip)			
b. By Car (estimated per mile)			
c. Lodging and Meals (per diem)			
Total Travel Costs			
6. Communication			
a. Phone			
b. Internet Provider			
c. Postage			
d. Documentation (e.g., reports)			
Total Communication Costs			
Pre-Profit/Pre-F&A Estimated Costs			
Cost Sharing (if applicable)			
Profit/F&A Costs			
Taxes (if applicable)			
Total Costs			

devote a quarter of her time to the project over that six-month period. You would multiply her salary times .5 (for the six months) and .25 (for the quarter time) to come up with an amount of $15,000.

In business proposals and grants, top managers and principal investigators are named in the budget separately and their costs are estimated individually. You may ask yourself, "How do I know how much time per week this manager is going to spend on this project?" After all, managers spend some days on one project and other days on another. Nevertheless, you should estimate how much time *on average* a manager is going to spend on each project. Use that average percentage to calculate how much that person's time will cost.

Other management-related issues to keep in mind are benefits, training, and any outside consultants or specialists that your managers or principal investigators will require to do their jobs. Benefits might include health insurance, vacation, and leave. Your accountant should calculate the costs for these benefits. Training includes any special courses or learning tools your project managers would need to prepare for the project. If your managers or principal investigators need the help of outside consultants or specialists, build the costs of those consultants into this part of the budget. Consultants and specialists are usually compensated on a retainer or contract basis. When preparing the budget, you may need to designate a pool of cash out of which consultants or specialists will be paid, if needed.

Direct Labor

Direct laborers are paid on an hourly basis. In a factory, direct laborers are the people assembling the product. In a store, the direct laborers are the people who run the cash registers, stock the shelves, and help people at the customer service desk, among other tasks. In a nonprofit organization, these people are your staff, lab workers, or anyone you pay hourly to work on the project.

Direct labor is calculated on an hourly basis. First you need to estimate how many hours an average hourly employee will spend on the project. Then, multiply those hours by the average amount your hourly employees make. Of course, employees are paid on a variety of different levels, especially in larger companies. Sometimes it helps to identify these levels in the budget and their respective pay scales. Then calculate the costs of the employees at each level separately (Figure 8.1). For example, if you have ten "Level 3" employees working at an average of $18.25 per hour, each hour worked by these ten employees will cost the client $182.50. In a project that is estimated to take one thousand hours, these employees will cost the client $182,500. Meanwhile, twenty "Level 2" employees working at an average $15.75 per hour for one thousand hours will cost $315,000.

If your direct labor requires any special training or you will need to hire new employees for a particular project, you should build those costs into this part of the budget. It might seem odd to charge a client for training your employees, but that money needs to come from somewhere. If the client wants a special service, then they should be willing to pay for you to hire and train employees.

Direct labor also requires you to estimate *labor overhead*. Labor overhead includes fringe benefits, insurance, vacations, sick leave, and retirement.

Overhead is typically calculated from standard formulas that an accountant will have available. Again, it is best to leave these calculations to the accountants.

Indirect Labor

Indirect laborers are the people who support the direct labor. Indirect laborers might include salaried supervisors, repair and janitorial services, and office and clerical support. In a budget, indirect labor is usually broken down into subcategories and charged on a salaried or hourly basis. The costs of salaried labor, especially for larger projects, is estimated similarly to the costs of management, meaning salaries are multiplied by the percentage of time these employees will spend on the project.

Hourly indirect labor is handled similarly to hourly direct labor. To calculate hourly indirect labor, estimate how many hours your repair staff, janitors, office, and clerical workers will devote to a particular project. In the budget, list these subcategories and their costs separately (Figure 8.1).

As with direct labor, overhead should be calculated by an accountant and included with the costs for indirect labor.

Facilities and Equipment

The facilities and equipment section of the budget includes the fixed and semi-variable costs of the buildings, equipment, and machinery that will be used, bought, or leased during the project. Facilities costs include any construction, renovation, or retooling of your factories, laboratories, or workspaces to accommodate the needs of the project. Also, place any expenses like insurance and maintenance supplies in this part of the budget.

Any machines, tools, office or laboratory equipment, desks and chairs, and computer hardware or software that are leased or purchased would also be handled under this part of the budget. List the costs for larger pieces of equipment separately in the itemized budget, and group smaller items into subcategories (Figure 8.1). In most cases, it is assumed that you (the bidder or grantee) will keep the purchased equipment and tools after the project is completed; nevertheless, you should clarify with the client who owns the equipment and tools after the project is completed.

In this section of the budget, you should also include the costs of depreciation for preexisting and purchased facilities and equipment that are used for the project. Depreciation is the lost value of facilities and equipment due to wear and aging during the project. Your company or organization is entitled to charge that depreciation to the client. Depreciation is calculated according to a general formula that your accountant will have available. As with overhead, let the accountant handle these calculations for your budget.

Direct Materials

Direct materials include the materials that will make up the products or services you are developing for the client. For example, if you are proposing to produce a bike, the direct materials might include metal for the frame, tires, tape for the handlebars, and so on. In an office environment, direct materials might include paper and supplies that go into the production of reports, manuals, videotapes, or CD-ROMs. In construction, direct materials might include lumber, fabric, pipes, or windows. If you are a researcher, direct materials would involve any chemicals or materials that will be disposed of when the project is complete. Essentially, direct materials are the items that will be the client's property or disposed of after the project is completed.

In your budget, list the direct materials that will go into the products and services. Then multiply the costs of these direct materials by the amount of products you will produce (Figure 8.1).

One type of direct materials that is often forgotten is the *documentation* for the product. If your deliverables include a user manual or website, make sure you include those costs in the direct materials part of the budget.

Indirect Materials

Indirect materials are the items that are used to turn direct materials into the product. For instance, cleaning supplies or lubricants for machinery are indirect material costs, because they are materials that are used while producing the product. In an office, sometimes supplies like paper, pens, pencils, staplers, toner for the copy machine are put in this indirect materials category (Figure 8.1).

The section handling indirect materials is often the forgotten part of a budget, and many companies and nonprofit organizations have lost money because they didn't include these items. Supplies like paper, staples, and toner might sound like small things until you realize that they add up quickly.

Travel

Travel costs are often hard to estimate accurately, especially air travel costs. If your project involves travel for training, research, supervision, meetings, or conferences/conventions, you should build these travel costs into the budget.

- For travel by air, estimate how many trips will be needed. Then contact a nationally recognized airline and ask their standard business rate for travel to and from the places you will need to travel. Avoid using an airline's sale prices to estimate travel costs, because the prices often increase before you need to fly.
- Travel by train or bus is a bit easier to estimate because the rates do not fluctuate as wildly as airline rates. When estimating these costs, call up the bus or train company and ask for their standard business rate for travel to and from the places you will need to travel. Then enter those total costs in the budget.
- Travel by car—yours or your company's—is charged by the mile. Most organizations have a set rate for reimbursing mileage. Otherwise, the U.S. government publishes a standard rate that is a low but widely accepted figure. When you estimate the mileage for a project, make a generous estimate of how many miles you or your colleagues might be asked to travel during

the project, keeping in mind that your actual mileage usually ends up higher than estimated mileage from Point A to Point B. Then, multiply those miles by the per-mile rate provided by your organization or the government. If you plan on renting cars, you should only plan to charge the clients the cost of the rental and the gas. With rental cars, you should not charge mileage.

- If you need to stay at any hotels or other kinds of short-term lodgings, make sure you build those costs into the travel portion of the budget. To estimate these costs, call up the major hotel near the place you might stay. Ask for their standard *rack rate* for a night. The rack rate is usually higher than the rate they actually charge their guests, but this rate can be documented for the client or funding source. If you end up staying at the hotel for less than the standard room rate, you can use the savings to offset travel costs, which are usually more than you expected.

It is wise not to underestimate travel costs. These costs can fluctuate wildly, especially with the volatile costs of airfare, so don't budget for the cheapest possible rates.

Communication

Another hidden project expense is communication costs. Almost certainly, you are going to need access to phone, fax, letter, and the Internet. Even though these items may seem free to the average employee, they cost your company or organization money. Your accountant should be able to estimate how much a project's phone calls, faxes, postage, and Internet provider will cost. Otherwise, you may need to look at your records from past projects to help you estimate how much it will cost to communicate with others.

Communication also includes any costs to *disseminate* your findings, especially with grant-funded projects. Funding sources want any discoveries or new concepts sent out to journals, magazines, or universities. If the funding source wants you to communicate with others, build those costs into this part of the budget.

Profit (Business Proposals Only)

You or your company deserves to make a profit for providing your products or services to the clients. In proposals, profits are handled two ways. First, the profit can be built into the cost of the product or service. For example, let us say one unit of a company's product costs fifty dollars to produce. The budget submitted to the client, however, charges fifty-five dollars per unit. In this case, the bidder has chosen to use the product as the source of his profit, because each package/participant will yield five dollars in profit.

The second way to handle profit, especially when you are providing the client with an itemized budget, is to simply include a "profit" line in the budget (Figure 8.1). If you are submitting a proposal to a government agency, you will often be required to disclose the profit you are making on the product or service. The profit then becomes an additional charge based on a flat rate or a percentage of the actual costs. An accountant should be able to help you develop a fair estimate of the profit you will receive.

There are advantages to both ways of calculating profit. Building the profit into the costs of the product or service is a hidden way to create a profit margin in a proposal. But you might find yourself defending the costs of your seventy-dollars per-unit product when the client argues it should only cost sixty dollars to produce. The advantage of a separate profit line is that it clearly shows the clients how much money beyond the costs you would like to make for your products or services. However, the profit line is also an obvious addendum in a budget, making it a prime target for negotiation.

In most proposals, profit is not expressed directly in the budget. Companies often consider their profit calculations to be "confidential" and are reluctant to submit them to the client. Also, some larger companies consider their profit margin nonnegotiable, even though everything in a proposal is ultimately open for negotiation.

Whichever way you choose to create a profit margin in your budget, you should remember two things when it comes to estimating your profit. First, your profit is the cushion in your proposal's budget. No matter how good you and your accountant are at estimating costs, the actual costs always end up being different. If the final costs are higher, then those overruns will come out of your profit. If the costs are lower than you expected, you can add those savings to your overall profit. In the end, the profit can often be your safety net when your estimates are off, so make sure the profit offers a sufficient cushion to handle overruns. Also, avoid cheating yourself out of a fair profit for your work. Sometimes bidders end up working for costs alone, leaving them nothing on which to grow their company.

Second, the profit is often the primary negotiating point between the client and bidder. Clients realize your company needs to make a profit; nevertheless, they are going to do their best to pay you as little as they can for your products and services. The profit in a budget is often the most obvious place to negotiate. After all, we may not be able to debate the costs of equipment or salaries, but profit is usually just a sum of cash calculated from a formula or flat rate. The clients will often ask you to reduce your profit percentage or your flat rate. It's up to you whether you will consider it.

Again, there is no substitute for a good accountant when you are working out these kinds of issues in a budget. An accountant can help you come up with the best way to express the profit in your budget.

Facilities and Administrative Costs (F&A) (Grant Proposals Only)

Nonprofit organizations, especially universities, will often include a budget line called *facilities and administrative costs* (F&A) or *indirect costs*. These costs cover the overhead costs of your university or nonprofit organization. At many research universities, these costs are about half the pre-F&A costs of any project completed on campus. In other words, after all the project's costs are calculated, they are multiplied by about 50 percent. That additional amount is then added to the budget. Projects done off campus are usually calculated at a lower rate.

These kinds of costs are usually not under your control, so let your organization's accountant figure them out. But, you should keep these costs in mind, because they will significantly inflate the total costs of your project.

Cost Sharing (Grant Proposals Only)

Another wrinkle in a grant proposal budget is the opportunity (or requirement) for cost sharing, meaning your organization or another funding source will share some of the costs of the project. These costs are usually handled with *matching funds* and *in-kind contributions*.

Matching Funds

A funding source may require your organization to fully or partially match the funds offered. For example, a foundation may ask you to match their grant 1 to 1, meaning you need to match each of the foundation's dollars with a dollar from your organization or another source. Or, a funding source may tell you they will only pay for 50 percent of equipment costs. If so, your organization would be responsible for supplying or finding the other 50 percent to pay for those costs.

Nonprofit organizations raise matching funds in a few ways:

- Withdraw cash from an endowment or similar fund
- Promise to do a fundraiser if the grant is awarded
- Match the funds with grants from other funding sources

Matching with cash can be problematic for nonprofit organizations, so you should be careful about grant opportunities that require cash matching. A funding source may award you a large grant, but you need to be realistic about whether your organization can raise the cash to match that amount.

In-kind Contributions

In-kind contributions are non-cash gifts and services that can often be used to match the funds provided by a funding source. These contributions can come in many forms, including volunteer time, donated goods and services from patrons, and donated space. For example, you can calculate the value of your volunteers' time (usually by the hour) and use that time as cost sharing. Similarly, if supporting businesses donate goods and services, such as materials or accounting services, you can add those to your in-kind contribution.

Some excellent sources for in-kind contributions are your facilities. If your organization has a facility that is already paid for, you can often contribute some of the costs of that facility to the grant. For example, let's say a gallery in your building will house a display of some kind. You can calculate the potential rent and upkeep of that gallery to use as in-kind contributions. No money is actually changing hands, because you already own the building and you would pay for the electricity, heat, water, and janitorial services anyway. Nevertheless, you can use those costs to offset the match.

In your budget sheet, cost sharing can be represented two ways. You might include a line in the budget called "cost sharing" in which you sum up all of the matching and in-kind contributions. Or, many nonprofits like to add a column in their budget sheet that helps them itemize the costs that will be shared.

Even if the funding source does not specifically ask for cost sharing, it's not a bad idea to show that your organization will find ways to share the cost burden. Cost sharing shows the organization's financial commitment to the project, which will make the funding source more comfortable about putting up its own resources.

Writing the Budget Rationale or Budget Section

In most cases, the budget should be written as a stand-alone section. As discussed in Chapter 7, some proposal writers prefer to sandwich a Budget section between the Qualifications section and the Costs and Benefits section. Other proposal writers prefer to only mention the bottom-line costs of the project in the Costs and Benefits section. Then they move the larger discussion of the budget, called a "budget rationale," to an appendix.

There are, of course, pros and cons to both approaches. A Budget section placed inside the body of the proposal ensures that the readers will look over your cost figures. On the other hand, a Budget section can run on for pages, bogging down the readers in numbers and perhaps causing them to forget the merits of your project. Placing the budget and a budget rationale in an appendix is a good way to avoid these problems. However, once in awhile, readers will complain that the budget is being "hidden" in the appendix.

Wherever you choose to include the budget, you should think of it as an argument that stands on its own. It is usually not sufficient to say, "Here is our budget," as though the table of expenses speaks for itself. Rather, you should explain your reasoning in coming up with your figures.

Like any other section in a proposal, the Budget section or rationale has an opening, body, and conclusion. The opening paragraph identifies the subject of the section (the budget) and the purpose of the section (to present and discuss the costs of the project). It should also include a main point that the Budget section will prove. For example, you might claim, "By keeping expenses low, we offer the most efficient fabrication services in this industry." This kind of claim will focus your discussion of the budget, giving the section something to prove.

The body of the Budget section backs up that kind of claim with a table of expenses and explanatory remarks that highlight the important parts of the budget. The aim of this budget rationale is to anticipate some of the readers' questions about the costs. Most readers are not as familiar with equipment, facilities, and materials as the company or organization submitting the proposal, so a little explanation can go a long way toward helping the readers feel confident about the cost of the project. A table of budget figures like the one shown in Figure 8.1 is the heart of a Budget section or rationale. Your discussion of the budget should refer to specific lines in the budget table, at times illustrating how and why the figures were calculated in a particular way.

The closing of a Budget section or rationale should restate the main point you made in the opening paragraph. The closing, usually only a sentence or two, is designed to round off the section and reinforce the soundness of your cost estimates.

As mentioned in Chapter 7, you should suppress any urges to be apologetic or defensive about the costs of your proposal. The budget is where you need to sound most confident. Otherwise, the readers will doubt the soundness of your figures, or they will detect a place where they can negotiate from a position of strength. The best approach is to just discuss the budget in a straightforward way.

The Budget for the Overture Designs Proposal

The RFP from Overture Designs stated, "At this stage, exact cost estimates are not expected; however, pre-proposals should include a cost estimate. Overture will negotiate for a final fee with the firm that submits the most feasible final proposal." Lisa Miller knew this statement meant that Overture was only looking for a general idea of how much the project would cost. In the conclusion of her proposal, she would mention a bottom-line figure. However, she also wanted to include a nonitemized budget that would highlight some of the major expenses of the project.

With her team of engineers, Lisa went over the project as described in her Project Plan section. She had the engineers estimate the costs involved with their part of the project. She also asked them to break the costs down into fixed, variable, and semivariable costs to help her and the in-house accountant at Insight Systems anticipate how costs might fluctuate with any alterations to the plan.

Later that week, Lisa worked with the accountant to draw up a rough budget for the project. Figure 8.2 shows the nonitemized budget table she placed in Appendix A. The figure also shows how she provided concise explanations of the costs of her proposal.

Lisa's budget includes an opening, body, and conclusion like any section in the body of the proposal. The opening explains the purpose of the section and offers some background information. The body explains the more significant items in the budget table. The conclusion rounds out the budget discussion by reinforcing the main point of the proposal and offering contact information.

Of course, Lisa's Budget section could have just as easily been placed in the body of the proposal. After all, her appendix offers a brief discussion of the budget, and it is not overly distracting. Nevertheless, Lisa sensed that the two principal architects at Overture (her proposal's primary readers) were mostly interested in the plan and a bottom-line cost. Lisa wanted to include a breakdown of the budget, but she also wanted to avoid distracting the readers from her plan. If Overture accepted her pre-proposal, she would write up an itemized budget that would break down the costs into greater detail.

The advantage of including a stand-alone budget like the one Lisa wrote to Overture is that it provided a self-contained argument. The readers would be able

FIGURE 8.2
A Nonitemized Budget for the Overture Designs Proposal

Appendix A: Budget

At Insight Systems, we pride ourselves on developing low-cost solutions for managing limited office space. In this appendix, we would like to go over some of the major costs of the telecommuting plan discussed in this proposal. These figures are estimates, as you requested in your RFP. We will provide a fully itemized budget with a formal proposal. Table A offers a summary of our estimated costs for the Overture Designs project.

Table A: Budget Summary

Item	Cost
Management and Labor	$55,982
Equipment Rental and Purchase	7,250
Hardware and Software	70,482
Materials	20,340
Travel	2,298
Communications	700
Costs Before Profit	$157,052
Profit (10% of before-profit costs)	15,705
Taxes (Gross Receipts)	4,854
Total Costs	$177,611

As shown in Table A, management and labor are our primary costs. These costs represent two full-time managers, three computer engineers, two carpenters, and an electrician who will all be committed full time to the Overture project.

Hardware and software make up the other significant expense in our budget. Where possible, we will utilize Overture's existing computer infrastructure. However, additional hardware and software will be needed to upgrade the current infrastructure and create a LAN server.

Finally, our estimates for materials are dependent on the amount of carpentry required to hardwire the LAN system into your current operations. Our materials estimate in Table A is based on similar-sized projects we have handled in the past.

Overall, you should find that these costs are a small investment in your company's infrastructure that will help you manage your limited office space while allowing you to maintain financial flexibility. If you have any questions about these figures, please call Lisa Miller at 1-800-555-3864 or e-mail her at lmiller@insight_systems.com.

to consider the money issues separately from the solution Lisa described in the Project Plan section.

Looking Ahead

Never underestimate the importance of the budget in a proposal or grant. Consider how you go about purchasing any product. You closely evaluate the merits of the product and take its drawbacks into account. But almost always, the last thing you think about before buying something is the price. The last question you need to answer is, "Do I feel as though this item is worth the asking price?" The more information you have about the product, the less you will hesitate to say yes or no.

Readers evaluate proposals and grants in much the same way. They look over the whole proposal, but in the end it all comes down to the money. The more information the readers have about how the budget was developed, the more likely they are to make a firm decision about whether your proposed plan suits their needs.

The next few chapters will discuss the style and design of proposals and grants. At this point, you should have drafted your entire proposal. Now, it's time to revise and design the proposal to make it easier to read and more persuasive.

CASE STUDY **Money Issues**

George accepted the always-difficult task of working out the budget for the Cool Campus grant proposal. He had learned long ago that involving a financial specialist as early as possible was a good idea, so he scheduled a meeting with Bill Vonn, the development officer for the College of Engineering. George had written several successful grant applications to the U.S. government, but this was the first grant he intended to send to a private foundation. He was uncertain about how to handle the budget issues.

As soon as George called him, Bill was enthusiastic about the Cool Campus Project. Durango University had not sent a grant application to the Tempest Foundation for six years, so he was eager to re-establish connections with the foundation. He thought the grant had a good chance of being funded.

George was still concerned. "I'm just not sure how we divide up these costs," he said. "What will the foundation pay for and what are they going to balk at?"

Bill replied, "George, I think you're getting ahead of yourself. Let's go through the grant and identify the specific costs in the project."

George and Bill began underlining the major costs of the project:

- Fee for an urban planner or urban planning firm
- Salaries for the project leaders and participants in the project
- Rental of ballroom and breakout rooms for the charrette
- Promotional materials and activities to invite stakeholders to the charrette
- Supplies for the charrette
- Food and refreshments for the charrette
- A room at the library to archive and store materials
- A webmaster to develop and maintain a website
- Projectors for presentations at the charrette and other meetings
- Equipment for creating podcasts of the meetings

- Postage to send items to the Tempest Foundation
- Funding for phone calls
- Travel costs for project leaders, urban planners, and project reviewers
- Costs to disseminate results of the project
- Honoraria for project evaluators

George looked at the list. "There's no way they are going to pay for all these things," he groaned.

Bill smiled and said, "You're right. But that's not all bad. The university will need to pay for some of these items. We will put those items in the 'cost-sharing' and 'in-kind' columns in the budget. Plus, we can count items like salaries and volunteer time toward cost-sharing, too."

"I see," said George. "Writing a grant to a foundation is a little different than writing a grant to the National Science Foundation or the Department of Energy."

"True. Private foundations are going to expect the university to foot some of the bill for this project. We can do much of the cost-sharing by taking advantage of stuff we're already paying for, like renting the ballroom in the union."

"Rent?" asked George.

"Yeah, the ballroom would cost $1000 to rent for the weekend. So, we can put that in-kind cost on our side of the ledger."

"That's helpful."

Bill then added, "And, if President Wilson is really behind this project, he'll promise to put some of the university's money into the budget. That will show the Tempest Foundation that the University is really serious about this project."

Bill pulled out a budget worksheet and began filling it out. After crunching the numbers, Bill and George wrote up a tentative budget and budget rationale, shown in Figure 8.3.

As Bill added up the numbers, George started getting concerned again. "Wow, that added up quick," he said.

"It always does," said Bill. "Private foundations don't have bottomless pockets of money, but they are willing to dig deeper for significant projects. If they like this project, the Tempest Foundation will be willing to put in a significant amount. If they can't afford to give us the full amount, they will tell us what they can afford. At that point, we may need to find someone else, like a donor, who can make up the difference."

"What about F&A costs? Will they pay those?" asked George.

"I doubt it. The university will need to waive those costs. This project, though, really isn't research, so persuading the university to waive F&A shouldn't be too difficult."

"We'll keep our fingers crossed."

FIGURE 8.3

A Draft Budget Rationale and Summary for the Cool Campus Project

---

Appendix A: The Cool Campus Project Budget

The start-up expenses for the Cool Campus Project will be modest, and Durango University is committed to sharing the costs with the Tempest Foundation. The major costs will include hiring an urban planner to organize and facilitate the charrette. We will also ask the Tempest Foundation for funding to promote the charrette, provide supplies, support expenses and honoraria for reviewers, and fund travel for project leaders. Minor costs will include items like funding for phone calls, postage, and materials for disseminating the results of our project.

Durango University will cost-share by paying the salaries of project leaders and participants, purchasing food and refreshments for the charrette, and providing equipment and space. We will also calculate as in-kind contributions the time of volunteers and our webmaster. Table A shows our budget and how we arrived at the costs for this phase of the Cool Campus Project.

FIGURE 8.3
(Continued)

Table A: The Budget

Item	Tempest Foundation	Durango University
Project Leaders' Salaries and Benefits		
George Tillman (20 percent time)		$20,650.00
Anne Hinton (10 percent time)		14,120.00
Major Participants' Salaries and Benefits		
Diane Smith, urban planner	$12,000.00	
Gina Sanders, librarian (10 percent time)		6,800.00
Staff and Assistants		
3 facilitators	10,000.00	
5 research assistants (50 percent time)	11,450.00	
Clerical assistance (100 hours @ 15.00/h)	9,000.00	3,000.00
Volunteers (200 hours @ 15.00/h)		
Services and Facilities		1,500.00
Rental of ballroom in student union		2,550.00
Room at library to house materials		540.00
Projector rental		450.00
Podcasting equipment rental		200.00
Space on server for website		
Materials		
Supplies for charrette	430.00	
Promotional materials	980.00	4,000.00
Food and Refreshments		
Travel and Housing Expenses		
Project leaders	3,200.00	
Urban planners	3,000.00	
Evaluators	2,000.00	
Communications and Dissemination		
Phone	230.00	
Postage	310.00	
Documentation	930.00	
Evaluation		
Honoraria for 2 evaluators	1,000.00	(waived)
Indirect Costs (F&A)		$53,810.00
Total Costs	$54,530.00	

Bill made a copy of the budget sheet and the rationale. He then said, "OK, you finish writing up your budget. I'm going to put in a call to the university's head development officer. She'll be able to tell us how much the university can put into this project and how much donor money we could raise for it. Then I'm going to call the point of contact at the Tempest Foundation to see how he or she feels about some of these costs."

"Thank you," said George as Bill began walking toward the door.

Bill laughed, "Hey, that's my job. I'm just glad you didn't run in here the day before the grant's due date. The extra time gives me some flexibility to work with the university and the foundation. Your project looks great. Let's keep our fingers crossed."

Questions and Exercises

1. Using your own personal finances, divide your expenses into fixed, variable, and semivariable costs. List these costs in a budget table in which you show yourself as management or labor (depending on whether you receive a salary or are paid hourly). Then, write a one-page budget rationale to your parents, spouse, or friend in which you justify the major expenses in your budget.

2. Find a proposal or grant on the Internet, at your workplace, or from your campus that includes an itemized budget. Where does the budget appear in the proposal? How does the placement of the budget influence the reading of the whole proposal? How does the budget itemize costs? Does the proposal include a rationale that explains parts of the budget to the readers?

3. Write a budget for a practice or real proposal or grant. First, decide whether you need a fixed or flexible budget. Second, list your major costs, dividing them into fixed, variable, and semivariable categories. Third, place these costs in a budget worksheet, breaking them down according to the larger categories described in this chapter. Finally, write a short budget rationale in which you lead the readers through the highlights of your budget.

4. Ask your local Small Business Association representative about the budget requirements for a business plan to start a new business. Ask the representative what kinds of information investors or banks need in order to consider lending money. When you are finished, report your findings to your class.

5. Ask a grants officer on your college campus about the process for writing a budget for a grant. Ask how his or her office likes writers of grants to be involved in the budgeting process. Ask about the typical mistakes in budgeting made by writers of grants. When you are finished, report your findings to your class.

Writing with Style

Overview

This chapter discusses the use of stylistic techniques to clarify writing while making it more persuasive. This chapter will meet the following objectives:

1. Discuss the importance of style in proposals and grants.

2. Define style and the role of style in writing.

3. Show how to use the plain style.

4. Show how to use the persuasive style.

Good Style Is a Choice, Not an Accident

Some people believe that style is not important to writing proposals and grants. After all, they say, the content of the proposal is what counts. Style just makes that content sound better.

Actually, style is a critical feature of any proposal. Style expresses the attitude of your company or organization toward the work. Style also reflects character by signifying the relationship your company or organization wants to build with the readers (Laib 1993, p. 21). In a word, style is about quality. Style is about your company's or organization's commitment to excellence and attention to detail.

Good style is a choice you can and should make. This chapter will discuss two types of style that are prevalent in proposals and grants. The *plain style* involves writing strong sentences and paragraphs that express your ideas clearly to the readers. The *persuasive style* is used to motivate the readers by appealing to their emotions and values. Both the plain and persuasive styles have their place in any given proposal. The challenge is to balance these two styles in ways that will inform the readers successfully and move them to action.

What Is Style?

Style operates at a few different levels in a proposal. On the sentence level, good style might involve choosing the right words or forming sentences that are easy to read. On the paragraph level, style could involve weaving sentences together in ways that emphasize your main points and lead the readers comfortably through your ideas. At the document level, style involves setting an appropriate tone and weaving themes into your work that appeal to your readers' emotions and values. In his book *Technical Writing Style,* Dan Jones defines style the following way:

> Style affects or influences almost all other elements of writing. Style is your choices of words, phrases, clauses, and sentences, and how you connect these sentences. Style is the unity and coherence of your paragraphs and larger segments. Style is your tone— your attitude toward your subject, your audience, and yourself—in what you write. Style is who you are and how you reflect who you are, intentionally or unintentionally, in what you write (p. 3).

Style does more than make the content easier to read and more persuasive. In many ways, it illustrates your clear-headedness, your emphasis on quality, and your willingness to communicate and work with the readers.

Style is not embellishment or ornamentation. Some people mistakenly believe that style is the spice sprinkled over a proposal to make the content more palatable to the readers. They throw in some extra adjectives and an occasional metaphor to perk up the bland parts of the proposal. But, just as spices are most flavorful when they are properly cooked into food, style needs to be carefully worked into the proposal. Indeed, a proposal that uses stylistic devices to embellish the content might really be hinting to the readers that the proposal lacks substance. Style enhances and amplifies content, but it should never be used to artificially embellish or hide a lack of content.

Writing Plain Sentences

As a student, you were more than likely advised to "write clearly" or "write in concrete language," as though simply making up your mind to write clearly or concretely was all it took to do so. In reality, writing plainly is a skill that requires practice and concentration. Fortunately, once you have learned and mastered a few simple guidelines, writing plainly will become a natural strength in your writing.

To start, let us consider the parts of a basic sentence. From your grammar classes, you learned that a sentence typically has three main parts: a subject, a verb, and a comment. The subject is what the sentence is about. The verb is what the subject is doing. And the comment says something about the subject. For example, consider these three variations of the same sentence.

Subject	Verb	Comment
The Institute	**provides**	**the government with accurate crime statistics.**

Subject	Verb	Comment
The government	**is provided**	**with accurate crime statistics by the Institute.**

Subject	Verb	Comment
Crime statistics	**were provided**	**to the government by the Institute.**

FIGURE 9.1
Sentence Guidelines

Guideline 1: The subject should be what the sentence is about.

Guideline 2: Make the "doer" the subject.

Guideline 3: State the action in the verb.

Guideline 4: Put the subject early in the sentence.

Guideline 5: Eliminate nominalizations.

Guideline 6: Avoid excessive prepositional phrases.

Guideline 7: Eliminate redundancy.

Guideline 8: Make sentences "breathing length."

The content in these sentences has not changed. Nevertheless, the emphasis in each sentence changes as we replace the subject slot with different nouns. Sentence A is *about* the "Institute." Sentence B is *about* the "government." Sentence C is *about* the "crime statistics." By changing the subject of the sentence, we essentially shift the focus of the sentence, drawing our readers' attention to different issues.

This simple understanding of the different parts of a sentence is the basis for eight guidelines that you can use to write plainer sentences in proposals (Figure 9.1). We will discuss these sentence guidelines in more detail in the following pages.

Guideline 1: The Subject Should Be What the Sentence Is About

At a very simple level, weak style often occurs when the readers cannot easily identify the subject of the sentence, or the subject of the sentence is not what the sentence is about. For example, what is the subject of the following sentence?

1. Ten months after the Hartford Project began in which a team of our experts conducted close observations of management actions, our final conclusion is that the scarcity of monetary funds is at the basis of the inability of Hartford Industries to appropriate resources to essential projects that have the greatest necessity.

This sentence is difficult to read for a variety of reasons, but the most significant problem is the lack of a clear subject. What is this sentence about? The word *conclusion* is currently in the subject position, but the sentence might also be about the *experts*, the *Hartford Project*, or *scarcity of monetary funds*. Many other nouns also seem to be competing to be the subject of the sentence, such as *observations*, *management*, *structure*, *conclusion*, *inability*, and *company*. These nouns bombard the readers with potential subjects, undermining their efforts to identify what the sentence is about.

When the sentence is restructured around *experts* or *scarcity*, most readers will find it easier to understand:

1a. Ten months after the Hartford Project began, <u>our experts</u> have concluded through close observations of management actions that the scarcity of monetary funds is at the basis of the inability of Hartford Industries to appropriate resources to essential projects that have the greatest necessity.

1b. The <u>scarcity of monetary funds</u>, our experts have concluded through close observations of management actions ten months after the Hartford Project began, is at the basis of the inability of Hartford Industries to appropriate resources to essential projects that have the greatest necessity.

Both of these sentences are still rather difficult to read. Nevertheless, they are easier to read than the original because the noun occupying the subject slot is the focus of the sentence—that is, what the sentence is about. We will return to this sentence about Hartford Industries after discussing the other guidelines for plain style.

Guideline 2: Make the "Doer" the Subject
Guideline 3: State the Action in the Verb

In your opinion, which revision of sentence 1 above is easier to read? Most people would point to sentence 1a, in which *experts* is in the subject slot. Why? In sentence 1a, the experts are actually doing something. In sentence 1b, *scarcity* is an inactive noun that is not doing anything. Whereas experts take action, scarcity is merely something that happens.

Guidelines 2 and 3 reflect the tendency of readers to focus on who or what is doing something in a sentence. To illustrate, which of these sentences is easier to read?

2a. On Saturday morning, the paperwork was completed in a timely fashion by Jim.

2b. On Saturday morning, Jim completed the paperwork in a timely fashion.

Most people would say sentence 2b is easier to read because Jim, the subject of the sentence, is actually doing something, while the paperwork in sentence 2a is inactive. The active person or thing usually makes the best subject of the sentence.

Similarly, Guideline 3 states that the verb should contain the action in the sentence. Once you have determined who or what is doing something, ask yourself what that person or thing is doing. Find the action in the sentence, and make it the verb. For example, consider these sentences:

3a. The detective investigated the loss of the payroll.

3b. The detective conducted an investigation into the loss of the payroll.

3c. The detective is the person who is conducting an investigation of the loss of the payroll.

Sentence 3a is easier to understand because the action of the sentence is expressed in the verb. Sentences 3b and 3c are increasingly more difficult to understand, because the action, *investigate,* is further removed from the verb slot of the sentence.

Guideline 4: Put the Subject Early in the Sentence

Subconsciously, readers start every sentence looking for the subject. The subject anchors the sentence, because it tells the reader what the sentence is about. So, if the subject is buried somewhere in the middle of the sentence, the readers will have greater difficulty finding it, and the sentence will be harder to read. Consider these two sentences:

4a. If deciduous and evergreen trees experience yet another year of drought like the one observed in 1997, the entire Sandia Mountain ecosystem will be heavily damaged.

4b. The entire Sandia Mountain ecosystem will be heavily damaged if deciduous and evergreen trees experience yet another year of drought like the one observed in 1997.

The problem with sentence 4a is that it forces the readers to hold all those details (i.e., trees, drought, 1997) in short-term memory before the sentence identifies its subject. Readers almost feel a sense of relief when they find the subject, because until they locate it they cannot figure out what the sentence is about. Quite differently, sentence 4b tells the readers what the sentence is about up front. With the subject early in the sentence, the readers immediately know how to connect the comment with the subject.

Of course, introductory or transitional phrases do not always signal weak style. But when these phrases are used, they should be short and to the point.

Guideline 5: Eliminate Nominalizations

Nominalizations are perfectly good verbs and adjectives that have been turned into awkward nouns. For example, look at these sentences:

5a. Management has an expectation that the project will meet the deadline.

5b. Management expects the project to meet the deadline.

In sentence 5a *expectation* is a nominalization. Here, the perfectly good verb *expect* is being used as a noun. After turning the nominalization into a verb, sentence 5b is shorter than sentence 5a, and it also has more energy because the verb *expect* is now an action verb.

Consider these two sentences:

6a. Our discussion about the matter allowed us to make a decision on the acquisition of the new X-ray machine.

6b. We discussed the matter and decided to acquire the new X-ray machine.

Sentence 6a includes three nominalizations *discussion, decision,* and *acquisition,* making the sentence hard to understand. Sentence 6b turns all three of these nominalizations into verbs, making the sentence much easier to understand. An additional benefit to changing nominalizations into verbs is the energy added to the sentence. Nouns tend to feel inert to the readers, while verbs tend to add action and energy.

Why do writers use nominalizations in the first place? First, humans generally think in nouns, so our first drafts are often filled with nominalizations, which are nouns. While revising, an effective writer will turn those first-draft nominalizations into action verbs. Second, some people believe that using nominalizations makes their writing sound more formal or important. In reality, though, nominalizations only make sentences harder to read. The best way to sound important is to write sentences that readers understand.

Guideline 6: Avoid Excessive Prepositional Phrases

Prepositional phrases are necessary in writing, but they are often overused in ways that make writing too long and too tedious. Prepositional phrases follow prepositions (e.g., *in, of, by, about, over, under*), and they are used to modify nouns. For example, in the sentence "Our house by the lake in Minnesota is lovely," the phrases *by the lake* and *in Minnesota* are both prepositional phrases. They modify the nouns *house* and *lake.*

Prepositional phrases are fine when used in moderation, but they are problematic when used in excess. For example, in sentence 7a the prepositions have been italicized and prepositional phrases underlined. Sentence 7b is the same sentence with fewer prepositional phrases:

7a. The decline *in* the number *of* businesses owned *by* locals *in* the town *of* Artesia is a demonstration *of* the increasing hardship faced *in* rural communities *in* the Southwest.

7b. Artesia's declining number of locally owned businesses demonstrates the increased hardship faced by southwestern rural communities.

Don't eliminate all the prepositional phrases in a sentence. Rather, look for places where prepositional phrases are chained together in long sequences. Then try to condense the sentence by turning some of the prepositional phrases into adjectives. For example, in sentence 7b the phrase *in the town of Artesia* was reduced to the adjective *Artesia's.* The phrases *in rural communities in the Southwest* were reduced to *by southwestern rural communities.* The resulting sentence 7b is much shorter and easier to read.

Guideline 7: Eliminate Redundancy

In our efforts to stress our points, we often use redundant phrasing. For example, we might write *unruly mob,* as though some mobs are orderly, or we might talk about *active participants,* as though someone can participate without doing anything. Sometimes buzzwords and jargon lead to redundancies like, "We should collaborate together as a team" or "Empirical observations will provide a new understanding of the subject." In some cases, we might use a synonym to modify a synonym by saying something like, "We suggested important, significant changes."

Redundancies should be eliminated because they use two words to do the work of one. As a result, the readers need to work twice as hard to understand one basic idea.

Guideline 8: Make Sentences "Breathing Length"

A natural sentence is one that can be spoken in one breath. When a text is read out loud, the period at the end of each sentence is our signal to breathe. Of course, when reading silently, we do not actually breathe when we see a period. Nevertheless, we do take a mental pause at the end of each sentence. A sentence that runs on and on forces us to hold our breaths, mentally. By the end of an especially long sentence, we are more concerned about getting through it than deciphering it.

The best way to think about sentence length is to imagine how long it takes to comfortably say a sentence out loud. If the written sentence is too long to say out loud in one breath, it probably needs to be shortened or cut into two sentences. After all, you don't want to asphyxiate your readers. On the other hand, if the sentence is very short, perhaps it needs to be combined with one of its neighbors to make it a more comfortable breathing length. You also want to avoid hyperventilating the readers with a string of short sentences.

A Simple Method for Writing Plainer Sentences

To sum up the eight sentence guidelines, here is a process for writing plainer sentences. First, write your draft as usual, paying little attention to the style. Then, as you revise, identify difficult sentences and apply the six steps shown in Figure 9.2.*
With these six steps in mind, let us revisit sentence 1, the example of weak style offered at the beginning of our discussion of plain style.

Original

1. Ten months after the Hartford Project began in which a team of our experts conducted close observations of management decisions, our final conclusion is that the scarcity of monetary funds is at the basis of the inability of Hartford Industries to appropriate resources to essential projects that have the greatest necessity.

Revision

1a. After a ten-month study, our experts concluded that Hartford Industries' budget shortfalls limit its support for priority projects.

FIGURE 9.2
Six Steps to Plainer Writing

1. Identify who or what the sentence is about.
2. Turn that who or what into the subject, and then move the subject to an early place in the sentence.
3. Identify what the subject is doing, and move that action into the verb slot.
4. Eliminate prepositional phrases, where appropriate, by turning them into adjectives.
5. Eliminate unnecessary nominalizations and redundancies.
6. Shorten, lengthen, combine, or divide sentences to make them breathing length.

---

*In his book *Revising Business Prose*, Richard Lanham offers a simpler technique that he calls the "paramedic method." His method is less comprehensive than the one shown here, but it works well also.

In the revision, the subject (*our experts*) was moved into the subject slot, and then it was moved to an early place in the sentence. Then, the action of the sentence (*concluded*) was moved into the verb slot. Prepositional phrases like *to appropriate resources to essential projects* were turned into adjectives. Nominalizations like *conclusion* and *necessity* were turned into verbs or adjectives. And finally, the sentence was shortened to breathing length. The resulting sentence still offers the same content to the readers—just more plainly.

Writing Plain Paragraphs

Some simple methods are available to help you write plainer paragraphs in proposals and grants.

The Elements of a Paragraph

Paragraphs tend to include four kinds of sentences: a transition sentence, a topic sentence, a support sentence, and a point sentence. Each of these sentences plays a different role in the paragraph.

Transition Sentence

The purpose of a transition sentence is to make a smooth bridge from the previous paragraph to the next paragraph. For example, a transitional sentence might state, "With these facts in mind, let us consider the current opportunity available." The *facts* mentioned were explained in the previous paragraph. By referring to the previous paragraph, the transition sentence provides a smooth bridge into the new paragraph. Most paragraphs, however, do not need a transition sentence. These kinds of sentences are typically used when the new paragraph handles a significantly different topic than the previous paragraph. The transition sentence is used to redirect the discussion from the previous topic to the new topic.

Topic Sentence

The topic sentence is the claim or statement that the rest of the paragraph is trying to prove or support. In a proposal, topic sentences typically appear in the first or second sentence of each paragraph. They are placed up front in each paragraph for two reasons. First, the topic sentence sets a goal for the paragraph to reach by telling the readers the claim you are trying to prove. Then, the remainder of the paragraph proves that claim with facts, examples, and reasoning. If the topic sentence appears at the end of the paragraph, the readers are forced to rethink all the details in the paragraph now that they know what the paragraph was trying to prove. For most readers, all that mental backtracking is a bit annoying.

The second reason for putting the topic sentence up front is that it is the most important sentence in any given paragraph. Since readers tend to pay the greatest attention to the beginning of a paragraph, placing the topic sentence up front guarantees they will read it closely. Likewise, scanning readers tend to concentrate on the beginning of each paragraph. If the topic sentence is buried in the middle or at the end of the paragraph, they will miss it.

Support Sentences

The support in the body of the paragraph can come in many forms. In Chapter 4, you learned that there are two ways to argue logically (i.e., using reasoning and using examples). Sentences that use reasoning tend to make if/then, cause/effect, better/worse, greater/lesser kinds of arguments for the readers. Sentences that use examples illustrate points for the readers by showing them situations or items that support your claim in the topic sentence. For the most part, sentences that contain reasoning and examples will make up the bulk of a paragraph's support sentences. Other support will come in the form of facts, data, definitions, and descriptions. Support sentences are intended to help prove the claim made in the paragraph's topic sentence.

Point Sentences

Point sentences usually restate the topic sentence at the end of the paragraph. They are used to reinforce the topic sentence by restating the paragraph's original claim in new words. Point sentences are especially useful in longer paragraphs where the readers may not fully remember the claim stated at the beginning of the paragraph. These sentences often start with transitional devices like *therefore, consequently,* or *in sum* to signal to the readers that the point of the paragraph is being restated. Point sentences are optional in paragraphs, and they should be used only occasionally when a particular claim needs to be reinforced for the readers. Too many point sentences will cause your proposal to sound too repetitious and even condescending to the readers.

Of these four kinds of sentences, only the topic sentence and the support sentences are needed for a good paragraph. Transitional sentences and point sentences are useful in situations where bridges need to be made between paragraphs or specific points need to be reinforced.

Here are the four kinds of sentences used in a paragraph:

8a. How can we accomplish these five goals? (transition) Universities need to study their core mission to determine whether distance education is a viable alternative to the traditional classroom (topic sentence). If universities can maintain their current standards while moving their courses online, then distance education may provide a new medium through which nontraditional students can take classes and perhaps earn a degree (support). Utah State, for example, is reporting that students enrolled in their online courses have met or exceeded the expectations of their professors (support). If standards cannot be maintained, however, we may find ourselves returning to the traditional on-campus model of education (support). In the end, the ability to meet a university's core mission is the litmus test to measure whether distance education will work (point sentence).

8b. Universities need to study their core mission to determine whether distance education is a viable alternative to the traditional classroom (topic sentence). If universities can maintain their current standards while moving their courses online, then distance education may provide a new medium through which nontraditional students can take classes and perhaps earn a degree (support). Utah State, for example, is reporting that students enrolled in their online courses have met or exceeded the expectations of their professors (support). If standards cannot be maintained, however, we may find ourselves returning to the traditional on-campus model of education (support).

As you can see in paragraph 8b, a paragraph works fine without transition and point sentences. Nevertheless, these additional sentences can make texts easier to read while amplifying important points.

Aligning Sentence Subjects in a Paragraph

Have you ever needed to stop reading a paragraph because each sentence seems to go off in a new direction? Have you ever run into a paragraph that actually feels bumpy as you read it? More than likely, the problem was a lack of alignment of the paragraph's sentence subjects. To illustrate, consider this paragraph:

9. <u>The lack</u> of technical knowledge about the electronic components in automobiles often leads car owners to be suspicious about the honesty of car mechanics. Although they might be fairly knowledgeable about the mechanical workings of their automobiles, <u>car owners</u> rarely understand the nature and scope of the electronic repairs needed in modern automobiles. For instance, the <u>function and importance</u> of a transmission in a car is generally well known to all car owners, but the <u>wire harnesses and printed circuit boards</u> that regulate the fuel consumption and performance of their car are rarely familiar. <u>Repairs</u> for these electronic components can often run over <u>four hundred dollars</u>—a large amount for a customer who cannot even visualize what a wire harness or printed circuit board looks like. In contrast, a <u>four-hundred-dollar charge</u> for the transmission on the family car, though distressing, is more readily understood and accepted.

There is nothing really wrong with this paragraph—it's just hard to read. Why? It is difficult to read because the subjects of the sentences change with each new sentence. Look closely at the underlined subjects of the sentences in this paragraph. These subjects are all different, causing each sentence to feel like it is striking off in a new direction. As a result, each new sentence forces the readers to shift focus to concentrate on something new.

To avoid this bumpy, unfocused feeling, line up the subjects so each sentence in the paragraph stresses the same issues. To line up subjects, first ask yourself what the paragraph is about. Then, restructure the sentences to align with that subject. Here is a revision of paragraph 9 that focuses on the "car owners" as subjects:

9a. Due to their lack of knowledge about electronics, some <u>car owners</u> are skeptical about the honesty of car mechanics when repairs involve electronic components. Most of our <u>customers</u> are fairly knowledgeable about the mechanical features of their automobiles, but <u>they</u> rarely understand the nature and scope of the electronic repairs needed in modern automobiles. For example, most <u>people</u> recognize the function and importance of a transmission in an automobile, but the average <u>person</u>

knows very little about the wire harnesses and printed circuit boards that regulate the fuel consumption and performance of their car. So, for most of our customers, a <u>four-hundred-dollar repair</u> for these electronic components seems like a large amount, especially when <u>these folks</u> cannot even visualize what a wire harness or printed circuit board looks like. In contrast, most <u>car owners</u> think a four-hundred-dollar charge to fix the transmission on the family car, though distressing, is more acceptable.

This paragraph is easier to read because *car owners* and related subjects are in the subject slot of each sentence. This makes the paragraph sound more focused. In this revised paragraph, you should also notice two things. First, *car owners* are not always the exact words used in the subject slot. Synonyms and pronouns should be used to add variety to the sentences. Second, not all the subjects need to be related to car owners. In the middle of the paragraph, for example, *four-hundred-dollar repair* is the subject of a sentence. This deviation from *car owners* is fine as long as the majority of the subjects in the paragraph are similar to each other. In other words, the paragraph will still sound focused, even though an occasional subject is not in alignment with the others.

Of course, the subjects of the paragraph could be aligned differently to stress something else in the paragraph. Here is another revision of paragraph 9 in which the focus of the paragraph is *repairs*.

9b. <u>Repairs</u> to electronic components often lead car owners, who lack knowledge about electronics, to doubt the honesty of car mechanics. The <u>nature and scope of these repairs</u> are usually beyond the understanding of most nonmechanics, unlike the typical mechanical repairs with which customers are more familiar. For instance, the <u>importance of fixing</u> the transmission in a car is readily apparent to most car owners, but <u>adjustments</u> to electronic components like wire harnesses and printed circuit boards are foreign to most customers—even though these electronic parts are crucial in regulating their car's fuel consumption and performance. So, <u>a repair to these electronic components,</u> which can cost four hundred dollars, seems excessive, especially when the repair can't even be visualized by the customer. In contrast, <u>a four-hundred-dollar replacement</u> of the family car's transmission, though distressing, is more readily accepted.

In this paragraph, the subjects are aligned around words associated with repairs. It is important to notice that paragraph 9a is easier for most people to read than paragraph 9b. Paragraph 9a is more readable because it has "doers" in the subject slots throughout the paragraph. In paragraph 9a, the car owners are active subjects, while in paragraph 9b the car repairs are inactive subjects. Much like sentences, the best subjects in a paragraph are people or things that are doing something.

The Given/New Method

Another way to write plain paragraphs is to use the *given/new method* to weave sentences together. Developed by Susan Haviland and Herbert Clark in 1974, the given/new method is based on the observation that readers will try to fit new information into what they already know. Therefore, every sentence in a paragraph will begin with something the readers already know (i.e., the given) and end with something new that the readers do not know. To illustrate, consider these two paragraphs:

10a. New Mexico is a beautiful place. Artists sometimes choose to strike off into the mountains. Studios around the state are another favorite place to work. The southwestern landscapes are wonderful in this enchanted state.

10b. New Mexico is a beautiful place for artists to work. Some artists choose to strike off into the mountains. Other artists enjoy working in the many studios around the state. Both the mountains and the studios offer places to paint the wonderful southwestern landscapes of this enchanted state.

Both of these examples are readable, but paragraph 10b is easier to read because each new sentence carries over something from the previous sentence.

Typically, the given information should appear early in the sentence and the new information should appear later in the sentence. Placed early in the sentence, the given information will provide a familiar anchor or context for the readers. Later in the sentence, the new information builds on that familiar ground. Consider this larger paragraph:

11. Recently, an art gallery exhibited the mysterious paintings of Irwin Fleminger, a modernist artist whose vast Mars-like landscapes contain cryptic human artifacts. One of Fleminger's paintings attracted the attention of some young schoolchildren who happened to be walking by. At first, the children laughed, pointing out some of the strange artifacts in the painting. Soon, though, the artifacts in the painting drew the students into a critical awareness of the painting, and they began to ask their bewildered teacher what the artifacts meant. Mysterious and beautiful, Fleminger's paintings have this effect on many people, not just schoolchildren.

In this paragraph, the beginning of each sentence provides something given, usually an idea, word, or phrase drawn from the previous sentence. Then, the comment of each sentence adds something new to that given information. By chaining together given and new information, the paragraph builds the readers' understanding gradually, adding a little more information with each sentence.

In some cases, however, the previous sentence does not offer a suitable subject for the sentence that follows it. In these situations, transitional phrases can be used to provide the readers given information in the beginning of the sentence. To illustrate,

12. This public relations effort will strengthen Gentec's relationship with leaders of the community. With this new relationship in place, the details of the project can be negotiated with terms that are fair to both parties.

In this sentence, the given information in the second sentence appears in the transitional phrase, not the subject. Transitional phrases are a good place to include given information when the subject cannot be drawn from the previous sentence.

To sum up at this point, there are two primary methods available for developing plain paragraphs: (1) aligning the subjects of the sentences and (2) using the given/new method to weave the sentences together. Both methods are useful in proposal writing and should be used interchangeably. In some cases, both methods can be employed in the same paragraph as the writer uses various techniques to weave the paragraph into a coherent whole.

When Is It Appropriate to Use Passive Voice?

Before discussing the elements of persuasive style, we should expose one important boogie monster as a fraud. Since childhood, you have probably been warned against using passive voice. Teachers or supervisors may have told you that passive voice was off-limits, period. It's bad for you, they said. Never use it.

Passive voice can be problematic because it removes the doer from the sentence. For example, consider this passive sentence and its active counterpart:

13a. The door was closed to ensure privacy. (passive)

13b. Frank Roberts closed the door to ensure privacy. (active)

Written in passive voice, sentence 13a lacks a doer. The subject of the sentence, the door, is being acted upon, but it's not really doing anything.

Despite dire warnings about passive voice, it does have a place in proposals, especially highly technical or scientific proposals. Either of the following conditions makes a passive sentence appropriate:

- The readers do not need to know who or what is doing something in the sentence.
- The subject of the sentence is what the sentence is about.

For example, in Sentence 13a, the person who closed the door might be unknown or irrelevant to the readers. Is it important that we know that *Frank Roberts* closed the door? Or, do we simply need to know the door was closed? If the door is what the sentence is about and who closed the door is not important, then the passive is fine.

Consider these other examples of passive sentences:

14a. The shuttle bus will be driven to local care facilities to provide seniors with shopping opportunities. (passive)

14b. Jane Chavez will drive the shuttle bus to local care facilities to provide seniors with shopping opportunities. (active)

15a. The telescope was moved to the Orion system to observe the newly discovered nebula. (passive)

15b. Our graduate assistant, Mary Stewart, moved the telescope to the Orion system to observe the newly discovered nebula. (active)

In both these sets of sentences, the passive sentence may be more appropriate, unless there is a special reason Jane Chavez or Mary Stewart need to be singled out for special consideration.

When developing a focused paragraph, passive sentences can often help you align the subjects and use given/new strategies. For example, consider the following two paragraphs:

16a. The merger between Brown and Smith will be completed by May 2008. Initially, Smith's key managers will be moved into Brown's headquarters. Then, other Smith employees will be gradually worked into the Brown hierarchy to eliminate any redundancies. During the merger process, employees at both companies will be offered all possible accommodations to help them through the uncertain times created by the merger.

16b. Brown and Smith will complete their merger in May 2008. Initially, Bill's Trucking Service will move the offices of key managers at Smith into Brown's headquarters. Brown's human resources manager will then gradually move Smith's other employees into the Brown hierarchy to eliminate any redundancies. During the merger, vice presidents, human resources agents, and managers at all levels will offer accommodations to employees at both companies to help them through the uncertain times created by the merger.

Most people would find Paragraph 16a more readable because it uses passive voice to put the emphasis on *employees*. Paragraph 16b is harder to read because it includes irrelevant doers, like Bill's Trucking Service, and it keeps changing the subjects of the sentences, causing the paragraph to seem unfocused.

In scientific and technical proposals, the passive voice is often the norm because *who* will be doing *what* is not always predictable. For example, in Sentence 15b, we might not be able to predict in our proposal that Mary Stewart will actually be the person adjusting the telescope on a given evening. More than likely, all we can confidently say is that *someone* at the observatory will move the telescope on a particular day. So, the passive is used because *who* moves the telescope is not important. On the other hand, the fact that the telescope will be moved is important.

Used properly, passive voice can be a helpful tool in your efforts to write plain sentences and paragraphs. Passive voice is misused when the readers are left wondering who or what is doing the action in the sentence. In these cases, the sentence should be restructured to put the doer in the subject slot of the sentence.

Persuasive Style

Persuasive style can help motivate readers to say yes to your ideas. Designed to move readers to take action, persuasive style is best used at strategic points where you are trying to emphasize or amplify specific ideas. As a rule of thumb, this style is best used in places where you expect the readers to make decisions.

There are, of course, many ways to be persuasive. In proposals and grants, though, the following four persuasion techniques will give your writing more impact:

- Elevating the tone
- Using similes and analogies
- Using metaphors
- Changing the pace

Let us consider each of these techniques separately.

Elevating the Tone

Tone is essentially the resonance or pitch that the readers will "hear" as they are looking over your proposal. Most people read proposals silently to themselves, but all readers have an inner voice that vocalizes the words as they move from sentence to sentence. By paying attention to tone, you can influence the readers' inner voice to read the proposal with a specific emotion or attitude. You can also use tone to establish a sense of character that will reassure the readers about your, your team's, or your company's credibility. Tone puts a human face on the text, if only momentarily, to appeal to the readers on an emotional and character level.

Writers will often choose to elevate the tone at strategic places in the proposal, especially in introductions, openings, closings, and conclusions. For the most part, the plain style, which is used in the bulk of the proposal, sets a rather neutral, professional tone. As you near the closing paragraph of larger sections or the conclusion of the proposal, however, you should gradually elevate the tone of your writing to express a particular emotion or character. Effective public speakers use this tone elevation technique all the time. Their speech may start out with a good amount of energy, but it soon settles into a rather plain style. When the speaker nears important transition points or the conclusion, he elevates the tone. Hearing this elevated tone, the audience knows the speaker is nearing an important point, so they listen more closely.

One easy way to elevate tone in written texts is to first decide what feelings of emotion or character you want to heighten at important points in the proposal. Then map out those feelings on a piece of paper. For example, let us say we want to convey a sense of excitement as the readers are looking over the proposal. We would first put the word *excitement* in the middle of a sheet of paper. Then, as shown in Figure 9.3, we would map out the feelings associated with that emotion.

To insert this tone of excitement in your proposal, you can weave these words into the text at strategic moments. Subconsciously, the readers will detect this elevated tone in your work, and their inner voice will begin reinforcing the sense of excitement you are trying to convey.

Similarly, if you want to add in a particular sense of character, map out the words associated with that character trait. For instance, let us say you want your proposal to convey a sense of security. A map around the word *security* might look like the diagram in Figure 9.4. If you weave these words associated with *security* into strategic places in the proposals, your readers will perceive the sense of security that you are trying to convey.

FIGURE 9.3
Mapping a Tone That Shows Emotion

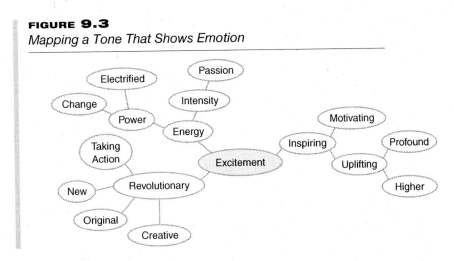

FIGURE 9.4

Mapping a Tone That Shows Character

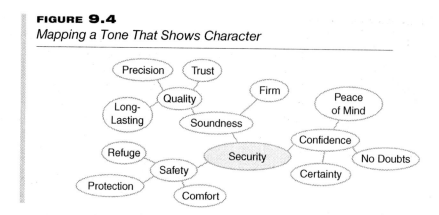

Of course, writers can overdo the use of a particular tone. To avoid this problem, decide on one emotion and one character for the entire proposal. Multiple emotional or character tones will only confuse and overwhelm the readers. Also, use these words only sparingly. Just like adding spices to food, you want to avoid overseasoning your proposal.

Using Similes and Analogies

Similes and analogies are rhetorical devices that help writers define difficult concepts by comparing them to simpler things. For example, let us say a proposal we are writing needs to describe a "semiconductor wafer" to people who know almost nothing about semiconductors. A simile could be used to describe the wafer this way: "A semiconductor wafer is like a miniature Manhattan Island crammed on a silicon disk that is only three inches wide." In this case, the simile ("X is like Y") not only clarifies the concept by putting it into familiar terms, it also creates a visual image that helps the readers understand the complexity of the semiconductor wafer.

Analogies are also a good way to help your readers visualize difficult concepts. An analogy follows the structure "A is to B as X is to Y." For example, a medical analogy might be, "Like police keeping order in a city, white blood cells seek to control viruses in the body." In this case, both parts of the analogy are working in parallel. *Police* is equivalent to *white blood cells* and *keeping order in the city* is equivalent to *control viruses in the body.*

Similes and analogies are primarily used to provide the readers with a quick, visual understanding of something unfamiliar by comparing it to something familiar. A good rule of thumb is to use similes and analogies more often when the readers are less experienced with your subject. Reduce the use of similes and analogies when the readers are experts.

Using Metaphors

Though comparable to similes and analogies, metaphors work at a deeper level in a proposal or grant. Metaphors are used to create or reinforce a particular *perspective* that you want the readers to adopt toward your subject or ideas.

Familiar Metaphors

Some metaphors are familiar to your readers, making them particularly useful. For example, a popular metaphor in Western medicine is the "war on cancer." If we were writing a grant proposal to request funding for cancer research, we might weave this metaphor into our proposal. We could talk about *battles with cancer cells, new weapons against cancer,* and the *front line of cancer research.* By employing this metaphor throughout the grant proposal, we would reinforce a particular perspective about cancer research. A metaphor such as *war on cancer* would add a sense of urgency to our proposal, because it suggests that cancer is an enemy that must be defeated, at almost any cost. Of course, cancer research is not really a war. And yet, we accept this metaphor with little question or dispute.

Commonly used metaphors are very powerful tools in proposal writing because they tend to work at a subconscious level. In other words, the use of the *war on cancer* metaphor should not be obvious to the readers. Instead, the metaphor should be used in key places throughout the proposal to gradually shift the readers' point of view, turning cancer into an enemy in their minds.

New Metaphors

But what if a familiar metaphor, like the *war on cancer,* is not appropriate for our proposal? In these cases, we can create a new metaphor and use it to invent a new perspective for the readers. For example, perhaps we want our readers to view cancer as something to be managed, not fought. Our new metaphor, *managing cancer* would allow us to talk about *negotiating* with cancer cells or using drugs that *mediate* between cancer cells and regular cells. We might speak of patients as *managers* who set goals and priorities that their body will aim to reach. Doctors might become *consultants* who offer patients advice on managing their illnesses.

This new metaphor creates a quite different perspective than the *war* metaphor. It shifts the readers' perspective, urging them to think differently about how patients will handle their illnesses.

Using Common and New Metaphors

To use metaphors in proposals, you should first look for the common metaphors that are widely used in your field. For example, perhaps you notice that "drugs are a disease in our city" is prevalent in the media. You can then use this metaphor to create a theme in your grant proposal. Extending the metaphor, you might say, "Our city needs treatment," or "We need to control the illness first; then we can begin recovering." By playing off the original metaphor, you can create more metaphorical phrases that reinforce the perspective you want.

In some cases, new metaphors need to be created from scratch. For instance, a proposal that is arguing for the construction of a new office building might use a metaphor such as "Harmon Industries needs a new home." This *home* metaphor could then be used to invent a theme in which words associated with homes, like *comfort, security, garden,* and *family,* are woven into the text. In this case, we could use this *home* metaphor to shift the readers' perspective from "the office building is the workplace" to "the office building is our home."

Changing the Pace

You can also regulate the readers' pace as they work through your proposal or grant. Longer sentences tend to slow the reading pace down, while shorter sentences tend to speed up the pace. By paying attention to the length of sentences, you can increase or decrease the intensity of your writing. For instance, let us say you believe a problem is urgent and needs to be handled right away. The best way to increase the intensity in your proposal would be to use short sentences while you describe that problem. As the pace increases, the readers will naturally feel impelled to do something, because they will sense the problem is rapidly growing worse. On the other hand, if you want the readers to be cautious and deliberate, longer sentences will decrease the intensity of the proposal, giving the readers the sense that there is no need to rush.

Sentence length is a great way to convey the intensity you want without saying something such as "This opportunity is slipping away!" or "We really need to take action now!" Sentence length can also soothe anxious readers by slowing down the pace a bit.

Looking Ahead

After reading through this chapter, some people may wonder about the ethics of using stylistic devices to influence the readers. Most people would not question the use of plain sentences and paragraphs to help the readers to understand the ideas in a proposal or grant, but the use of persuasive style might sound a bit like manipulating the readers.

To be candid, you *are* manipulating the readers when you are trying to persuade them. That's what proposals and grants do. The challenge is to match your proposal's style to the readers' needs. Plain style is best for instructing the readers, giving them the facts in a straightforward way. Persuasive style is used to motivate the readers to take action. Motivating people is ethical if you are urging them to do what is best for them. When persuasive style is used properly, it matches tone, choice of words, and pace to the situation that the readers face. It stresses important ideas at important points in the proposal.

CASE STUDY **Revising for Clarity and Power**

While George was handling the budget, Anne decided to edit the Cool Campus Project grant proposal. She was more than happy to edit the grant. She often struggled to write a first draft, but once it was written, she enjoyed working with sentences and paragraphs to make them clearer and easier to read.

When looking over the proposal, Anne immediately noticed that some of the sentences were hard to read because they did not have clear subjects

and action verbs. Several paragraphs did not have good topic sentences and their sentences did not flow together very well. But Anne knew these stylistic problems were typical for a first draft.

In particular, one paragraph from the Current Situation section caught her interest (Figure 4.9). The paragraph originally read:—

So, the legacy of Old Betsy lives on. Today's plant, the Young Power Plant (Figure 1), still burns coal to make steam, which is pushed through tunnels under the campus to keep buildings warm. Electricity mostly comes from the Four Corners Power Plant, a massive coal-fire plant that is located west of Farmington, New Mexico. With the increase in electricity-using devices on campus like televisions and computers, the electricity needs of the campus outstripped the generating capacity of its own power plants in the mid-1970s.

She noticed that each sentence in the paragraph used a different subject, and the subjects of some sentences were not always easy to identify.

Anne began revising the paragraph by asking what the paragraph was about. She decided the paragraph was about the campus's current reliance on coal for energy. She then restructured the sentences in the paragraph to focus on the campus as a subject.

So, the legacy of Old Betsy lives on. Presently, the campus is heated by the Young Power Plant (Figure 1), which still burns coal to make steam and then pushes it through tunnels under campus. Meanwhile, the campus draws its electricity from the Four Corners Power Plant, a massive coal-fire plant that is located west of Farmington, New Mexico. The campus's electricity needs outstripped the generating capacity of its own power plants in the 1970s, mainly because of new electricity-using devices on campus like televisions and computers.

Anne decided that the overall organization of the paragraph was fine. A transitional sentence started off the paragraph by referring to the previous paragraph. The second sentence was the topic sentence, because it provided a claim that the paragraph would prove. The remainder of the paragraph used facts and logical reasoning to support the topic sentence.

After Anne finished revising all the paragraphs in the proposal to make them more readable, she decided to amplify parts of the proposal with persuasive style. First, she began thinking about the tone she wanted the proposal to convey. She found herself returning to the word *innovative* as a possible tone for the whole document.

Putting the word *innovative* in the middle of a sheet of paper, she mapped out some words associated with this concept (Figure 9.5).

With her map finished, Anne wove some of these words into the introduction, opening paragraphs, closing paragraphs, and the conclusion

FIGURE 9.5

Using Tone to Make a Proposal Sound Innovative

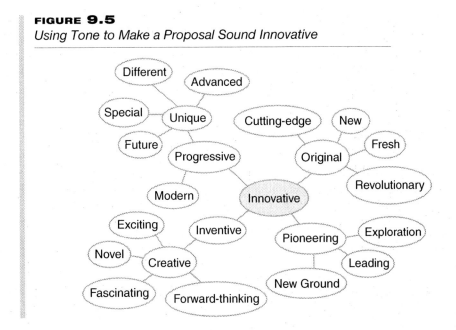

of the proposal. She hoped her readers would sense that something new and innovative was being proposed.

Finally, Anne decided she needed a metaphor that would add a visual image to the grant proposal. She began to think of Durango University as a "community" that was trying to become self-sustaining. She wrote "Durango University is a community" and began using this metaphor to come up with some new ways of describing campus. She used the thesaurus function of her word-processing software to come up with some variations of the metaphor:

- Campus as a community
- Faculty, staff, and students as neighbors
- Growing independence
- A sense of unity and cooperation
- Relying on ourselves and each other

- Many cultures in one place
- Working together for the common good
- Looking out for each other
- Common identity among our differences

The metaphor added a sense of warmth to the proposal by drawing on these words and phrases associated with community.

When Anne was finished revising, the proposal included basically the same content as before. However, her attention to sentences and paragraphs had made the text much clearer and more readable. Meanwhile, her attention to tone and the inclusion of the community metaphor gave it more depth and energy.

The final Cool Campus Project grant proposal appears in Chapter 12 of this book. There, you can see the other revisions Anne made to the style of the proposal.

Questions and Exercises

1. Using the six steps outlined in Figure 9.2, revise the following sentences to make them more readable:

   a. According to our survey that we conducted last Friday after the president gave his speech on crime on campus, the collection of data offers a demonstration on how much of importance this issue is to women of college age.

   b. The meeting over the project for Guilford simply gave us confirmation that we may find it necessary to pursue the hiring of an engineer who can program in the computer languages of Visual Basic and C++.

   c. Due to concerns about the large amounts of flammable items in close proximity to the location of the fire, it was necessary that an investigation of the blaze in the southwest corner of the building be conducted by an inspector from the fire department.

2. Find three sentences that are hard to read. Use the six steps outlined in Figure 9.2 to make these sentences easier to read. Then, in a memo to your instructor, describe the steps you followed to improve the sentences' readability.

3. Use subject alignment and given/new techniques to make the following paragraph more readable:

   Because clear writing is equated with sincerity and trustworthiness by most readers, style is important in proposal writing. The soundness and honesty of an argument will be questioned by the readers, if the meaning of proposal is hard to interpret. After all, they wonder, perhaps the argument in the proposal is not clear to the writers if their ideas cannot be expressed in plain language. Even worse, important assumptions or facts might be hidden in the twists and turns of the sentences and paragraphs, they might suspect. On the other hand, the writers show the readers that they know what is needed and how to provide it when they submit a plainly written proposal. In my experience, the clients are more easily won over by writers who submit a plain proposal rather than a proposal that is hard to read.

4. On campus or in your workplace, find a couple paragraphs that seem difficult to read. First, align the subjects in each paragraph to see if this technique improves readability. Then, use given/new strategies to revise each paragraph. Which method works better? Would a combination of subject alignment and given/new be more appropriate in some cases?

5. Study the style of a proposal or grant found on the Internet or in your workplace. What is the tone used in the proposal? Does the proposal use any similes or analogies to help the readers visualize difficult concepts? Can you locate any metaphors/themes that are woven into the text? How might the techniques of persuasive style discussed in this chapter be used to improve this proposal?

6. A common metaphor in our society is the "war on illegal drugs." With a team, think up some common phrases that demonstrate this metaphor in use. What does this metaphor imply about people who use and sell drugs? What police tactics does the metaphor suggest? What does the metaphor imply about our interactions with countries who export illegal drugs? If we wanted to handle the drug problem from a different perspective, what might be some other appropriate metaphors? How might these metaphors imply different approaches to illegal drugs?

7. While revising some of your own writing (perhaps your Current Situation or Project Plan sections from earlier chapters), try to create a specific tone by mapping out an emotion or character that you would like the text to reflect. Weave a few concepts from your map into your text. At what point is the tone too strong? At what point is the tone just right?

8. Using the text from Exercise 7, revise by shortening all the sentences. How do these shorter sentences change the pace of your writing? Now, revise the text by lengthening the sentences. How do these longer sentences change the pace of your writing?

10 | Designing Proposals

Overview

This chapter discusses how to develop persuasive visual designs for proposals and grants. The chapter will meet the following objectives:

1. Discuss the importance of design in a proposal or grant.
2. Discuss the application of gestalt theory to design.
3. Define four principles of design for crafting effective page layouts.
4. Describe the use of a five-step "design process" for inventing, revising, and editing pages.

"How You Say Something . . ."

The old saying, "How you say something is what you say," is truer now than ever in writing effective proposals and grants. Not long ago, document design was considered a luxury in proposals, not a necessity. Today, readers *expect* proposals to be visually interesting and engaging. They expect proposals to make a positive first impression. And they expect the design of a proposal to help them read the document more efficiently by highlighting important ideas. Readers cringe when a proposal with little or no design crosses their desks or computer screens, because they quickly realize that their needs as readers were not anticipated by the writers.

Design is more than simply making a proposal or grant look nice. An effective design increases the readability of the text by highlighting important information and allowing the readers to process the text in a variety of different ways. Moreover, the design of a proposal establishes a particular tone for the document—an image. Much as clothing and body language establishes an image for a public speaker, a proposal's design signals the attitude, the competence, and the quality of people submitting the proposal or grant.

Of course, the content is still the most important feature of your proposal or grant. Even the best design will never hide a weak understanding of the current situation or a flawed plan. However, design can make a positive impression on the readers while emphasizing your ideas. Good design can incline the readers favorably toward your document before they even read a word.

How Readers Look at Proposals

Usually reviewers read through proposals strategically, skimming some sections and paying closer attention to sections that directly affect their interests. Most readers, for example, make an initial surface-level scan of the proposal. They look at the executive summary, read the introduction, and then scan each major section's headings and opening paragraphs. Their aim is to gather an overall sense of the structure and argument of the proposal. Eventually, the reviewers may read the proposal from front to back, especially if it is a finalist for the bid or the funding.

The challenge of good design is to permit the readers to choose how *they* want to read the proposal. The proposal should be designed in a way that helps them process the text at different levels, while making the text usable in a variety of different possible contexts. Good design gives the readers easy "access points" where they can enter the text from a variety of places for a variety of reasons.

Four Principles of Design

Good design is not something to be learned in a day. Nevertheless, you can master some basic principles of document design that will help you make better decisions about how your proposal or grant should look. In this section, we will discuss four rather simple principles of design that were derived from *gestalt psychology,* which has deeply influenced the graphic arts (Bernhardt 1986; Moore and Fitz 1993). The basic assumption of gestalt design is that humans do not view their surroundings passively (Arnheim 1964, p. 28). Rather, they instinctively look for relationships among objects, creating wholes that are more than a sum of their parts. For example, in Figure 10.1, most people see a square, and they might even see an X in the middle of the square. Why? Gestalt design would explain that people viewing this graphic see a whole that is more than the sum of the parts. As in this diagram, the design of a proposal allows readers to visualize larger relationships among parts. Visual design can help them draw the natural connections among these parts to see the proposal as a greater whole.

The four design principles we will discuss in this chapter are *balance, alignment, grouping,* and *consistency*. These principles are based on gestalt psychology, especially Kurt Koffka's work in the area. As a synthesis of gestalt theory, the four

FIGURE 10.1
The Whole Is More Than a Sum of the Parts

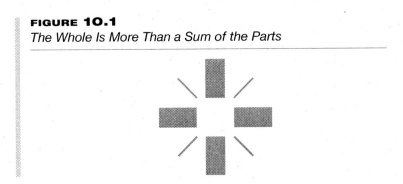

principles in this chapter are designed to provide a simple handlist of terms with which you can master document design for proposals.

Design Principle 1: Balance

On a page that is balanced, the design elements offset each other to create a stable feeling in the text. Imagine a page is balanced on a point. Each time we add something to the left side, we need to add something to the right side to maintain balance. Similarly, when we add something to the top of the page, we need to add something to the bottom. Figure 10.2, for instance, shows an example of a balanced page and an unbalanced page. The page on the right is unbalanced because the items on the right side of the page are not offset by items on the left. Meanwhile, the page is top-heavy because the text is bunched up toward the top of the page. The page on the left, however, feels stable because the design elements have been balanced evenly on the page. Whereas readers would find the unbalanced page uncomfortable to read, they would have little trouble viewing the balanced page on the left.

One thing to note, however, is that a balanced page is not necessarily a symmetrical page. In other words, as shown in the left page in Figure 10.2, the two halves of the page do not need to mirror each other, nor do the top and bottom need to be identical. Instead, the sides of the page should simply offset each other to create a sense of balance.

When balancing a page layout, graphic designers will talk about the "weight" of items on a page. What they mean is that some items on a page attract the readers'

FIGURE 10.2
Balanced and Unbalanced Pages

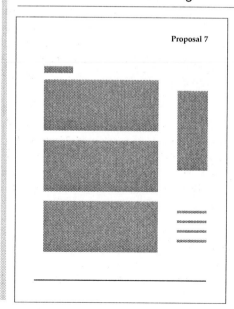

eyes more than others. A picture, for example, has more weight than printed words because readers' eyes tend to be drawn toward pictures. Likewise, colored text or graphics weigh more than black and white, because readers are attracted to color.

Here are some general guidelines for weighting the elements on a page:

- Items on the right side of the page weigh more than items on the left.
- Items on the top of the page weigh more than items on the bottom.
- Big items weigh more than small items.
- Pictures weigh more than written text.
- Graphics weigh more than written text.
- Colored items weigh more than black and white.
- Items with borders around them weigh more than items without borders.
- Irregular shapes weigh more than regular shapes.

When designing a standard page for a proposal, the challenge is to create a layout that allows you to keep the text as balanced as possible.

Using Grids to Balance a Page Layout

A time-tested way to devise a balanced page design is to use a page "grid" to evenly place the written text and graphics on the page. Grids divide the page vertically into two or more columns. The examples in Figure 10.3 show some standard grids and how they might be used.

In most cases, as shown in Figure 10.3, the columns on a grid do not translate into columns of written text. The grid is simply used to structure the text evenly, allowing columns of text or larger pictures to overlap one or more columns.

Why use a grid in the first place? It might be tempting to merely expand the margin on the right or left side in an *ad hoc* way. The problem with this approach is that readers subconsciously sense the page's irregular spacing. As gestalt design implies, the readers will subconsciously look for regular patterns or shapes. If no grid is used, the readers will try to imagine a grid anyway, thus creating more reading tension than necessary. Furthermore, in the long run, a grid-based page design offers more flexibility. An *ad hoc* layout may work for a couple pages, but as charts, margin text, and graphics are added, the page design will grow increasingly difficult to manage.

One solution, of course, is to use a simple one-column design. In a one-column format, graphics and text are usually centered in the middle of the column (Figure 10.4). There is, of course, nothing wrong with a one-column grid. A one-column grid tends to be rather traditional and word-dominant, and it provides limited flexibility on the placement of graphics. For example, as shown in Figure 10.4, few options exist for the placement of a graphic on the right page. Nevertheless, this page design is easy to use.

Other Balance Strategies

With the advent of desktop publishing, we now have the ability to use design features that were once available only to large publishers. In proposals, writers now use design features like pullouts, margin comments, and sidebars to enhance the reading of the body text.

FIGURE 10.3

Grids and Their Uses

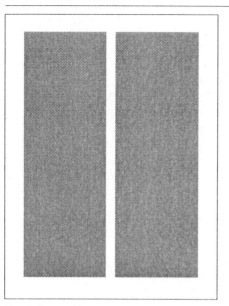 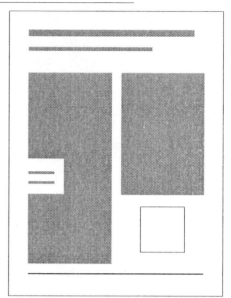

Two-Column grid

 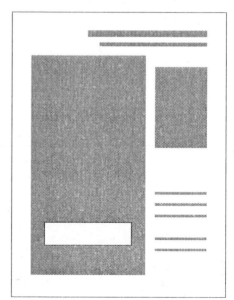

Three-Column grid

FIGURE 10.3
(Continued)

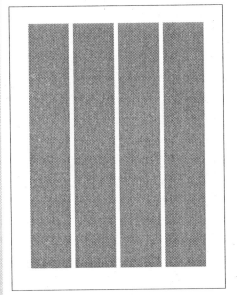
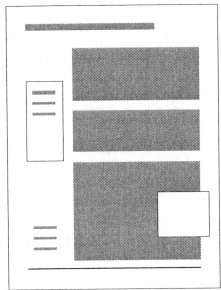

Four-Column grid

FIGURE 10.4
A One-column Page Design

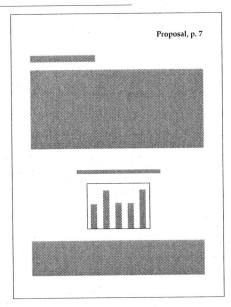

One-Column grid

FIGURE 10.5

Other Visual Techniques Used to Balance Pages

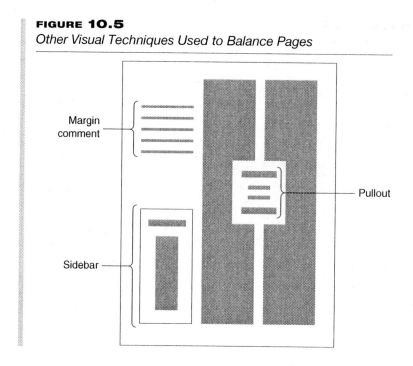

Pullouts   Quotes or paraphrases can be *pulled out* of the body text and placed in a special text box to catch the readers' attention. Essentially, pullouts are used to break up large blocks of text and create access points for the readers. Magazines, for example, frequently use pullouts when a picture or graphic is not available to break up a page of words. A pullout should draw its text from the page on which it appears. Often, the pullout is framed with rules or a box, and the text wraps around it (Figure 10.5).

Margin Comments   Key points or highlight quotations may be summarized in the margin of the proposal. When a grid is used to design the page, one of the margins often leaves enough room to include an additional list, offer a special quote drawn from the body text, or provide a simple illustration. In a large proposal, margin comments might even be used to remind the readers where they are in the proposal by restating the outline of the proposal and highlighting the main points of the section they are about to enter (Figure 10.5).

Sidebars   Examples or anecdotes can be placed in sidebars to reinforce the main text. In a magazine article, for example, a sidebar might include a special profile of an important person who is mentioned in the main article, or it might provide a "story within the story" that illustrates an important point made in the body text.

FIGURE 10.6

Using Lists as Alignment Tools

In proposals, sidebars could be used to explain a process in more detail or describe a previous project that was a success. Sidebars should never contain essential information. Rather, they offer supplemental information that enhances the readers' understanding.

Pullouts, margin comments, and sidebars can be used to balance a text and break up large blocks of words. Meanwhile, they enhance the readability of the proposal by reinforcing main points and providing supplemental information.

Design Principle 2: Alignment

Alignment is the use of vertical *white space* to help the readers identify the various levels of information in a proposal. The simplest alignment technique is the use of an indented list to offset a group of items from the body text. An indented list signals to the readers that the listed items are intended to supplement the text in the surrounding paragraphs. In Figure 10.6, for example, the page on the left gives no hint about the hierarchy of information in the text, making it difficult for a reader to scan the text. The page on the right, meanwhile, uses indented lists to clearly signal the hierarchy of the text. The indented material is easily recognized as supplemental information.

In a proposal, blocks of text can be aligned to show the hierarchy of information. Examples or explanatory information can be indented to signal that they are to be considered separately from the body text. Figure 10.7 illustrates how information can be indented to signal various levels in the text.

FIGURE 10.7
Alignment That Shows Hierarchy of Information

Essentially, alignment uses white space to create vertical lines in the text. The readers will mentally draw the vertical lines into the page, seeing aligned elements as belonging to the same level of importance.

Design Principle 3: Grouping

Even the most patient readers find it difficult to trudge through large, undivided blocks of text. Grouping techniques help break down the text into smaller parts that are more comprehendible, especially for readers who are scanning the document.

The principle of grouping is based on the assumption that readers comprehend better when information is divided into smaller chunks. A large block of text, perhaps a one-column page with no headings and no indentation, feels uninviting to a reader and difficult to read. Grouping allows you to break up the page by providing the readers more white space and giving them a variety of access points at which to enter the text.

The simplest type of grouping is paragraphing, because paragraphs break a larger stream of written text into blocks of ideas. There are more advanced ways, however, to group information on a page, including using headings, rules, and borders.

Using Headings

The primary purpose of headings is to signal new topics to the readers, but they also cue the readers into the overall organization of the proposal. With a quick

FIGURE 10.8
Levels of Headings

FIRST-LEVEL HEADING

This first-level heading is 18 pt. Times, boldface with small caps. Notice that it is significantly different from the second-level heading, even though both levels are in the same typeface. This heading is also *hanging*, because it is placed further into the margin than the regular text. Use consistent spacing above and below each head (e.g., 24 pts. above and 18 pts. below).

Second-level Heading

This second-level heading is 14 pt. Times with boldface. Usually, less space appears above and below this head (perhaps 18 pts. above and 14 pts. below).

Third-level Heading
This third-level heading is 12 pt. Times italics. Often no space appears between a third-level heading and the body text, as shown here.

Fourth-level Heading. This heading appears on the same line as body text. It is designed to signal a new layer of information without standing out too much.

scan of the headings in the document, the readers should be able to easily identify how the information in the proposal is organized.

In a larger document like a proposal, headings should highlight the various levels of information for the readers. A first-level heading, for example, should be sized significantly larger than a second-level heading. In some cases, first-level headings might use all capital letters (all caps) or small capital letters (small caps) to distinguish them from the font used in the body text. To make the first-level heading stand out, some writers even prefer to put them inside the left-hand margin or "hanging" into the left-hand margin (Figure 10.8).

Second-level headings should be significantly smaller and different than the first-level headings. Whereas the first-level headings might have used all caps, the second-level headings might capitalize only the first letter of each word (excluding articles and short prepositions; e.g., "Marketing for Generation Next"). First- and second-level heads are often boldface. Third-level headings might be italicized or placed on the same line as the body text itself. Figure 10.8 shows various levels of headings.

Early in the proposal-writing process, you should decide how the proposal will use headings. Headings are powerful tools for breaking information into groups; however, when used improperly they can create unneeded chaos in a proposal. They need to be used consistently throughout the document.

FIGURE 10.9
Using Rules to Divide a Page into Groups

Using Horizontal and Vertical Rules

In page design, horizontal and vertical rules are straight lines that can be used to carve the proposal into larger blocks. Rules should be used judiciously in a proposal, because they can impede the progress of the reader through the text. Too many rules make the document look like it has been chopped up into small bits and pieces. When used properly with headings or to set off an example, horizontal and vertical rules can help the readers identify the larger groups of information in a proposal.

Figure 10.9 illustrates how rules can be used to divide a page into larger parts. As shown in the figure, the horizontal and vertical rules carve the text into larger chunks, ensuring that the readers will see them as groups. On the other hand, rules can restrict how the reader views the page by framing off text into isolated blocks of information.

Using Borders

Like rules, borders are also used to group text into units. Borders, however, tend to be even more isolating than rules, because they enclose text completely, setting it off from the rest of the information on a page. Borders are best used to set off examples, graphics, pullouts, and sidebars that supplement the body text. For example, Figure 10.10 shows how a border can be used to set off an example or sidebar on a typical page.

Borders are helpful tools for grouping information. However, like rules, they can be overused. If borders are used sparingly in a proposal, they will draw the readers' attention to the information inside the border. When borders are used too

FIGURE 10.10
Misusing Borders to Group Information

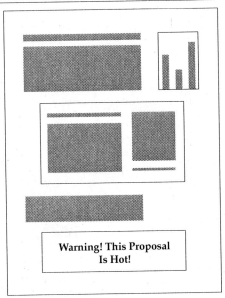

often, however, the readers will grow immune to their grouping effects, and they will tend to skip reading the information inside.

Design Principle 4: Consistency

The final design principle, consistency, simply suggests that each page should be designed consistently with other pages in the document. Specifically, each page should follow a predictable pattern in which design features are used uniformly throughout the proposal. There are four techniques available for giving each page a consistent look: headers and footers, typefaces, labeling, and lists.

Headers and Footers

Even the simplest word-processing software can put a header or footer consistently on every page. As their names suggest, the header is text that runs across the top margin of the page, and the footer is text that runs along the bottom of the page. In many proposals, headers and footers include the title of the proposal and perhaps the bidding company's name. They also invariably include a page number. Page numbers are critical in proposals, because they help the readers refer to various parts of the proposal with ease. If there are no page numbers available, the readers find themselves struggling to tell others where to look in the proposal, instead of merely saying "go to page X."

Headers and footers can also include design features like a horizontal rule or even a company logo. If these items appear at the top or bottom of each page of the proposal, the document will tend to look like it follows a consistent design.

FIGURE 10.11

Serif and Sans Serif Typefaces

This paragraph uses the Palatino typeface. Serif typefaces are often used in traditional-looking texts, especially for the body text. Studies have suggested inconclusively that serif typefaces like Palatino are more legible, but there is some debate as to why. Some researchers claim that the serifs create horizontal lines in the text that make serif typefaces easier to follow (White, p. 14). These studies, however, were mostly conducted in the United States, where serif fonts are common. In other countries, such as Britain, where sans serif fonts are often used for body text, the results of these studies might be quite different.

This paragraph uses Helvetica, a sans serif typeface. A sans serif typeface tends to look more modern and progressive to most readers. However, sans serif text tends to be harder to read at length, at least for readers in the United States. Generally, sans serif typefaces are best used in titles and headings.

Typefaces

As a rule of thumb, a proposal should not use more than two different typefaces. Most page designers will choose two typefaces that are very different from each other, usually one *serif* typeface and one *sans serif* typeface. A serif typeface, like Times or Bookman, has small tips (serifs) at the ends of main strokes in the letters. A sans serif font is one that does not include these small tips. Figure 10.11 shows the difference between a serif font (Palatino) and a sans serif font (Helvetica). Notice how the letters in Palatino include the additional tips on each letter while Helvetica does not.

There are no rules for typeface usage, just guidelines. To readers in North America, serif fonts like Times or Palatino tend to look more formal and traditional, while sans serif fonts like Helvetica seem informal and modern. Because sans serif fonts look modern, some page designers will use them in headings, headers, and footers to make their proposal look more progressive. Designers often prefer serif fonts in the body text, because North American readers usually report that they find sans serif fonts harder to read at length.

To complicate matters further, international readers like those from the United Kingdom are accustomed to sans serif fonts like Helvetica appearing in the body text. They, consequently, find sans serif fonts easier to read at length.

Of course, your choices of typefaces are up to you, but you should use them consistently throughout the proposal.

Labeling of Graphics

Graphics, such as tables, charts, pictures, and graphs, should be labeled consistently throughout the proposal. In most cases, the label above a graphic will include a number (e.g., Table 5) and a title (e.g., Forecast of Future Sales). In some cases, though, the number and title might appear below the graphic. Again, the important thing is to be consistent. You should always choose a consistent typeface for labeling and then locate the labels consistently on each graphic. In Chapter 11, we will further discuss how to use graphics in proposals.

Sequential and Nonsequential Lists

In proposals, lists are useful for showing a sequence of tasks or a group of similar items. A simple way to design lists is to remember that they tend to fall into two basic categories: sequential and nonsequential. Sequential, or numbered, lists are used to present items in a specific order. For instance, in a proposal, sequential lists might handle a list of tasks or they might rank various objectives. In these lists, numbers or letters are used to show the order or hierarchy of the items. Nonsequential lists, on the other hand, use bullets, checkmarks, or other icons to show that the items in the list are essentially equal in value.

Lists are handy tools for making information more readable, and you should look for opportunities in your proposal to use them. When you include a list, though, make sure you are consistent in your usage of sequential and nonsequential lists. In sequential lists, numbering schemes should not change in the proposal except for good reason. For example, you might choose a numbering scheme like 1), 2), 3). If so, do not number the next list 1., 2., 3., and others A., B., C., unless you have a good reason for changing the numbering scheme. Similarly, in nonsequential lists, use similar icons when setting off lists. Do not use bullets with one list, checkmarks with another, and pointing hands with a third. These inconsistencies only confuse the readers while making your proposal seem unpolished.

To avoid these problems with lists, decide up front how your proposal will use lists. Choose one style for sequential lists and another for nonsequential lists and stick with those two styles throughout the proposal.

The Process of Designing Proposals

Balance, alignment, grouping, consistency—once you know these four basic principles, designing proposals and grants becomes much easier. These four principles form the basis of a "process" that you can use to design almost any text. In their book *Designing Visual Language,* Charles Kostelnick and David Roberts (1998) suggest that a design process "includes several kinds of activities, beginning with invention, followed by revision, and ending with fine-tuning" (p. 23). Kostelnick and Roberts point out that, like writing, designing a text is a fluid process in which the designer cycles among the different parts of the process until the design is completed.

Following a design process becomes especially important when you are working with a team on a proposal. Your team should start by making some or all of the design decisions *before* team members go off to write their parts. With design issues settled up front, each team member can then conform his or her part to the overall design of the proposal, making assembly much easier at the end. Moreover, each team member can help find or create visual items like the graphics or sidebars that will make up the proposal's design. If your team waits until the proposal's due date to consider the design of the proposal, chances are good that you will need to resort to the lowest common denominator—that is, little or no design.

To create effective layouts for proposals, follow this five-step process:

1. Consider the rhetorical situation.
2. Thumbnail a few example pages.
3. Create a design stylesheet.
4. Develop a few generic pages.
5. Edit the design.

Step 1: Consider the Rhetorical Situation

Start the design process by revisiting your understanding of the *rhetorical situation,* which you developed at the beginning of the proposal-writing process. Specifically, pay attention to the unique characteristics of the primary readers and the physical context in which they will read the proposal.

Different readers will respond to a document's design in different ways, so you want your proposal or grant to align with the primary readers' values and attitudes. For instance, if the primary readers are rather traditional, the proposal should use a conservative design that includes a simple layout, a classic font like Times, and limited amounts of graphics. If the readers are more progressive or trendy, the design can be a little more creative. In these situations, perhaps you might use more graphics. You might consider using an unusual font for the headings. If you know the topic is an emotional one for the readers, positive or negative, perhaps some photographs might reinforce or defuse those emotions by showing the people or issues involved in the proposed project.

Second, the context in which the proposal will be used is also important. Pay special attention to the physical factors that will influence the reading of the proposal. For example, if you know that the readers will look over the proposal in a large board meeting, then you will want to make the text as scannable as possible with clearly identifiable headings, plenty of lists, and a generous use of graphics to reinforce the proposal's main ideas. You might also add pullouts or margin comments to state your main points in ways that pop off the page. On the other hand, if you think your proposal will receive a close reading, perhaps fewer graphical elements and more paragraphs would give the text a more detailed, grounded feel.

Step 2: Thumbnail a Few Example Pages

With the readers and context in mind, sketch out a few possible page layouts that would suit the rhetorical situation. Graphic artists will often start designing pages by sketching a few "thumbnails" freehand or on a computer (Figure 10.12). Thumbnails take a few moments to draw, but they will allow you to look over possible designs before you commit to a particular page layout—saving you time in the long run.

While thumbnailing designs, pay special attention to the balance of the page. Will the page use two, three, or four columns? Where will graphics appear on a page? Will there be space for margin comments, pullouts, or sidebars? How large will the headings be on the page? Where will a header or footer be placed? Most designers sketch a few different possible layouts and then decide which one seems to best suit the rhetorical situation. If you are working with a team, provide the other team members with a few different possible layouts and let them choose the best one.

FIGURE 10.12
Thumbnails

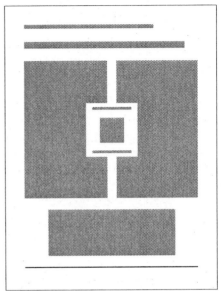

Once you have developed a basic pattern for the body pages, thumbnail a few possible cover pages for the proposal. Be bold with the cover. Nothing puts readers in a positive mood better than an active, professional cover (the "everything centered" cover is a real yawner). Add energy by increasing the size of the text, moving the text to the left or right side of the page, adding in a graphic, and so on. All these features will give momentum to the proposal while reassuring the readers that the proposal is not going to be boring.

Step 3: Create a Design Style Sheet

Style sheets are records of your design decisions. After sketching out some thumbnails or creating a page layout, write down some of your decisions about various design elements of the document. These features can be handled on five levels:

Line Level—font, font size, and use of italics, bolding, and underlining

Paragraph Level—spacing between lines (leading), heading typefaces and sizes, indentation, justification (right, center, left, full), sequential and nonsequential lists, column width

Page Level—columns, headers and footers, rules and borders, use of shading, placement of graphics, use of color, pullouts, sidebars, page numbers, use of logos or icons

Graphics Level—captions, labeling, borders on graphics, use of color, fonts used in tables, charts, and graphs

Document Level—binding, cover stock, paper size, color, weight, and type (glossy, semi-gloss, standard), section dividers

Sometimes, making all these design decisions can be a daunting task. Nevertheless, in a larger proposal, a style sheet actually saves time, because writers can refer to it when they have a question about specific design issues. When working with a team of other writers, you can simplify the writing process considerably by asking each writer to follow the style sheet as closely as possible. That way, when the whole proposal comes together, the final draft will require far less editing of the design.

Style sheets are living documents that can be modified as the proposal is developed. The style sheet should be modified as the writing of the proposal creates new challenges for the design.

Step 4: Develop a Few Generic Pages

Graphic designers will tell you that the best time to design a document is before the words are written. In most cases, though, writers start thinking about design after they have completed an outline or drafted a few pages of the proposal. At this point in the writing process, they can bend and shape the text into a generic page layout. They can create a *template* that can be used to structure all the pages in the proposal.

With your thumbnails sketched and a style sheet created, use some or all of the proposals' content to create a template that each page in the proposal will follow. As you add content to your design, you will likely discover that some of your earlier style decisions need to be modified to fit the needs of a real document. Mark these modifications in your style sheet.

Each page should follow the same basic pattern as the other pages. Avoid the temptation to make small alterations to accommodate the demands of individual pages. Instead, if one page's design needs to be changed, you might need to go back and alter the overall template to accommodate these modifications. By creating a few generic pages, you can find places where alterations are needed *before* you start designing the whole proposal.

Step 5: Edit the Design

Editing is an important part of design. After you have completed designing the pages and adding the written text and graphics, you should commit some time exclusively to revising and editing the proposal's design. While adding text and graphics, you more than likely stretched your original design a bit. Now it is time to go back and correct some of the smaller inconsistencies that came about as you put the text together.

To help you edit, look back at the rhetorical situation, your thumbnails, and your style sheet. Does the final design fit the readers and the context in which they will read the proposal? Does the final design reflect the visual qualities you wanted as you sketched out your thumbnails? Are there any places where the final design needs to be revised to fit the style sheet? Or does the style sheet need to be modified to fit decisions you made as text and design were meshed together? In the end, make sure the final, edited design fits the rhetorical situation with which you started the writing process.

Looking Ahead

In the struggle to pull together a proposal or grant, often at the last minute, there is a tendency to see design as a luxury that can be ignored in a pinch. It's the content, not the design that is important, right?

In these moments of weakness, remind yourself that "how you say something is what you say." If you hand in a proposal that uses a one-column format with double spacing and underlined headings, the readers are going to wonder whether your company or organization has the creativity and commitment required for their project. After all, how a proposal looks says a great amount about how your company or organization does business. In the long run, it is worth the effort to spend the few hours required to design an attractive, functional proposal.

In the next chapter, we will look at graphics, another important design element in proposals and grants.

CASE STUDY Creating a Look

Calvin was thinking about the proposal's design well before the team had completed the rough draft. As a contractor, he had learned the importance of how something looked. When designing or remodeling a house, Calvin knew that the appearance of the house is critical to its function and visual appeal.

Likewise, he realized, the design of documents also made a big difference. When Calvin wrote proposals to bid on building contracts, his clients always seemed to place a high value on how the document looked and how easy they could find the information they needed.

Calvin also appreciated any well-designed proposals he received from his subcontractors. He was very busy and did not have time to struggle through badly designed proposals with dense blocks of text. Proposals that included an organized table of contents and design features such as balanced pages, columns, headers and footers, as well as captions, labels, graphics, and color, were much easier to read and nicer to look at.

Tim was creating the graphics for the proposal, so he and Calvin decided they should get together to talk about the design of the proposal.

Calvin and Tim began designing the proposal by reviewing the rhetorical situation. "All right, let's look at our readers. What design would most appeal to them?"

"Well, the primary readers are the reviewers at the Tempest Foundation," replied Tim, "but we have quite a few other readers to consider too, like President Wilson, the Board of Regents, students, faculty, staff, and others."

"Yeah, and we can't forget about people in the community," said Calvin.

"I don't know how we are supposed to design a document for all these different people," Tim said. "President Wilson probably wants something more formal and academic, but people in the community aren't going to want to read something that has too much text."

"OK, maybe we should concentrate on our primary readers. The reviewers at the Tempest Foundation are the decision makers. Above all, we will need to design the document so these reviewers can quickly locate the information they need. What are their needs, and how do their busy schedules affect our design decisions?"

Looking over their notes about the reviewers' characteristics, Tim and Calvin thought about the kind of design that would suit the reviewers and the contexts in which they would consider the proposal. They guessed that most of the reviewers would be busy professionals who volunteered to be on the board of the Tempest Foundation. These people would only have limited time and energy to read a proposal.

Calvin and Tim also guessed that the reviewers were likely progressive due to the mission of the foundation, but the subject matter of the proposal was rather serious. So, they decided that the design would need to balance the reviewers' progressiveness with the grave importance of doing something about global warming.

Calvin pointed out that the readers' physical context would be important to the design of the grant proposal. The primary readers would probably discuss the grant at a meeting with other reviewers, so important information needed to be easy to find. The proposal would also be used by the secondary readers on campus and at the charrette, so it needed to be easy to scan.

Specifically, the design of the proposal would need to accommodate a scanning reader who was not going to have the time or energy to commit full attention to the text.

With these readers and contexts in mind, Calvin began thumbnailing a few possible pages for the proposal (Figure 10.13). He decided to use a two-column design on a three-column grid, because that layout would decrease the width of each column, making the text easier to scan. It would also allow him to add in some pullouts in a wider margin to highlight important points and ideas in the proposal.

As Calvin sketched the designs, Tim made a few comments about how to handled titles and headings. Tim also suggested, "Why don't we include a prominent quote on every page, which would highlight an important concept from that page?"

"I like that," Calvin responded. He drew boxes for quotes on each page.

Then they decided that the first page of the proposal would double as the cover page. That way, the readers would be put right into the proposal itself. The table of contents could appear on the first page.

Looking at Calvin's thumbnails, Tim said, "I like how you did that. Avoiding a formal cover page makes the proposal look more inviting—not as stodgy. That large title on the first page really draws the readers into the text. A picture on the front page would really help, too."

"Good idea," Calvin replied. He integrated Tim's suggestions into the thumbnails.

Tim needed to go to class, so Calvin took his thumbnails back to his office. At his computer, he began typing up a simple style sheet that

FIGURE 10.13
Thumbnails for Cool Campus Project

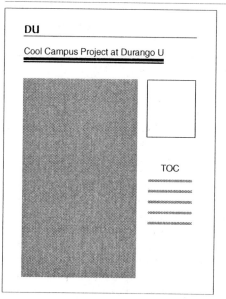

FIGURE 10.14
Calvin's Style Sheet

Line Level
Body Text: 12 pt. Times
Italics: Use with titles and to emphasize

Paragraph Level
Leading: Single Space
Headings: Level 1, 16 pt. Arial; Level 2, 12 pt. Arial bold; Level 3, 12 pt. Arial italics
Justification: Full
Sequential lists: 1. 2. 3.
Nonsequential lists: boxes

Page Level
Columns: One-column or three-column grid
Header: none
Footer: centered page number on each page, including cover
Borders: around information box only, 1 pt. lines
Pullouts: quote on side of each page, 18 pt. Arial, centered
Graphics: Tables and graphs fit into one column, or go across both columns at
             top or bottom of page.

Graphics Level
Font: Arial 10 pt.
Labeling: Title and number across top of graphic in 12 pt. Arial bold
Borders: 1 pt. border around each graphic, if needed
Captions: none

Document Level
Binding: Plastic Comb
Cover stock: Same as body paper
Paper: 25 lb, off-white standard (Ivory), 8.5 x11 in.

---

would guide the grant-writing team's decisions about design (Figure 10.14).

The style sheet would be especially helpful as they revised and put the whole proposal together, because it would help the team create a consistent design.

From prior experience, Calvin knew his decisions in the style sheet would need to be modified as the final version of the proposal was written. But creating a style sheet took only a couple of minutes, and it would give the group a good idea of the how the proposal would look.

When he finished his thumbnails and style sheet, Calvin created a template for the proposal in his word-processing software. He then began filling the template with some text from the first draft of the proposal.

As he designed the pages, it became obvious that he would need to collect more information before he could completely design the proposal. First, he wanted to add some pullouts that featured quotes from President Wilson, global warming experts, and people in the community.

Second, the proposal needed some photographs, charts, and tables for the body pages. Tim was collecting those graphics, so Calvin left spaces where he thought they might appear.

Now Calvin needed to wait for the others to finish their parts of the proposal. When the rest of the proposal was finished, the design would need to be adjusted to fit the text and graphics they wanted to include.

You can see Calvin's final design for the Durango University Cool Campus proposal in Chapter 12.

Note: *The Case Study segments for Chapters 10 and 11 were co-written with Allen Brizee.*

Questions and Exercises

1. Choose three full-page advertisements from a magazine. How did the designers use balance, alignment, grouping, and consistency to design these advertisements? How is the rhetorical situation (subject, purpose, readers, context of use) reflected in the design of these pages?

2. Analyze the design used in a proposal or grant. Write a memo to your instructor in which you discuss how the proposal's design uses the principles of balance, alignment, grouping, and consistency. Then, note where the proposal strays from these principles. Based on your observations, do you think the proposal's design is effective? How might it be improved?

3. Many proposals and grants are now being reviewed on-screen through the Internet or in CD-ROM format. Find a proposal on the Internet. How did the writers handle the proposal's on-screen design (if at all)? How does the design of a screen-based proposal differ from paper-based proposals? What are some strategies writers might follow to make proposals more readable on a computer screen?

4. For a practice or real proposal of your own, go through the five-step design process discussed in this chapter. Study the rhetorical situation from a design perspective, then thumbnail a few pages for your proposal. Write out a basic style sheet. Develop some generic pages for your proposal. And finally, add content into your design.

5. Study the page layouts used in other kinds of documents (newsletters, posters, or books). Can any of these designs be adapted for use as models for designing proposals? Why might you try different designs that break away from the more traditional designs used in proposals?

6. Look at the designs of the example proposals in Chapter 12. How do these significantly different designs change the tone and readability of the text?

Using Graphics

Overview

This chapter discusses the use and design of graphics in proposals and grants. The chapter will meet the following objectives:

1. Discuss the importance of graphics in proposals and grants.
2. Offer four guidelines for using graphics appropriately.
3. Illustrate the proper use of graphs, tables, and charts.
4. Discuss the proper use of photography and drawings.

The Need for Graphics

Given the ease with which today's computers create graphics, writers of proposals and grants routinely use visuals like graphs, charts, tables, and even pictures. We live in an increasingly visual society. Consequently, most people rely on what they can see in a proposal, not only what they can read. In many cases, graphics not only enhance the story you are trying to relate in your proposal or grant, but they also tell a large part of the story itself.

For example, consider the paragraph shown in Figure 11.1. The data points in this paragraph soon become a jumble of numbers that are difficult to process and almost impossible to remember. And yet, the simple table that follows this paragraph presents this same data in a highly accessible format.

Figure 11.1 illustrates how graphics can provide the readers with a great amount of information at a glance. Graphics help you avoid bogging the readers down in data, keeping them reading instead of giving them an excuse to just skip ahead to parts of the proposal where they will not be overwhelmed by numbers. Graphics also help you and the readers compare numbers and identify trends. In Figure 11.1, for instance, the figures in the paragraph are difficult to compare. However, when the figures are put into the table, the numbers are easy to compare. Later in this chapter, you will see how graphs and charts can be used to show trends in the data.

There are also other benefits to graphics:

- Graphics can keep a reader from simply scanning the proposal. When readers who scan come across an interesting visual, they will typically look into the written text to find an explanation for the data being displayed. The graphics

FIGURE 11.1
Text vs. Table

Example Text

According to the 2006 Sales Figures Report (p. 21), adults from ages 20–29 were responsible for purchasing an average of 30 meals per person per year, spending an average of $7.50 per visit, and accounting for 35 percent of our total sales. Meanwhile, teenagers (ages 10–19) purchased 120 meals per person per year, spending an average of $6.15 per visit and accounting for 40 percent of our total sales. Children under 10 years accounted for 10 percent of our overall sales, purchasing 50 meals per person per year at an average of $3.10 per visit. Adults ages 30-39 bought an average of 15 meals per year, spending $5.17 per visit and accounting for 10 percent of our overall sales. And finally, adults ages 40 years and above accounted for only 5 percent of our total sales, spending only an average of $4.94 per visit and purchasing only 10 meals per person per year.

Example Table

Table 24 Sales of Meals by Customer Age

Customer Age	Average Number of Meals per Year	Average Dollars Spent per Visit	Percent of Total Sales
Under 10	30	$2.10	10
10–19	120	$5.15	40
20–29	30	$6.50	35
30–39	15	$4.17	10
Over 40	10	$3.94	5

Source: 2006 Sales Figures Report, p. 21.

---

serve as "access points" at which readers can begin reading the written text.

- Graphics break up large blocks of written text, providing the readers with resting places while they look over the proposal. A proposal that force-marches readers through pages of written text is not a pleasure to read. Visuals give the readers opportunities to pause and consider the ideas in the text.
- Graphics visually reinforce your argument in the proposal. In our visual age, readers tend to trust what they can see, so a well-placed graphic can often bolster the proposal's argument with a simple glance.

In this chapter, you will learn how to use graphics effectively in your proposals and grants. We will begin by going over some basic guidelines and then showing you examples of some commonly used types of graphics.

Guidelines for Using Graphics

Graphics capture the readers' attention. When used properly, they reinforce and clarify your message, often slicing through the details and numbers to create a powerful image in the readers' minds. Spatially, they can highlight relationships among data points, organizations, and people.

There are four guidelines you can follow when using graphics in a proposal. A graphic should do the following:

- Tell a simple story
- Reinforce the written text, not replace it
- Be ethical
- Be labeled and placed properly

Let us consider each of these guidelines more closely.

A Graphic Should Tell a Simple Story

When you glance at a graphic in a proposal or grant, you should immediately know what "story" it is designed to tell. In a line graph, for example, a rising line might indicate an increase in sales. In a bar chart, a tall column next to a short column might show that one factory produced more product than another factory. In a pie chart, a large slice might indicate where the majority of the last year's budget was spent. These kinds of graphics tell a simple story that the readers can immediately recognize.

When planning a graphic, first ask yourself what story you want the graph, chart, table, or picture to tell. Do you want to illustrate a trend in sales? Do you want to compare levels of growth among test subjects and a control? Do you want to show how the budget should be divided? Once you have articulated the story you want the graphic to tell, write it down in one sentence. For instance, you might write, "This graph will show how different amounts of water affect the growth of hybrid Roma tomato plants." Once you have written down the story you want to tell, you can then identify the appropriate way to illustrate that story. The graph in Figure 11.2 demonstrates how a graphic can tell a simple story about tomatoes.

If a graphic does not tell a *simple* story, the readers will often not be able to figure out what message it is trying to convey. Readers tend to glance at graphics, not study them in depth, so if the graphic's story is not immediately apparent, the graphic will waste their time and it will waste space in your proposal.

A Graphic Should Reinforce the Written Text

A graphic can be used to clarify and reinforce, but it cannot replace the written text. Instead, the written text and the visual text should play off each other. The written text should refer the readers to the graphic, and the graphic should reinforce what is said in the written text. The two should work hand-in-hand. For example, the written text might claim, "The chart in Figure 5 illustrates Carson

A Graph That Tells a Simple Story

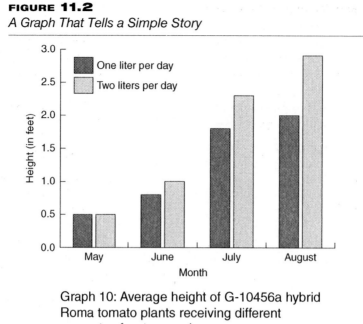

Graph 10: Average height of G-10456a hybrid
Roma tomato plants receiving different
amounts of water per day

Industries' rise in productivity over the last ten years. We believe this rise, in part, demonstrates that our new flextime program is having a positive effect on employee morale." The written text in this case accomplishes two goals. First, it refers the readers to the figure, using the figure as a supportive example. Second, the written text clearly identifies the story the graph is designed to tell.

Graphics should never be used simply to decorate a text. Not long ago, pie charts and clip art were novelties in proposals, making them interesting for that reason alone. But today, excess pie charts and clip art have become annoying eyesores in proposals, especially when they are being used to merely add decoration or color. Used appropriately, pie charts can be helpful, as we will discuss later in this chapter. However, when pie charts are used as decoration, they suggest a dumbed-down proposal that lacks substance.

A Graphic Should Be Ethical

In the effort to strengthen a proposal's message, there is always a temptation to use graphs, charts, and tables to hide facts or exaggerate trends. For example, it might be tempting to use a table to hide important data points that do not support the proposal's argument. In a line graph, it might be tempting to leave out data points that resist attempts to draw a smooth sloping line. Or, perhaps the scales on a bar chart might be altered to suggest more growth than is actually the case.

A good rule of thumb with graphics—and a good principle to follow in proposal writing altogether—is to always be absolutely honest with the readers. Your readers are not fools, so they will usually detect attempts to use graphics to stretch the truth. Moreover, a lack of honesty can come back to bite you later. After all, a proposal or grant is just the beginning of a relationship, not the end. In the long run, honest words and graphics keep you out of trouble.

Kostelnick and Roberts (1998) warn that unethical graphics can erode the credibility of an entire document (pp. 300–302). Even if the readers only suspect deception, they will grow suspicious of the graphic, the document, and the writers themselves. Also, in his book *The Visual Display of Quantitative Information* (1983), Edward Tufte offers an insightful discussion of ethical and unethical uses of graphics. His discussion of visual ethics provides helpful tips about staying honest when using graphics.

A Graphic Should Be Labeled and Placed Properly

Proper labeling and placement of graphics helps the readers move back and forth between the written text and the visual displays. Each graphic in a proposal should be sequentially numbered and labeled with an informative title. For example, the graph in Figure 11.2 includes a number (Graph 10) and a title (Average height of G-10456a hybrid Roma tomato plants receiving different amounts of water per day). This labeling allows the reader to quickly locate the graphic in the proposal.

Other parts of the graphic should also be carefully labeled:

- The x and y axes of graphs and charts should display standard units of measurement.
- Columns and rows in tables should be labeled so the readers can easily locate specific data points.
- Important features of drawings or illustrations should be identified with arrows or lines and some explanatory text.

Captions can help reinforce the story the graphic is trying to tell. Captions should include names of any sources if the data or graph was taken from another text.

When placing a graphic, try to put it on the page where it is mentioned or on the following page. Readers will rarely flip more than one page to look for a graphic. Even if they *do* make the effort to hunt down a graphic that is pages away, the effort will take them out of the flow of the proposal, urging them to start skimming the text. In almost all cases, a graphic should appear after the point in the text at which it is mentioned. When a graphic appears before it is mentioned, it often confuses the readers because they lack the context to interpret what the graphic shows.

Using Graphics to Display Information and Data

A variety of different graphics are available for displaying information and data. Each type of graphic allows you to tell a different story with the information you are presenting.

Line Graphs

In proposals and grants, line graphs are typically used to show trends over time. The y-axis (vertical) displays some kind of measured quantity like income, sales,

FIGURE 11.3

A Line Graph

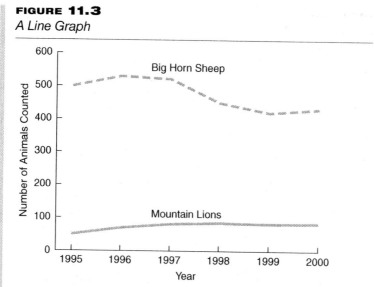

Figure 17.2: Relationship Between Populations of Mountain Lions and Big Horn Sheep in the Manzano Mountains

production, and so on. The *x*-axis (horizontal) is divided into even time increments like years, months, days, or hours. For example, Figure 11.3 shows a line graph that plots the population changes in mountain lions and bighorn sheep over a five-year period.

As you can see, the line graph allows the readers to easily recognize the trends in animal populations. The drawback of line graphs is that they don't offer the readers exact figures. For instance, in Figure 11.3, can you tell exactly how many mountain lions were sighted in 1997? Line graphs are strongest when the trend is more important than the exact figures behind that trend.

Bar Charts

Like line graphs, bar charts can be used to show trends over time. Bar charts are also well suited to show increases in volume. For example, Figure 11.4 demonstrates how a bar chart can plot a volume.

The advantage of a bar chart over a line graph is that the vertical columns suggest a physical quantity. In other words, the columns allow readers to make easier comparisons among data points because one column is physically larger or smaller than the others. A line graph, in contrast, only plots vertical points without providing a sense of the volume that is being measured.

Something you should also notice is that the *y*-axis in a bar chart must always start at zero. If the *y*-axis does not start at zero, the differences among columns will be exaggerated artificially, giving the readers the impression that the differences in amounts are greater than they really are. In almost all bar charts, it is unethical to start the *y*-axis at any number other than zero.

FIGURE 11.4

A Simple Bar Chart

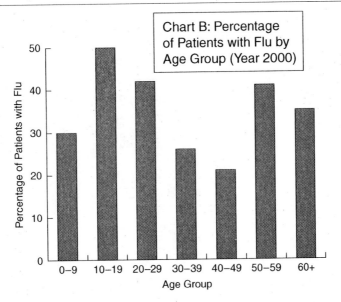

Chart B: Percentage of Patients with Flu by Age Group (Year 2000)

Tables

Tables offer the most efficient way to display a large amount of data in a small amount of space (Figure 11.5). The number and title of the table should appear above the table. Along the left column, the *row titles* should list the items being measured. Along the top row, the *column titles* should list the qualities of the items being measured. Beneath the table, if applicable, a citation should identify the source of the information.

FIGURE 11.5

A Basic Table

Table 2: Observations of Perching Birds at Peterson Pits during Month of June

Birds Sighted from 6:00–9:00 a.m.	1997	1998	1999	2000
Robins	370	380	420	443
Purple Finches	284	293	305	321
Cardinals	84	92	100	113
Blue Jays	79	92	105	103
Goldfinches	27	33	25	37

Source: A. Lawler, (2001). "Habitat Restoration Strengthens Perching Bird Populations," *Central Iowa Ornithology Quarterly 73*, pp. 287–301.

In proposals, tables tend to be used two ways. First, they are used in Current Situation sections to provide baseline data that offer a numerical snapshot of the past or present situation. Figure 11.5, for example, might be used to show the current situation regarding bird populations in Story County, Iowa. Second, tables are used to present budgets, breaking down costs into cells that can be easily referenced.

Pie Charts

Pie charts are often overused in proposals. Nevertheless, a good pie chart can be used to demonstrate how a whole was cut into parts. In proposals and grants, pie charts are often used to illustrate how income or expenses are divided. For example, the two pie charts in Figure 11.6 show the estimated sources of income and expenses for a nonprofit organization.

When labeling a pie chart, you should try to put category titles and specific numbers in the graphic itself. For instance, in Figure 11.6, each slice of the pie charts is labeled and includes a measurement to show how the pie was divided. Without these labels, these pie charts would not be nearly as helpful to the readers.

One thing to remember about pie charts is that they use a large amount of space to display only a small amount of data. The pie charts in Figure 11.6, for instance, use half a page to plot a mere six and five points, respectively. If you decide to use a pie chart, make sure the story you are illustrating is worth that much space in your proposal.

Organizational Charts

In proposals, organizational charts are used to illustrate the relationships among people, companies, and divisions (Figure 11.7). Usually, these charts are placed in

FIGURE 11.6
Pie Charts

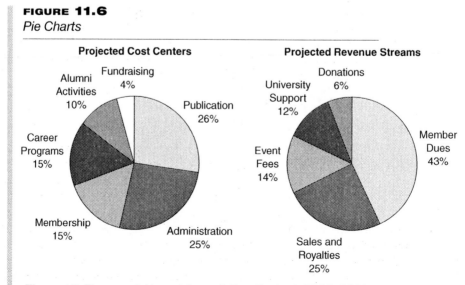

Figure 15: Proposed Alumni Association Budget, 2000–2001

FIGURE 11.7

An Organizational Chart

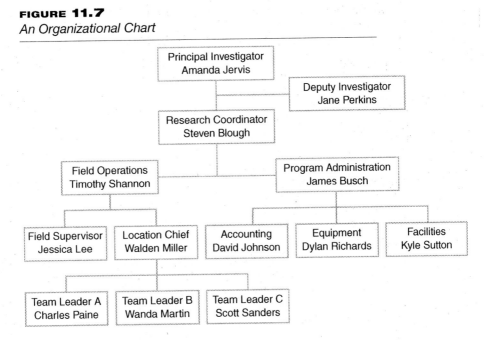

Figure 16: Research Team Hierarchy

the Qualifications section of a proposal or an appendix, though occasionally they may be used in the discussion of the plan. Essentially, they are designed to show the chain of command in a project or organization.

Organizational charts can be helpful, especially when there are many people and divisions involved in a project. In proposals for smaller projects, however, organizational charts often waste too much space. When deciding whether to include an organizational chart, ask yourself whether the chart has a specific purpose. Does including an organizational chart tell the readers something they need to know to make a decision? If your organizational chart does not have a clear purpose, then you should move it to an appendix or not use it at all.

Gantt Charts

Gantt charts have become quite popular in proposals and grants, especially now that project-planning software regularly includes graphing tools to create these charts. Gantt charts, like the one in Figure 11.8, are used to illustrate a timeline, showing when various phases of the project will begin and end.

There are two primary benefits to including a Gantt chart. First, the chart shows how different stages of a complex project will overlap and intersect. Second, it gives the readers an overall sense of how the project proceeds from start to finish. The Gantt chart in Figure 11.8 demonstrates both of these benefits.

Readers are beginning to expect Gantt charts in business proposals, especially in highly technical proposals, and they are being used increasingly in grant

FIGURE 11.8
A Gantt Chart

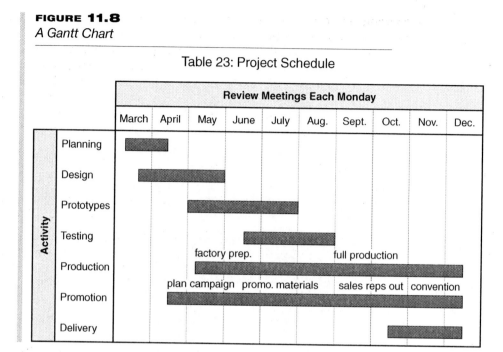

Table 23: Project Schedule

	Review Meetings Each Monday									
	March	April	May	June	July	Aug.	Sept.	Oct.	Nov.	Dec.
Planning										
Design										
Prototypes										
Testing										
Production	factory prep.						full production			
Promotion		plan campaign	promo. materials				sales reps out	convention		
Delivery										

proposals that describe large projects. These charts are typically used to reinforce the discussion of the proposal's plan, offering a visual sense of how the project will progress.

Pictures

Digital cameras and scanners are making the placement of photographs in proposals and grants easier than ever. When used properly, pictures can visually reinforce claims made in the written text. But, like those slides of your last vacation, photographs rarely capture the essence of what you are trying to show. In many cases, photographs leave the readers wondering what story the writers are trying to illustrate.

To use a photograph appropriately, make sure it tells a clear story, and never use photographs to merely decorate the proposal. If you decide to include photographs, the readers should be able to determine exactly what story the photograph is trying to illustrate.

Photographing People

When photographing people, a good rule of thumb is to only include people doing what they actually do in the workplace (people rarely huddle in a cubicle, pointing at a computer screen). If you need to include a picture of a person or a group of people standing still, take them outside and photograph them against a simple but scenic background. Photographs taken in the office tend to look dark, depressing, and dreary. Photographs taken outdoors, on the other hand, imply a personality of openness and free thinking.

If you need to photograph people inside, put as much light as possible on the subjects. If your subjects will allow it, use some facial powder to reduce the glare off their cheeks, noses, and foreheads. Then, take their picture against a simple backdrop to reduce background clutter that may distract the readers from the subjects of the photograph. If you are photographing an individual, take a picture of their head and shoulders. People tend to look uncomfortable in full-body pictures.

Photographing Equipment

When taking pictures of equipment, try to capture a close-up shot of the equipment at work. If the equipment has moving parts, try to focus the picture on those parts doing something. After all, a machine sitting alone on a factory floor looks pretty boring. A machine in action implies progress.

If you need to show a machine doing nothing, put a white dropcloth behind it to block out the other items and people in the background. Again, make sure you put as much lighting as possible on the machine so it will show up clearly in your photograph.

Photographing Places

Places are especially difficult to photograph, as you may have noticed from your vacation photos. A photograph rarely captures the spirit of a place.

A good strategy is to show people doing something in the place you are photographing. If you want to include a picture of your company's facilities, make sure you include someone doing something in that place. If you want to take a picture of a research site, like an archeological dig, you should include someone working at that site. The people you include will add a sense of action to the photograph, and they will also help your readers determine the scale of the place.

Drawings

Line drawings are often superior to pictures for illustrating machines, buildings, and designs. Whereas pictures usually include more detail than needed, a drawing limits the graphic to only the basic feature of the subject. A drawing allows you to show close-ups of the parts in a machine, the details of a building, or the schematics of electronic components. Drawings also allow you to show "cut aways" of buildings or machines, illustrating features that are not visible from the outside. Figure 11.9 shows a drawing that might appear in a proposal written by Lisa Miller for her pre-proposal to Overture Designs.

Unless you are an artist yourself, it is probably a good idea to hire a professional illustrator to handle the drawings in your proposal. Before meeting with the illustrator, sketch (thumbnail) the drawing you have in mind. Then, when you meet with the illustrator, explain what story you want the drawing to tell or what point you want it to make. With this information, the illustrator will be better able to draw a graphic that suits your proposal's needs.

FIGURE 11.9
A Drawing

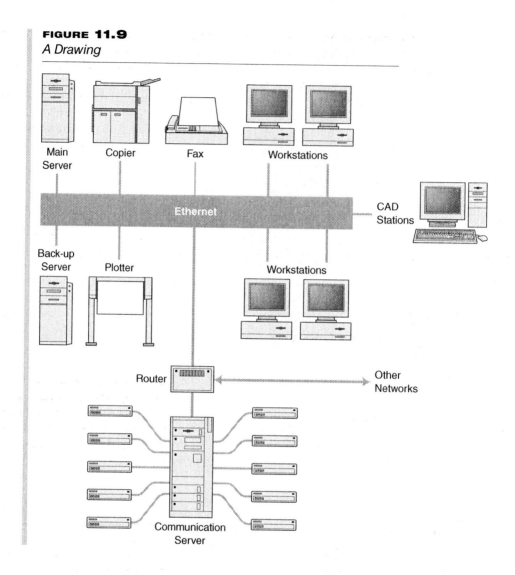

The primary drawback of using drawings is the time and expense required to create them. You should plan to use drawings only when they are absolutely needed to make an important point in the proposal.

Other Kinds of Graphics

Of course, there are countless other ways to visually present information and data. The graphics discussed in this chapter are only the most prevalent ones used in proposals and grants. In special cases, you may find yourself needing radar plots, maps, flowcharts, blueprints, scatterplots, pictographs, logic trees, screen shots, and other graphics. Also, each of the graphics discussed in this chapter can be altered to suit different needs. A bar chart alone, for example, can employ a variety of formats, such as a horizontal bar chart, stacked-bar chart, 100-percent bar chart, and deviation bar chart.

If you need to create a more specialized graphic, there are books available to walk you through their development. Tufte's *The Visual Display of Quantitative Information* (1983) is especially informative, and Kostelnick and Roberts offer a thorough discussion of graphics in their book *Designing Visual Language* (1998). See the References at the end of this book for more information on these texts.

Looking Ahead

Graphics are often the sign of a professional, quality proposal. As you are writing your proposal or grant, look for places where a graphic might be used to reinforce the message in the written text.

In most cases, it is best to create each graphic *as* you are writing the proposal, or find someone else to do the graphics while you are composing. Why? Invariably, if you wait until the last moment to create the graphics, you will run out of time and end up including no graphics at all. In today's competitive environment, the absence of graphics in a proposal or grant can often be the difference between success and failure.

Keep in mind that our society is becoming increasingly visual. Graphics can be used to reinforce your main points, help the readers make comparisons among ideas, and illustrate trends. The old adage that "a picture is worth a thousand words" won't allow you to replace a thousand words of your proposal with a graphic. However, a graphic can be used to clarify or drive home an important point to the readers. They are powerful tools that you should plan to use.

CASE STUDY Inventing Visuals

Tim jumped at the opportunity to develop the graphics for the Cool Campus proposal. That sounded like more fun than doing the budget or editing sentences and paragraphs.

When he and Calvin met to talk about the page designs of the grant proposal, Tim began to gain a clearer sense of the kinds of graphics he would need for the document. Obviously, some pictures would help make the text seem more realistic to the reviewers. Also, some graphs would help illustrate energy usage trends on campus.

Tim knew these visuals would be important, especially since many of the reviewers at the Tempest Foundation would scan the proposal before reading it closely. The graphics would invite the readers into the text.

He decided to gather some photographs and then create a few graphs and charts. Gathering photographs was the easiest task. He grabbed his digital camera and hopped on his bike. He decided to snap pictures of the Young Power Plant and a few pictures of people on campus. These photographs would help the readers visualize the campus.

He also wanted pictures of alternative energy sources to show the reviewers the types of renewable energy sources that the campus might use. How would he find pictures of solar panels and wind farms?

He e-mailed George, the engineer on the Cool Campus grant-writing team, to ask his advice. George responded with a rather simple solution. He said Tim could take pictures off U.S. government websites. Copyright law would allow them to use the pictures as long as they were properly cited.

Searching on government websites, Tim soon found a bunch of pictures that he could use. He also came across a picture of a hybrid bus built by General Motors. He wondered if he could use that picture, too, so he e-mailed George again.

"That's a little more difficult," replied George in his e-mail. "You are going to need to ask their permission to use that picture, because they own it. But I don't see why they wouldn't let you use it. Why don't you e-mail GM's public relations department and ask? I'm sure they would like the free publicity."

Tim downloaded the picture of the hybrid bus and wrote an e-mail to General Motors asking permission to use it. He explained how the photograph would be used and how it would be cited. A few days later, he received an e-mail message that gave him permission to use the photograph at no cost.

Now Tim had a bigger problem. At the moment, he didn't have any data to graph. So, he began thinking about the stories he wanted his graphs and charts to tell. On a sheet of paper, he wrote down the information he wanted to illustrate:

- Show the increased energy usage on campus.
- Show the increased cost of energy on campus.
- Show that there is broad support on campus for converting to renewable energy sources.

He realized that the only place that would have figures on energy usage and costs was the Department of Physical Facilities, which was supervised by Anne Hinton, one of his partners on the Cool Campus grant-writing team.

Tim reached her by phone. She said, "Oh, sure, we can get you that data. I'll send you our annual report."

Tim also asked Anne how he might generate some numbers to show broad support for the Cool Campus Project.

"Maybe we can just survey the college deans and department chairs through e-mail. The survey wouldn't be scientific, but we could use the data to show that the powerbrokers on campus would support the project."

"That sounds great," said Tim.

Anne said, "You send me the survey questions and some text to introduce the survey, and I'll have our webmaster put the survey on our website. When the survey is ready to go, I'll send out an e-mail that asks the deans and chairs to complete the survey. Not everyone will take the time to do it, but we should get enough response to generate some useful data." The survey Tim sent Anne included the four questions shown in Figure 11.10.

A week later, Anne sent Tim the data from the survey. About 80 percent of the deans and chairs responded. Tim tabulated the responses to the survey questions and entered them into his spreadsheet program. He decided to display the responses as a horizontal bar chart, which illustrated the answers to each response (Figure 11.11).

Tim then used the annual report Anne sent him to gather information on the three primary energy sources at Durango: coal, electricity, and petroleum. Based on data from the annual report, Tim developed the line graph shown in Figure 11.12

Lastly, Tim found a graph in the annual report that showed the increasing costs of energy on campus (Figure 11.13). He was startled by what he found. Now he understood why President Wilson was so nervous about energy costs on campus. They were skyrocketing.

Tim redesigned the graph to make it visually similar to the others, but he kept the data the same.

He needed a couple of hours to finish making the graphs, and he collected all the photographs in one folder on his hard drive. Then, he sent them all to Calvin as e-mail attachments.

Tim realized that the time collecting photographs and making graphs was time well spent. These visuals would make the grant proposal seem much more realistic and professional.

FIGURE 11.10
Tim's Unscientific Survey

The Department of Physical Facilities is conducting an opinion poll about energy usage on campus. The campus's increasing energy bills have been responsible for many of our budget constraints, so we are seeking alternatives to our present energy sources.

To gauge your impressions of the issue, we have created a simple survey that will provide the university with some preliminary feedback. Please answer the following brief questions. We don't need names or specific information, just your responses to the questions.

Thank you for your help. When you click 'Submit' the survey will be sent to us automatically. If you have any questions, please call me at 555-1924 or e-mail me at anne.hinton@durangou.edu.

Dr. Anne Hinton
Vice President for Physical Facilities

Questions	Strongly Agree	Agree	Disagree	Strongly Disagree
The energy problems at Durango U. need to be addressed now, not later.	☐	☐	☐	☐
Our energy problems can be solved primarily through conservation of energy.	☐	☐	☐	☐
Durango U. should convert to renewable energy sources as soon as possible.	☐	☐	☐	☐
Durango U. has an obligation to take on a leadership role in the region regarding energy issues and issues of global warming.	☐	☐	☐	☐

FIGURE 11.11
Tim's Bar Chart

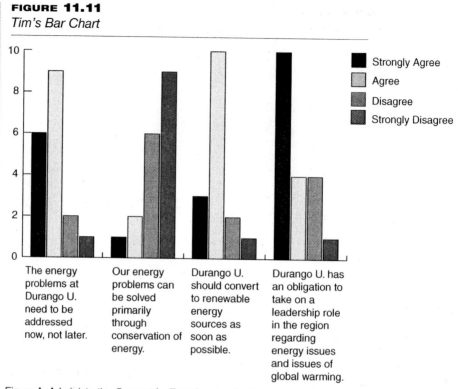

Figure A: Administrative Support for Transforming the Campus

FIGURE 11.12
Tim's Line Graphs

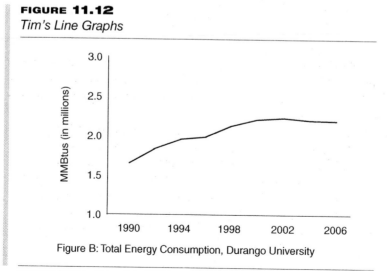

Figure B: Total Energy Consumption, Durango University

SOURCE: Durango University's 2006 Annual Report.

FIGURE 11.13
Tim's Line Graphs

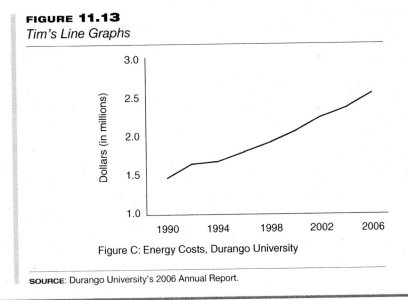

Figure C: Energy Costs, Durango University

SOURCE: Durango University's 2006 Annual Report.

Questions and Exercises

1. Find a graph, chart, or table in a printed document. Does the graphic tell a simple story? Does it reinforce the written text, not replace it? Is it ethical? Is it labeled and placed properly? Find one or more graphics that do not follow the guidelines discussed in this chapter. Are they still effective? How could you improve each graphic?

2. Find a document that includes minimal or no graphics. Looking through the document, can you find instances where a graphic might have helped reinforce or clarify the written text? Create a graph, table, or chart that might be included in this document.

3. Create a simple survey that asks questions about a local problem. Ask some people to fill out your survey (perhaps some people in your class). Then, use the data you gathered to create various different types of graphs, tables, or charts.

4. Look at pictures in your local newspaper. Can you articulate what story they were designed to tell, even if they were not accompanied by written text? Also, look for pictures that do not tell clear stories. How could the author have used better pictures to suit the needs of the document and its readers?

5. Use the data in Figure 11.5 to create a couple of different kinds of graphs. Try making a bar chart and a line graph. How do these different graphs allow you to tell a different story with this data set? Which graph do you think is more effective?

12 | The Final Touches

Overview

This chapter will discuss the development of front and back matter while describing how to revise proposals and grants. The chapter will meet the following objectives:

1. Discuss the importance of revising proposals and grants.

2. Show how to write the front matter.

3. Show how to write the back matter.

4. Describe the revision process to finish and polish the document.

Seeing the Proposal as a Whole Document

To this point in this book, you have learned how to plan, organize, style, and design proposals and grants, using time-tested rhetorical strategies. As you near the end of the proposal-writing process, it is time to take stock of your proposal as a whole document. You need to ask yourself whether your proposal achieves its purpose and addresses the needs of the readers. These kinds of questions can be difficult to ask, especially when a nearly finished draft of the proposal is sitting in front of you, but a committed effort to refine and polish the document is usually the difference between the successful proposal and the one that came close.

In this chapter, we are going to discuss how to pull the entire proposal package together. The proposal itself is the core of the package. Nevertheless, you will likely also include additional materials, such as a letter of transmittal, an executive summary, a table of contents, and appendices. These materials are called the *front matter* and *back matter*. You should also think about revising your proposal at least one more time. At this point it probably looks rather finished, but don't stop now. Here is where you can add that extra refinement that will persuade the clients or funding source that you have the right plan to address their needs.

This chapter also includes two final versions of proposals that have been used as case studies throughout this book: the Cool Campus proposal to the Tempest Foundation and Insight Systems' proposal to Overture Designs. In these final drafts, you can see how the writers put the final touches on their proposals.

Inventing Front Matter

Front matter consists of the materials that appear before the introduction of the main proposal. Like the introduction, the front matter is intended to set a context or framework for the proposal. Items in the front matter include some or all of the following items:

- Letter of transmittal
- Cover page
- Executive summary
- Table of contents

These materials are not mandatory, unless they are requested by the client or funding source. Nevertheless, they are often useful accessories that help the readers work more efficiently through your ideas. The inclusion of these front matter items also shows an attention to detail that the readers will appreciate.

Grant proposals may also require you to fill out forms that provide information about your organization, its nonprofit status, and other information. These forms are usually self-explanatory, but the point of contact (POC) at a funding source can answer your questions about filling them out.

Letters or Memos of Transmittal

The purpose of a letter of transmittal (or a memo of transmittal for internal proposals) is to introduce the readers to the proposal or grant. Even though a proposal may not need a letter of transmittal, there are a couple of reasons why you should include one. First, letters and memos are personal forms of correspondence, so they can add a personal touch to the proposal package. A letter of transmittal allows you to introduce yourself and shake hands with the readers before they start looking over your ideas. These letters tend to be lighter in tone than proposals, setting the readers at ease before they start considering your ideas.

A second reason why letters and memos of transmittal are important is their ability to steer your proposal into the right hands. In large companies and organizations, even the most important documents sometimes end up on the wrong desk, in the wrong mailbox, and ultimately in the wrong trash can or recycle bin. By identifying the proposal's readers and purpose up front, a letter of transmittal can steer your proposal into the right hands. If the wrong person receives your proposal, the letter of transmittal will help them send it to the exact person who should receive it.

For grant proposals, funding sources often do not ask for a letter of transmittal, but this kind of letter can be a nice addition to the package. Readers at private foundations seem to warm up to a transmittal letter that adds a personal touch. And, if they don't want the letter, they can always remove it before the package is reviewed.

Writing a Letter or Memo of Transmittal

Like other documents, letters and memos have an introduction, body, and conclusion:

Introduction The introduction of a letter of transmittal should offer some background information and state the purpose of the proposal. Specifically, you should mention the RFP to which the proposal is responding or the meeting at which the proposal was requested. This kind of opening will help the readers remember exactly why the proposal is being sent to them. Then, you should tell the readers the purpose of the proposal itself. You can even include the same purpose statement used in the proposal's introduction, though most writers prefer to paraphrase that sentence to avoid the feeling of repetition. An introduction to a letter of transmittal should run, at most, a few sentences.

Body The body of a letter of transmittal should highlight and summarize the important points of the proposal. You might describe your plan in miniature if you think it will grab the readers' interest. You might also mention some of the key benefits of your plan or briefly describe the qualifications of you, your team, or your company. Try not to run on; a letter of transmittal should be concise, saving the details for the proposal itself. As a rule of thumb, the body of this letter or memo should run about two or three paragraphs.

Conclusion The conclusion should thank the readers for their time and tell them who to contact if they have any questions or need further information. You might also tell the readers that you will be in touch with them by a specific date to follow up on the proposal. The conclusion should be concise, perhaps two or three sentences.

Stylistically, letters of transmittal should be simple and personal. The tone should be upbeat and friendly, yet respectful. A judicious use of *you* and *we* will make a personal connection between the readers and yourself.

Meanwhile, avoid using business-letter clichés like "enclosed please find," "pursuant to our agreement," or "as per your request." This kind of hackneyed business language will only make your letter or memo sound distant and aloof— an unfortunate tone to use if you want the readers to trust you. Instead of using clichés, simply write the letter as though you are talking to another person. After all, you *are* talking to another human being, not a corporation. In a face-to-face conversation, you would never use these tired clichés and strange phrases, so you should avoid using them in a letter or memo.

In most cases, a letter of transmittal should be limited to one page. Avoid the temptation to start arguing for your plan at this point. Instead, keep this letter or memo concise and positive. Let the proposal do the heavy lifting.

Lisa Miller's Letter of Transmittal to Overture Designs

A few chapters ago, Lisa Miller completed the first draft of her proposal to Overture. While she was waiting for comments on the draft from her boss and the other engineers at Insight Systems, she decided to write a cover letter for the proposal (Figure 12.1).

Lisa decided to write the letter from her boss, Hanna Gibbons, directly to Grant Moser, the point of contact for the RFP. Of course, she knew others at Overture would read this letter of transmittal, especially the principal architects at the firm, Susan James and Thomas Weber. But she had a hunch that a personalized letter to Mr. Moser might incline him more favorably toward her proposal. In her experiences with writing proposals, Lisa had found that POCs often have great

FIGURE 12.1
Cover Letter to Overture Designs

Insight Systems ■

15520 Naperville Rd., Naperville, Illinois 62000-1234 (630) 555-1298
www.insight_systems.com

April 21, 2006

Grant E. Moser, Office Manager
Overture Designs
300 S. Michigan Ave., Suite 1201
Chicago, Illinois 60601

Dear Mr. Moser,

Thank you for the opportunity to submit a pre-proposal in response to Overture Designs' "Request for Proposals for Managing Office Growth" (May 29, 2006). Our pre-proposal outlines a strategy that will help your firm preserve its current award-winning office on Michigan Avenue while supporting your continued growth in the Chicago architectural market.

Our plan for managing your growth is simple. We suggest Overture implement a telecommuting network that allows some employees to work from home or on-site. Telecommuting has several advantages. First, it will allow your company to maintain financial flexibility in the ever-uncertain Chicago market. Second, implementing a telecommunication network will create minimal disruption to Overture's current operations. Third, telecommuting will preserve Overture's already high employee morale, helping you retain and recruit top-level architects and staff.

We also look forward to building a lasting relationship with Overture. Insight Systems has been a leader in telecommunications for more than twenty years. We have the right combination of innovation and experience to address Overture's immediate and long-term needs.

Thank you for your time and consideration. Lisa Miller tells me she enjoyed meeting you and touring the Overture office. I am looking forward to meeting you in the near future. If you have any questions or need further information, please call me at 1-800-555-9823, ext. 001. Otherwise, Lisa Miller can be reached by phone or e-mail (lmiller@insight_systems.com).

Sincerely,

Hanna Gibbons, Ph.D.
Chief Executive Officer, Insight Systems

influence over the primary readers, even if they are not the decision makers themselves. If Mr. Moser did have some influence, Lisa hoped her letter would help win him over to her company's side.

Lisa kept the body of the letter short. In the second paragraph, she decided to stress the benefits of her plan rather than summarize her proposal at length. A long discussion of telecommuting would have just made the letter sound complicated, so she simply mentioned her plan and then stated some of its strengths. Then, in the third paragraph, she briefly pointed out Insight Systems' experience in the area. Again, though, she kept the discussion concise. She did not want to bog down the readers in details at this point.

The conclusion of the letter was meant to leave a positive image in the minds of Mr. Moser and the primary readers. At the end of the letter, she thanked the readers and provided a brief glimpse into the future. Finally, she provided them with contact information if they would have any questions or need more information.

Overall, Lisa's letter of transmittal did not add anything new to the proposal. Nevertheless, it set a personal tone that she hoped would carry over a positive feeling into the review of the proposal itself.

The Cover Page

The cover page of a proposal, like the letter of transmittal, is intended to identify the subject of the proposal and set a particular tone. The cover page typically includes the following items:

- Title of the proposal
- Name of the client's company or the funding source
- Name and logo of the company or organization submitting the proposal
- Date on which the proposal was submitted

Cover pages can be simple or elaborate. Like the rest of the proposal, the design of the cover page should fit the character of the project and the readers. For example, the cover page on the left in Figure 12.2 is intended to set a conservative tone for a proposal. Its use of a traditional serif font and a balanced page offers a feeling of security. The cover page on the right is a bit more progressive with its use of a sans serif font and a unique page layout.

Is a cover page mandatory? Of course not. But a cover page is an easy way to set a professional tone for the proposal. Like the cover of a book, cover pages provide a distinct starting point at which the readers will begin assessing the merits of your ideas.

Executive Summary

In our fast-paced culture, executive summaries are often expected in proposals and grants, especially large ones. The purpose of an executive summary is to boil down the proposal to a synopsis that can be read in minutes. In one to three pages, the executive summary goes over the current situation, the plan,

FIGURE 12.2
Two Different Cover Pages

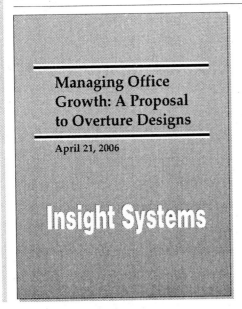

the qualifications, and even the costs. It provides an overall snapshot of the proposal, so your readers can quickly determine the proposal's major points and claims.

Executive summaries can be organized many different ways, but they tend to follow the structure of the proposal itself. The first paragraph in the summary identifies the purpose, subject, and main point of the proposal. The body paragraphs summarize the situation, plan, qualifications, and costs. The conclusion of the executive summary might mention a few benefits of the plan.

The importance of the executive summary should not be underestimated. Decision makers in most companies and funding sources are typically short on time, so they often rely on executive summaries to help them cut down the pile of competing proposals to a few proposals that they will read in depth. Also, readers often use the executive summary at meetings to help them quickly refresh their understanding of the proposal's main points. In some cases, the decision makers may end up reading the executive summary more closely and frequently than the proposal itself, so it needs to be well written.

Table of Contents

A table of contents is a standard feature in most proposals of more than ten pages. It provides the readers with an overview of the contents of the proposal, helping

FIGURE 12.3
An Ineffective Table of Contents

Table of Contents

them determine the most efficient way to read the text. It also forecasts the structure of the proposal, providing the readers with a mental framework into which the content of the proposal will be placed.

Ineffective tables of contents tend to use headings that lack meaning. For example, Figure 12.3 shows a table of contents that relies too heavily on nonspecific headings. This table of contents does not provide the readers with a solid understanding of the contents of the proposal. It also signals that the headings used in the proposal are not particularly descriptive or helpful.

An effective table of contents provides the readers with a meaningful outline of the contents of the proposal. Each title in the table of contents should be distinctive, specific, and long enough to give the readers a clear sense of what is in each section. To avoid a table of contents that lacks meaning, use the headings that are found in the proposal itself. List these headings in the table of contents in a way that highlights the structure of the proposal (Figure 12.4).

FIGURE 12.4
A More Effective Table of Contents

Table of Contents

Overall, the changes from Figure 12.3 to Figure 12.4 are small, but the revised table of contents offers more description of the contents of the proposal. The readers can now better anticipate the topics that will be discussed.

Inventing Back Matter

Back matter includes additional materials that support the information in the body of the proposal. Often called the *appendices*, the back matter in a proposal becomes a reference tool for the readers. It can include any or all of the following items related to the subject of the proposal:

- Itemized budget and budget rationale
- Resumés of management and key personnel
- Analytical reports or white papers
- News or magazine articles
- Prior proposals
- Formulas and calculations
- Glossary of terms
- Bibliography
- Personal or corporate references

Each appendix should be labeled with a number or letter, so it can be referred to in the body of the proposal. For example, in the body of the proposal, the readers might see the note, "The geothermal formulas and calculations used to determine these figures can be found in Appendix D." If the readers want to check those figures, they will know that they can then turn to that appendix in the back of the proposal.

In each appendix, an opening paragraph should introduce the contents that follow. For instance, if you decide to include copies of some magazine articles you collected on the subject, the appendix's opening paragraph might explain that you have included the articles to show the importance of the subject to the public. You might also briefly discuss how these articles reinforce the argument you are making in the body of the proposal. Even a glossary of terms should include some kind of short opening paragraph to help the readers understand the purpose of the glossary.

The most important form of back matter, the budget rationale, was discussed in Chapter 8. Let us look at some other kinds of back matter.

Resumés of Management and Key Personnel

It is becoming increasingly common to include the resumés of managers, principal investigators, and key personnel in an appendix to the proposal. Though your Qualifications section may have included biographies of the executives and researchers involved with the project, the readers may want to know more about their backgrounds. One- to two-page resumés for each executive or researcher will help the readers gather this additional information.

A typical resumé in the appendix will include the following information on each manager and key person on the project:

- Employment history
- Education
- Publications
- Special training or skills
- Awards
- Memberships in professional groups

The appendix should also include an introduction that states the purpose of the appendix (i.e., to provide resumés of managers and key personnel) and lists the people whose resumés follow.

Glossary of Terms and Symbols

As much as we try to avoid it, proposals and grants often include jargon words and symbols that are unfamiliar to the readers. In these cases, an appendix that includes an alphabetical listing of terms and symbols with definitions can help the readers work through the complex terminology of the proposal. Glossaries are especially helpful for readers who are not familiar with the technical aspects of the project.

Each item in a glossary should be written as a sentence definition. A sentence definition has three parts: (1) the name of the item, (2) the class to which the item belongs, and (3) the features that distinguish the item from its class. For example, here are a few items that might appear in a glossary.

cathode ray tube: a vacuum tube in which electrons are projected onto a fluorescent screen.

cyclotron: a particle accelerator in which charged particles (e.g., protons) are propelled in a circular motion by a magnetic field.

direct labor: the group of workers who are directly active in the production of goods and services.

Σ (sigma): the total number of electrons measured after one minute of testing.

Each of these definitions starts with the name of the item being defined. Then it names the class to which the item belongs (e.g., particle accelerator, vacuum tube, body of workers, total amount of electrons). The remainder of the definition tells how the item can be distinguished from its class.

Bibliography

The bibliography should include a list of printed sources, interviews, and other outside materials that were cited in the proposal or consulted during its development. The bibliography should list the sources of any quotations, graphics, data, or ideas that you took from another document. Also, if you conducted interviews, place the dates and times of these interviews into the bibliography.

The format of a bibliography should follow guidelines found in style manuals, such as those offered by the American Psychological Association (APA) or the Modern Language Association (MLA). APA style is widely used in scientific and technical proposals. MLA style is typically used in nontechnical proposals. Many reference books include examples of these styles. However, it is always helpful to consult the style guides themselves. Here are their official titles so you can track them down in a library or at a local bookstore:

- *Publication Manual of the American Psychological Association*
- *MLA Handbook for Writers of Research Papers*

Corporations and government bodies often develop their own style guides, which define specific rules for citations. In the end, the style chosen is usually not important (unless the client or funding source requests a citation style). Consistency in your citations, however, is important. Each item in your bibliography list should follow a predictable format.

Formulas and Calculations

In the body of a business proposal, formulas and calculations can be a momentum killer. And yet, these numerical tools are critical if the readers are going to assess the soundness of your proposal. In a research grant, formulas and calculations are important but can become overwhelming to nontechnical readers.

You may consider moving some or all of your formulas and calculations to an appendix, especially when you are addressing an audience that includes nontechnical readers. In the appendix, each formula and calculation should be properly labeled in a way that explains exactly how it is used. In some cases, an explanatory narrative should be included that leads the readers through any derivations of formulas or any calculations. Try to avoid dumping the readers into a maze of symbols and numbers. After all, if the clients or their experts cannot follow your derivations or calculations, they are not going to trust the conclusions you draw from them.

Related Reports, Prior Proposals, and FYI Information

In some cases, you might decide to include copies of documents that are discussed in the proposal. For example, a scientist may include an article or white paper that supports an important argument in the grant proposal, or a business proposal writer may include a recent magazine article that praises his company. Also, you may want to include prior proposals related to the subject.

Essentially, an appendix can include any number of additional documents as long as the readers aren't overburdened with unnecessary information. For each document you add, though, you should also include a small paragraph that identifies the background for the document. Tell the readers why the document is important, when it was written, who it was written for, and where it was used or appeared. This explanatory information is important, because you should not expect the readers to figure out why you decided to include additional documents in the appendix.

Revising the Proposal or Grant

In Chapter 1, you learned that writing a proposal involves a *process*. Even the best proposal writers and grant writers cannot sit down and crank out a proposal in one try—though you will certainly hear myths about the person who can write proposals without any revision. Myths aside, proposals usually require at least a few drafts before they are complete. To be successful, you should plan to devote significant time to revising and editing your documents.

Most writers revise their work as they finish each section of a proposal— always a good idea—but you should also rethink and revise the proposal as a whole text. Why? Because often, writing a proposal causes you to think more deeply about your subject. While writing, your original ideas about the situation, the plan, or the needs of the readers have almost certainly evolved or changed. During the revision phase of the writing process, it is time to rework all the sections of the proposal so they tell a consistent story.

The Rhetorical Situation

Start the revision process by looking closely over your notes about the rhetorical situation. Ask yourself the following questions, looking at each section in the proposal separately:

Subject

Is the subject of the proposal still the same? Does any content in the proposal drift outside the boundaries of the subject? Is the subject at the beginning of the proposal the same as the subject at the end?

Purpose

Does the proposal achieve the stated purpose? Do you need to refine or broaden the purpose statement to suit a deeper understanding of the situation?

Readers

Does the proposal address the motives, values, attitudes, and emotions of the primary readers? Will the secondary and gatekeeper readers be satisfied with the proposal? Does the proposal contain any information that hostile tertiary readers could use to damage you, your team, or your company or organization?

Context

Is the proposal appropriate for the physical, economic, political, and ethical situations in which it might be used? Can you make any changes to the format or design to make it more usable? Are any parts of your proposal politically or ethically vulnerable?

You need to be honest with yourself when looking over the rhetorical situation. Certainly, there is a tendency to ignore problems with the proposal now that you are reaching the end. But you should keep reminding yourself that the readers will not ignore these problems. The extra time and effort you spend rethinking the rhetorical situation will help you make the final adjustments needed to help you win the contract or receive the funding you need.

Rethinking the Problem or Opportunity

After reconsidering the rhetorical situation, look closely at your notes in which you identified the problem or opportunity that the proposal or grant was written to address. Often, especially in larger proposals, a writer's original understanding of the problem or opportunity evolved during the drafting and revision phases. As a result, the proposal is now handling a much more complex issue than was first defined. If so, perhaps you need to scale back the proposal to handle a smaller problem or opportunity. Or perhaps you need to rewrite parts of the proposal to suit that larger problem.

Reconsider the question "What changed?" as you rethink the problem or opportunity. As mentioned in Chapter 1, proposals and grants are tools for managing change, so, while revising the proposal, you should ask yourself whether your proposal is addressing the elements of change that are driving the current situation. Are you shaping change to the advantage of your company or organization? Are there any elements of change that you are *not* addressing in your proposal?

Then, think about the type of proposal or grant you were asked to write. Were you supposed to write a research proposal, planning proposal, implementation proposal, estimate proposal, or a combination of two of these kinds of proposals? Often during the proposal-writing process the project will experience a certain amount of "mission creep." For example, a research proposal will tend to creep ahead and start offering a strategic plan, or a planning proposal will begin describing implementation, offering details like schedules and personnel that typically would be found in an implementation proposal.

To avoid mission creep, give the clients exactly what they asked for—nothing more and nothing less. Clients usually want to handle a project one step at a time. If they asked for an assessment of their facilities' production capacity, they don't want you to tell them that you will be showing up with the heavy equipment in a month to start rebuilding their factory. If they asked for a cost estimate for recycling some post-production materials, they don't want a planning proposal that shows how you might restructure their factory to reduce waste.

Another reason for giving the readers exactly what they asked for is the simple fact that you do not want to give your ideas away for free. If you provide them a detailed implementation plan in addition to the strategic plan they asked for, you just gave them a blueprint for solving their problem without your help.

Rethinking the Rhetorical Elements

Finally, reconsider the rhetorical elements of your document, separately considering the content, organization, style, and design.

Content

Is the proposal's content complete? Is there any information missing that would help you persuade the readers? Are there any digressions in the proposal where you have included details that go beyond "need to know" information?

Organization

Does the proposal follow a logical order or the order specified by the client or funding source? Does it tell a story, leading the readers from the current situation, through a plan, to a beneficial conclusion? Does the introduction set an effective context for the body of the proposal by highlighting the subject, purpose, and main point while offering any helpful background information, stressing the importance of the subject, and forecasting the body of the proposal? Do the opening paragraphs of each section identify the purpose and point of their respective parts of the proposal?

Style

Does the proposal reflect an appropriate tone/persona for the readers and subject? Is the style plain where the proposal is instructing the readers and persuasive where you are trying to influence them? Can you use any stylistic devices like similes, analogies, or metaphors to make the text clearer or more powerful?

Design

Does the proposal follow an appropriate, consistent page design? Are the pages balanced? Does the proposal use alignment, grouping, and consistency appropriately? Have you used bulleted or numbered lists where appropriate? Does data appear in tables or charts? Are the graphics properly placed and labeled? Would more graphics help illustrate difficult points?

As the deadline looms and you grow tired of working on a proposal, it is tempting to cut revision time to a minimum. Sometimes you can actually convince yourself that the readers don't care whether the proposal is polished or not. In reality, readers *do* care, very much, about the final form of the proposal.

Often the difference between the successful proposal and the runners-up was the added time the winners put into revising the final document. Proverbs such as "The devil is in the details" and "Quality is found at the edges" are very true of proposals. Always set aside a significant block of time for revising the proposal. Often, the additional time spent on revising can be the difference between winning and losing the contract or funding.

Looking Ahead

A proposal or grant is the beginning of a relationship. Essentially, the readers are interviewing your company or organization, trying to determine whether a basis for a positive, constructive alliance exists. Your proposal is the face you are presenting to the client or funding source. If they feel comfortable with your proposal, they will feel comfortable with your company or organization. If something feels wrong about your proposal, they will accept another proposal that "just feels right."

In this chapter, we went over the endgame of the proposal-writing process. Once you finish with the proposal, you should be able to conceptualize the document as a whole. It should be complete, organized, easy to read, and well designed. If you feel comfortable with the proposal in its final form, with no regrets, chances are good your readers will feel comfortable with the proposal too.

CASE STUDY **Revising and Polishing**

The Cool Campus team decided to meet one last time to finish the proposal. As they put the parts of the proposal together, they soon realized that some of their ideas about the subject, purpose, and readers had evolved. They had developed a sharper understanding of the problem they were trying to solve and its potential solutions. George's budget and Tim's graphics added some new information that needed to be addressed in the written part of the grant proposal. Overall, though, it was obvious they had come a long way since their first meeting.

They began revising the grant proposal by looking over their notes about the rhetorical situation. They read through the proposal, marking places where they may have strayed from the subject or purpose. They also thought carefully about whether they were addressing the concerns and needs of the reviewers at the Tempest Foundation.

"It's interesting," said Calvin. "We started out talking about all the environmental issues on campus, including recycling and water usage. But, while writing this proposal, we have narrowed our subject down to just energy issues."

Anne said, "That's fine. We were thinking a little too broadly at the start, which would have made our grant sound too complex to the reviewers."

George laughed. "This one is complex enough already!"

"We do seem to be dreaming big, aren't we?" asked Karen.

"Why not?" said Anne. "If we were thinking small, we wouldn't need a grant. Anyway, a project like this one should appeal to the Tempest Foundation and other funding sources."

They worked on editing and proofreading the grant proposal. With all the parts in one place, it was easier to see how to fix problems with the proposal's organization. They also revised or crossed out any sentences that did not include need-to-know information. Meanwhile, Calvin made small changes in his page designs to help the written text work better with Tim's graphics. Calvin also edited for consistency, making sure the headings, rules, and lists were all handled in the same way.

As Calvin made a few last adjustments, George asked, "Are we finished?"

Tim said, "It looks done to me."

"Of course, I will be running a copy past President Wilson and some of our other gatekeeper readers, but it looks good for now," said Anne. "I'm sure they will have a few suggestions for changes."

"I'm glad we did this," said Karen. "I learned a great amount about energy, Durango University, and issues involved in global warming. I think we took a big step in the right direction by writing this grant."

George replied, "I hope this grant proposal is just the beginning of something special."

"Yeah, let's hope it is," said Calvin. "I really enjoyed working with all of you, and I look forward to having a chance to work together again soon."

A copy of the final Cool Campus Project grant proposal follows the Questions and Exercises for this chapter. A final version of Lisa Miller's final proposal to Overture Designs from Insight Systems is also included at the end of this chapter.

Questions and Exercises

1. Look over the two proposals included at the end of this chapter. How do they meet the purpose and the needs of their readers? Are there any further revisions you might make to these proposals? How could they be improved?

2. Find a proposal or grant on the Internet or at your workplace. Write an analysis of the proposal in which you discuss the content, organization, style, and design of the document. In your analysis, point out examples of the proposal's strengths, and then make some suggestions for improvement.

3. Write a letter or memo of transmittal for a real or practice business proposal or a grant proposal of your own. What information do you believe belongs in this letter or memo? What information should you save for the proposal itself? How can you write the letter with a positive, personal tone that puts the readers at ease?

4. Using a proposal from the Internet or your workplace, write a one-page executive summary that describes what is in the proposal. Your summary should cover all the major sections in the proposal. What did you decide to include? What did you leave out? How did you decide what to keep and what to leave out?

5. Using a proposal of your own, work through the revision process described in this chapter. Revise your work by reconsidering the subject, purpose, readers, context, and objectives of the proposal. Then check whether your understanding of the problem or opportunity changed as you wrote the proposal. Finally, edit the proposal by paying special attention to its content, organization, style, and design.

Example Proposals

Example Proposal: "Managing Office Growth: A Proposal to Overture Designs from Insight Systems"

Example Proposal: "The Cool Campus Project at Durango University: A Grant Request to the Tempest Foundation"

Managing Office Growth

A Proposal to Overture Designs from

Insight Systems

I

April 21, 2006

Table of Contents

Executive Summary

This pre-proposal was written to help Overture manage its office growth. In this pre-proposal, Insight Systems proposes to develop a telecommuting network that would allow selected employees at Overture to work from home. We believe this approach would provide Overture with adequate space to grow while avoiding expensive commitments to new facilities. Moreover, a telecommuting network will avoid any disruptions to Overture's current projects.

Overture's success is the main reason why it needs to develop a plan for managing its limited office space. Since 1982, when Overture moved into its current office, business at the firm has grown exponentially. With this growth, more employees and equipment have been needed. As a result, the current office space has started to feel a little snug.

Our plan to free up space at Overture's current office is simple. In four phases, we propose to build a telecommunication local area network (LAN) that allows selected employees to work outside the office. Here is our plan:

Phase One: We will study Overture's telecommuting options.

Phase Two: We will design a local area network (LAN) that will allow selected employees to telecommute from a home office.

Phase Three: We will train Overture's employees in telecommuting basics.

Phase Four: We will assess the success of the telecommuting program after it has been implemented.

The advantages of our plan are its flexibility and low cost. First, a telecommuting network would allow Overture to retain its current office space, avoiding a costly and disruptive move to other facilities. Second, employees at Overture would enjoy the flexibility of working at home or from a project site. Third, the investment in a telecommuting network would be minimal, allowing Overture to react quickly to the volatile architectural market in Chicago.

Insight Systems is uniquely qualified to handle this project. Since 1975, we have been providing flexible, low-cost telecommuting solutions to progressive companies like Overture. Our managers, engineers, and staff are all top people in this area. Our background and experience give us the ability to help Overture manage its needs for a more efficient, dynamic office space. Our keys to success are innovation, flexibility, and efficiency.

Thank you for the opportunity to write a pre-proposal for this project. We look forward to working with Overture in the near future.

Proposal to Overture Designs: Growth and Flexibility through Telecommuting

Founded in 1979, Overture Designs is one of the classic entrepreneurial success stories in the architectural field. Starting the firm with only a thousand dollars in the bank, Susan James and Thomas Weber began designing functional buildings for the Wrigleyville business community. Five years later, Overture cleared its first million dollars in revenue. Today, Overture is one of the leading architectural firms in the Chicago market with more than $50 million in annual revenue. The *Chicago Business Journal* has consistently rated Overture one of the top-five architectural firms in the city, citing the company's continued innovation and growth in the industry.

With growth, however, comes growing pains. Overture now faces an important decision about how it will manage its growth in the near future. The right decision could lead to more market share, increased sales, and even more prominence in the architectural field. However, Overture also needs to safeguard itself against over extension in case the Chicago construction market unexpectedly begins to recede.

To help Overture make the right decision, this proposal suggests an innovative strategy that will support the firm's growth while maintaining its flexibility. Specifically, we propose that Overture implement a telecommuting network that allows selected employees to work at home a few days each week. Telecommuting will provide Overture with the office space it needs to continue growing. Meanwhile, this approach will avoid a large investment in new facilities and disruption to the company's current operations.

In this proposal, we will first discuss the results of our research into Overture's office space needs. Second, we will offer a plan for using a telecommuting network to free up more space at Overture's current office. Third, we will review Insight Systems' qualifications to assist Overture with its move into the world of telecommuting. And finally, we will go over some of the costs and advantages of our plan. Our aim is to show you how telecommuting can help Overture grow while maintaining the innovative spirit that launched this firm two decades ago.

The Office Space Needs at Overture

Before describing our plan, let us first highlight some of the factors that created the current office space shortage at Overture.

In 1982, Overture moved into its current office space on Michigan Avenue. At the time, the firm employed five architects and fifteen staff members. The office was roomy and flexible, because Susan James designed it with functionality and growth in mind. The original architects at the firm each had a couple drafting tables and a large desk. Meanwhile, desks for staff members were placed strategically throughout the office to maximize the efficiency of the workspace. The design of Overture's office won accolades and awards as a masterpiece of modernist design. In a 1983 interview with *Architectural Review*, James explained that the workspace was designed to be "both aesthetic and pragmatic, a balance of form and function." She also pointed out that she wanted the office to demonstrate the advantages of the modernist design for clients.

Two decades later, the office is still considered a modernist masterpiece, but Overture's growth has made the workspace feel a bit cramped. This growth in business began in 1992 when the economy rebounded from recession. Soon, downtown businesses began renovating their neoclassical offices, adopting the modernist style. As a result, Overture found itself one of the firms leading a movement that the

Chicago Tribune dubbed the "Downtown Renaissance." The firm's revenues doubled from 1992 to 1999 and doubled again from 2000 to 2005. To meet this increased demand, Overture added ten architects and twenty new staff members during the 1990s and early 2000s. As a result, an office that once seemed roomy was becoming increasingly snug. More architects and staff also meant more drafting tables, more desks, and more equipment. Meanwhile, new kinds of equipment, like CAD systems, plotters, and large-format copiers, also began using up precious floor space, further restricting the limited area available.

Overture's office space shortage is simply a symptom of the firm's success and growing influence in the Chicago market. Now, the challenge faced by Overture is to free up office space without disrupting current projects or jeopardizing future growth. Left unaddressed, this lack of office space may create problems in the near future. One problem is that a restrictive office tends to undermine employee morale, leading to lower productivity and overall employee discomfort. Another problem is that the workspace will also become increasingly inefficient, wasting employees' time, while causing minor injuries to personnel and damage to equipment. A cramped office also presents a bad image to clients, especially since Overture prides itself on designing functional workspaces that enhance business activities.

Our Plan: Maintaining Flexibility through Telecommuting

Managing Overture's limited office space requires a solution that allows the company to grow but does not sacrifice financial flexibility. Therefore, we believe a successful solution must meet the following objectives:

- Minimize disruption to Overture's current operations
- Minimize costs, preserving Overture's financial flexibility
- Retain Overture's current office on Michigan Avenue
- Foster a dynamic workplace that will be appealing to Overture's architects and staff

To meet these objectives, Insight Systems proposes to collaborate with Overture to develop a telecommunication network that allows selected employees to work at home. The primary advantage of telecommuting is that it frees up office space for the remaining employees who need to work in the main office. Telecommuting will also avoid overextending Overture's financial resources, so the firm can quickly react to the crests and valleys of the market.

Our plan will be implemented in four major phases. First, we will study Overture's telecommuting options. Second, we will design a local area network (LAN) that will allow selected employees to telecommute from a home office. Third, we will train Overture's employees in telecommuting basics. And finally, we will assess the success of the telecommuting program after it has been implemented.

Phase One: Analyze Overture's Telecommuting Needs

We will start by analyzing the specific workplace requirements of Overture's employees and management. The results of this analysis will allow us to work closely with Overture's management to develop a telecommuting program that fits the unique demands of a dynamic architecture firm.

In this phase, our goal will be to collect as much information as possible, so the transition to telecommunication will be smooth and hassle-free.

- First, we will conduct surveys of your employees to determine which people might be willing and able to telecommute. These surveys will tell us about their work habits and the way in which a telecommuting network could be adapted to their individual needs.

- Second, we will interview Overture's management. These interviews will help us tailor the telecommuting network to your corporate culture and your managers' specific needs.

- Third, we will conduct empirical studies to help us understand the office dynamics at Overture. These empirical studies will allow us to replicate those office dynamics in a virtual environment.

We estimate this phase will require thirty days. At the end of that time period, we will submit a report to you in which we discuss the findings of our surveys, interviews, and empirical studies. In this report, we will also describe the various telecommuting options available and recommend the option that best suits your needs.

Phase Two: Designing a Computer Network for Telecommuting

Using our findings from Phase One, we will then work with Overture's management to design a telecommuting program that fits the specific needs of the firm.

The telecommunication network would be designed for maximum flexibility. We would begin by creating a LAN that would be connected to a main server and a back-up server at Overture's main office (Figure 1). These servers would be connected through an ethernet to all in-office workstations and peripherals (plotters, CAD systems, copiers, fax machines, etc.). The ethernet would allow each workstation to communicate with the main server, other workstations, and peripherals.

Using cable modems, employees working at home or remote sites will connect to Overture's LAN through a communication server and a router (Figure 1). The communication server will manage the modem connections. The router, meanwhile, will allow your telecommuting employees to access peripherals, like the plotters and copiers, through the ethernet. The router will also allow Overture's main office to connect easily with future branch offices and remote clients.

To ensure the security of the LAN, we will equip the network with the most advanced security hardware and software available. The router (hardware) will be programmed to serve as a firewall against intruders. We will also install the most advanced encryption and virus detection software available to protect your employees' transmissions.

Overall, the advantage of this LAN design is that Overture's telecommuting employees will have access to all the equipment and services available in the main office. Meanwhile, even traveling employees who are visiting clients will be able to tap easily into the LAN from their laptop computers.

Phase Three: Training Overture's Employees

Experience has shown us that employees adapt quickly to telecommuting. Initially, though, we would need to train them how to access and use the LAN from workstations inside and outside the office.

To fully train your employees in telecommuting basics, we will need two afternoons (eight hours total). We will show them how to communicate through the network and access peripherals at the main office. The training will also include time management strategies to help your employees adjust to working outside the office.

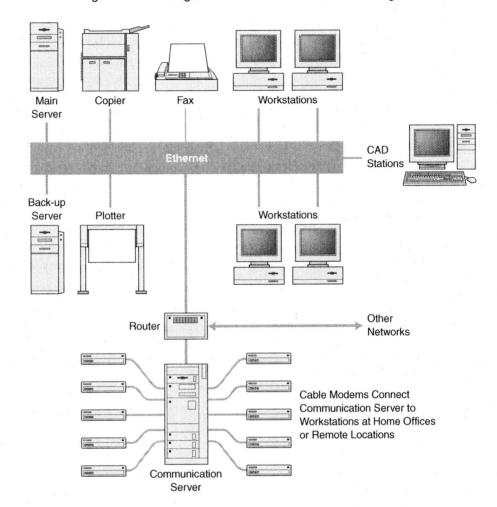

Figure 1: LAN Diagram for the Office at Overture Designs.

We have found that time management training helps employees work more efficiently at home—often more efficiently than they work in the office.

Insight Systems maintains a 24-hour helpline that your employees can call if they have any questions about using the LAN. Also, our website contains helpful information on improving efficiency through telecommuting.

Phase Four: Assessing the Telecommuting Program

To ensure the effectiveness of the telecommuting network, we will regularly survey and interview your managers and employees to solicit their reactions and suggestions for improvements. These surveys and interviews will be conducted every three months for two years.

We will be particularly interested in measuring employee satisfaction with telecommuting, and we will measure whether they believe their efficiency has increased since they began working at home through the LAN. The results of these assessments will help us fine-tune the LAN to your employees' needs.

After each three-month survey, we will submit a progress report to Overture that discusses our findings. At the end of the two-year period, we will submit a full report that analyzes our overall findings and makes suggestions for improving the telecommuting program in the future.

Qualifications at Insight Systems

At Insight Systems, we know this moment is a pivotal one for Overture Designs. To preserve and expand its market share, Overture needs to grow, but it cannot risk overextending itself financially. For these reasons, Insight Systems is uniquely qualified to handle this project, because we provide flexible, low-cost telecommuting networks that help growing companies stay responsive to shifts in their industry.

Management and Labor

With more than seventy combined years in the industry, our management team offers the insight and responsiveness required to handle your complex growth needs.

Hanna Gibbons, our CEO, has been working in the telecommuting industry for more than twenty years. After she graduated from MIT with a Ph.D. in computer science, she worked at Krayson International as a systems designer. Ten years later, she had worked her way up to vice president in charge of Krayson's Telecommuting Division. In 1993, Dr. Gibbons took over as CEO of Insight Systems. Since then, Dr. Gibbons has built this company into a major industry leader with gross sales of $15 million per year. Excited about the new innovations in telecommuting, Dr. Gibbons believes we are seeing a whole new workplace dynamic evolve before of our eyes.

Frank Roberts, chief engineer at Insight Systems, has thirty years of experience in the networked computer field. He began his career at Brindle Labs, where he worked on artificial intelligence systems using analog computer networks. In 1985, he joined the Insight Systems team, bringing his unique understanding of networking to our team. Frank is very detail oriented, often working long hours to ensure that each computer network meets each client's exact specifications and needs.

Lisa Miller, Insight Systems' senior computer engineer, has successfully led the implementation of thirty-three telecommuting systems in companies throughout the United States. Earning her computer engineering degree at Iowa State, Lisa has won numerous awards for her innovative approach to computer networking. She believes that clear communication is the best way to meet her clients' needs.

Our management is supported by one of most advanced teams of high-technology employees. Insight Systems employs twenty of the brightest engineers and technicians in the telecommunications industry. We have aggressively recruited our employees from the most advanced universities in the United States, including Stanford, MIT, Illinois, Iowa State, Purdue, and Syracuse. Several of our engineers have been with Insight Systems since it was founded. Also, we have forged an ongoing training relationship with Simmons Technical Institute to ensure that our employees stay at the forefront of their fields.

Corporate History and Facilities

Insight Systems has been a leader in the telecommuting industry from the beginning. In 1975, the company was founded by John Temple, a pioneer in the networking field. Since then, Insight Systems has followed Dr. Temple's simple belief that computer-age workplaces should give people the freedom to be creative.

Recently, Insight Systems earned the coveted "100 Companies to Watch" designation from *Business Outlook* magazine (May 2006). The company has worked with large and small companies, from Vedder Aerospace to the Cedar Rapids Museum of Fine Arts, to create telecommuting options for companies that want to keep costs down and productivity high.

Insight Systems' Naperville office has been called "a prototype workspace for the information age" (*Gibson's Computer Weekly*, May 2005). With advanced LAN systems in place, only ten of Insight Systems' fifty employees actually work in the office. Most of Insight Systems' employees telecommute from home or on the road.

Experience You Can Trust

Our background and experience gives us the ability to help Overture manage its needs for a more efficient, dynamic office space. Our keys to success are innovation, flexibility, and efficiency.

The Plan's Benefits and Project Costs

To conclude, let us summarize the advantages of our plan and discuss the costs. Our preliminary research shows that Overture Designs will continue to be a leader in the Chicago market. The strong economy, coupled with Overture's award-winning designs, will only increase the demand for your services. At Insight Systems, we believe the best way to manage Overture's growth is to implement a network that will allow some of the company's employees to telecommute from home or on-site.

Cost is the most significant advantage of our plan. As shown in the Appendix, implementation of our plan would cost an estimated $177,611. We believe this investment in Overture's infrastructure will preserve your company's financial flexibility, allowing you to react quickly to the market's crests and valleys. But the advantages of our plan go beyond simple costs:

■ *First, a telecommuting system will allow your current operations to continue without disruption.* When the telecommuting network is ready to go online, your employees will simply need to attend two four-hour training sessions on using the LAN. At these training sessions, we will teach them time-tested strategies for successful telecommuting from home. Your management can then gradually convert selected employees into telecommuters.

■ *Second, employee morale will benefit from using the telecommuting network.* With fewer employees at the office, there will be more space available for the employees who need to be in the office each day. Also, studies have shown that telecommuting employees not only report more job satisfaction, they also increase their productivity. Telecommuting would work especially well in your field, because architects often feel more comfortable working in less formal environments. The flexibility of telecommuting will allow Overture to recruit and retain some of the best people in the industry.

When the telecommuting system is in place, Overture will be positioned for continued growth and leadership in the Chicago architectural market. The key to Overture's success has always been its flexibility in a field that seems to change overnight.

Telecommuting will open up space at your current downtown office while maintaining the morale and productivity of your employees as your business continues to grow.

Thank you for giving Insight Systems the opportunity to work with you on this project. We look forward to submitting a full proposal that describes our plan in greater depth. Our CEO, Dr. Hanna Gibbons, will contact you on May 15 to discuss this pre-proposal with you.

If you have any suggestions for improving our plan or you would like further information about our services, please call Lisa Miller, our senior computer engineer, at 1-800-555-3864. Or, you can e-mail her at lmiller@insight_systems.com.

Appendix: Budget Rationale

At Insight Systems, we pride ourselves on developing low-cost solutions for managing limited office space. In this appendix, we would like to go over some of the major costs of the telecommuting plan discussed in this proposal. These figures are estimates, as you requested in your RFP. We will provide a fully itemized budget with the formal proposal. Table A offers a summary of our estimated costs for the Overture project.

As shown in Table A, management and labor are our primary costs. These costs represent two full-time managers, three computer engineers, two carpenters, and an electrician. These employees will be committed full time to the Overture project.

Hardware and software make up the other significant expense in our budget. Where possible, we will utilize Overture's existing computer infrastructure. However, additional hardware and software will be needed to upgrade your current infrastructure and create a LAN system.

Finally, our estimates for materials are dependent on the amount of labor required to hardwire the LAN system into your current operations. Our materials estimate in Table A is based on similarly sized projects we have handled in the past.

Overall, you should find that these costs are a small investment in your company's infrastructure. This investment will help you manage your limited office space while allowing you to maintain financial flexibility. If you have any questions about these figures, please call Lisa Miller at 1-800-555-3864 or e-mail her at lmiller@insight_systems.com.

TABLE A
Budget Summary

ITEM	COST
Management and Labor	$ 55,982
Equipment Rental and Purchase	7,250
Hardware and Software	70,482
Materials	20,340
Travel	2,298
Communications	700
Costs Before Profit	$157,052
Profit (10% of before-profit costs)	15,705
Taxes (Gross Receipts)	4,854
Total Costs	$177,611

DU

Durango University, 4446 Smithson Ave, Durango, Colorado, 81301

April 2, 2007

John Philips, Tempest Foundation Administrator
Tempest Foundation
1923 Camino del Oso
Santa Fe, New Mexico 87502

Dear Mr. Philips,

We are pleased to submit the enclosed grant proposal to the Tempest Foundation. Durango University is seeking funding for the Cool Campus Project, which will lead the conversion of our campus to renewable energy sources. We are currently seeking funding for the first phase of the project, the Cool Campus Strategic Plan.

I enjoyed speaking with you on the phone about this grant opportunity. We very much appreciate your help guiding the development of this proposal. Your comments helped us sharpen our ideas and develop a richer understanding of the problems we are trying to solve. We look forward to any comments from the Tempest Foundation's reviewers.

Your and the reviewers' time and efforts are greatly appreciated. If you have any questions or need more information, please contact me at (970) 555–1924. I can also be reached at georgtillman@durangou.edu.

Sincerely,

George Tillman

George Tillman
Professor of Environmental Engineering
Durango University

DU

The Cool Campus Project at Durango University: A Grant Request to the Tempest Foundation

The global warming problem can seem overwhelming. According to a 2007 report from the Intergovernmental Panel on Climate Change (IPCC), global warming will likely have the following dire effects on our planet:

- Global temperatures will rise from 2 to 11 degrees Fahrenheit in this century.
- Sea levels will rise from 7 to 23 inches, causing significant flooding of lowland areas.
- Heat waves and droughts will be more frequent and severe in the United States.
- Many parts of the world will experience much heavier rainfall.
- The polar icecaps will experience dramatic meltoffs, sending large iceshelves and icebergs into the ocean.
- Many species of animals will go extinct.

The report from the IPCC calls the evidence for global warming "unequivocal." It warns that unless humans dramatically cut emissions of greenhouse gases, the impact of global warming on this planet will be significant and, perhaps, catastrophic. These kinds of dire predictions might lead some people to conclude that we cannot do anything about this complex global problem.

At Durango University, we believe we *can* do something. Durango University has already made significant strides toward conserving energy, but we would like to fully convert our campus to sustainable energy sources. So, with this proposal, we are turning to the Tempest Foundation for a grant to help us develop a Cool Campus Strategic Plan. This strategic plan will guide the conversion of our campus to renewable and sustainable energy sources. With a long-term strategic plan in place, we believe Durango University's campus could eliminate or offset its emissions of greenhouse gases by 2025. Meanwhile, as we work toward converting our campus to renewable energy sources, we could help other universities around the world follow our lead.

Table of Contents

In this grant proposal, we will discuss Durango University's current energy usage and describe how we would use an urban planning charrette to develop and write the Cool Campus Strategic Plan. We will discuss our qualifications and the costs and benefits of the project. The finding provided by the Tempest Foundation would allow us to develop the Cool Campus Strategic Plan. With this plan in place, we can then devote our own resources toward making the Cool Campus Strategic Plan a reality.

Energy Issues at Durango University

Going green is not new on our campus. Durango University began its Green Campus Program in the year 2001 with a grant from its own Office of the President. The Green Campus Program has generated immediate benefits:

- increased conservation
- heightened environmental awareness on campus
- increased recycling
- purchase of renewable energy certificates to offset 30 percent of the campus's consumption of electricity
- use of compact fluorescent lightbulbs and Energy Star appliances

The Green Campus Program brought our community together and fostered a sense of independence, but the long-term energy challenges we face at Durango University go beyond the scope of the Green Campus Program.

> **"Our main challenge is now the campus infrastructure itself, which was built in 1914 with the available energy technologies."**

Our main challenge now involve the campus infrastructure itself, which was built in 1914 with the available energy technologies, specifically coal and oil. Our campus is bound to these nonrenewable energy sources, making us contributors to global warming and vulnerable to the increasing costs of energy.

The Legacy of Old Betsy

Our campus's reliance on coal for steam heat is the most difficult problem to solve. In 1914 when the university was founded, a small coal-fire plant nicknamed "Old Betsy" supplied steam heat and electricity from the eastern edge of campus (where the Student Union is today). Old Betsy's coal-fired boilers kept the campus warm by pushing steam through underground tunnels running to the buildings. The plant also used steam power to generate the small amount of electricity required by the campus (Philip, 28).

Of course, the campus has changed a great amount since then, but the technologies used to heat and power the campus have not. The campus now has twenty-four buildings, which are spread over a campus that covers eighty-six acres. Old Betsy was replaced in 1931 by a larger coal-fire plant, and successively larger coal-fire plants were built in 1954 and 1973. However, the newer plants only led to an expansion of the infrastructure originally designed for Old Betsy.

So the legacy of Old Betsy lives on today. Presently, the campus is heated by the Young Power Plant (Figure A), which still burns coal to make steam and then pushes it through tunnels under campus. The campus's electricity demands outstripped the generating capacity of its own power plants in 1970, mainly because of new electricity-using devices on campus like televisions

Figure A: The Young Power Plant at Durango University

and computers (Figure B). Today, the campus mainly draws its electricity from the Four Corners Power Plant, a massive coal-fire plant located west of Farmington, New Mexico. A small amount of our electricity is drawn from other regional power plants, which burn natural gas.

After thirty-five years of service, the Young Power Plant is due for replacement or a complete renovation. Its boilers are already expensive to run and maintain, compared to other sources of heat (James, 12). Steam is an inefficient way to heat a campus of our size. Moreover, burning coal adds carbon dioxide and other greenhouse gases into the atmosphere, contributing to global warming.

Oil, Cars, and Campus

Our next largest problem concerns the number of cars and trucks that travel to and around the campus every day. The campus was originally designed to be pedestrian-friendly. By the 1930s, though, automobiles were already a

Figure B: Total Energy Consumption, Durango University

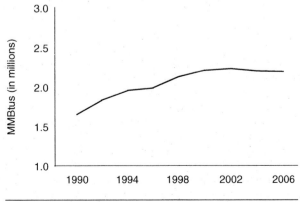

SOURCE: Durango University Annual Reports, 1990–2006.

common way to commute to and around campus. As a result, expansion plans for campus began to centralize the automobile. Public transportation eventually disappeared. The campus trolley, called the Dinky, stopped operating in 1931, and the campus bus service was discontinued in 1972.

Plans for expanding campus have routinely called for more parking lots and parking garages to accommodate more and more cars. Streets have been widened and major thoroughfares have been built to accommodate the greater flow of traffic. These changes have allowed university employees and students to commute from even further away, thus causing a cycle of more parking garages, even wider streets, and busier thoroughfares.

Today, the campus is over-reliant on automobiles and trucks for its transportation needs. The usual complaints about the shortage of parking conceal the much deeper problem that few alternatives are available for commuting to campus. In the past, the university has encouraged people to walk to campus or ride their bikes, but the design of the campus makes driving a car much more convenient and safer.

> **"Today, the campus is over-reliant on automobiles and trucks for its transportation needs."**

Worldwide, cars have been shown to be the single largest source of greenhouse emissions causing global climate change (Union of Concerned Scientists). Our campus's over-reliance on gasoline-powered cars is part of that problem. But currently there are few alternatives to driving, forcing even environmentally conscious people to rely on their automobiles.

Effects of Inaction

Doing nothing really isn't an option for Durango University. The Young Power Plant will need to be completely overhauled or replaced within the next decade. The burning of coal and gasoline will only continue adding to the problems of global warming. Meanwhile, the costs of energy are driving up expenses all around campus (Figure C). If we do nothing, more and more of the university's budget will be used to pay for heating, electricity, and gasoline. These additional costs will either be passed along to students or will lead to cuts in salaries, services, and staff. We also recognize that our

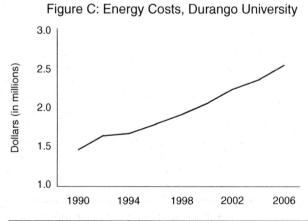

Figure C: Energy Costs, Durango University

SOURCE: Durango University Annual Reports, 1990–2006.

Figure D: Administrative Support for Transforming the Campus

Legend:
- Strongly Agree (black)
- Agree (light)
- Disagree (gray)
- Strongly Disagree (dark gray)

Categories:
- The energy problems at Durango U. need to be addressed now, not later.
- Our energy problems can be solved primarily through conservation of energy.
- Durango U. should convert to renewable energy sources as soon as possible.
- Durango U. has an obligation to take on a leadership role in the region regarding energy issues and issues of global warming.

own reputation is at stake as other universities take the lead in using renewable and sustainable energy sources.

Durango University's Green Campus Program has raised our community's awareness of environmental issues on campus, but we are ready to make the kinds of large-scale changes that will be needed for a sustainable future. In a recent poll of our deans and department chairs, the support for this kind of change was overwhelmingly positive (Figure D). We believe this kind of support opens the door for making lasting changes.

"Doing nothing really isn't an option for Durango University."

Our Plan: A Cool Campus Charrette

Converting a college campus to renewable energy will take careful planning and time. Therefore, our main goal is to develop a comprehensive Cool Campus Strategic Plan that will guide our campus's transformation into a net-zero carbon emission campus. To develop this plan, we will host a charrette that will invite the whole community into the planning process.

A charrette is a weekend retreat, facilitated by professional urban planners, that puts citizens and stakeholders into design teams (Figure E). These teams develop separate plans, drawing from their collective wisdom and their knowledge of the community. Then, the urban planners use the ideas generated by these teams to create professional designs and present them back to the community. The advantage of a charrette is that it works from the grass roots up, using the knowledge, desires, and experiences of the community, while encouraging all stakeholders to participate and buy into the project.

"To develop this plan, we will host a charrette that will invite the whole community into the planning process."

Figure E: A charrette draws on the experience
and creativity of the community.

SOURCE: Used with permission of Image Works.

Our objectives in the Cool Campus Charrette would be the following:

- Develop a comprehensive Strategic Plan that would guide Durango University's efforts toward energy conservation while shaping future decisions about renovation and construction.

- Create and foster a community dialogue about renewable energy that extends beyond the campus.

- Develop a new model of campus planning that shows how other campuses can use charrettes to work toward converting to renewable energy sources.

Step One: Create the Cool Campus Steering Committee, May 2008

To achieve these objectives, our first action would be to create a Cool Campus Steering Committee that would be responsible for making initial decisions about the charrette.

The members of the Steering Committee will work with Summers & Mondragon, an urban planning firm that has experience with issues of renewable energy and with facilitating charrettes. Summers & Mondragon will also help us meet LEED standards (Leadership in Energy and Environmental Design) developed by the U.S. Green Building Council (http://www.usgbc.org).

The purpose of the Steering Committee would be to lay a solid foundation for the charrette. The members of the Steering Committee would include a range of people, including executive-level university administrators, faculty and staff, student leaders, and local citizens. We envision a planning committee of about twelve people that would meet weekly for two months until the charrette was planned and scheduled.

When the charrette is scheduled, the Steering Committee will write a report to the Tempest Foundation and the university president that describes its actions and decisions. The Steering Committee would invite feedback from the Tempest Foundation on this report.

> "The purpose of the Steering Committee would be to lay a solid foundation for the charrette."

6

Step Two: Create a Charrette Library and Website, July 2008

The Steering Committee will work with Summers & Mondragon to assemble information about the campus and identify options for renewable energy, conservation, and public transportation.

Working with librarians from Durango University, Summers & Mondragon will create a library that brings together any information that might be useful during the charrette. That way, participants in the charrette would have the necessary information already at hand. The library would include documents, books, information from websites, archival materials, and any other data that participants might need. Durango University's librarians, led by Gina Sanders, would set aside a separate room for these materials and organize them into an accessible system that is cross-referenced and electronically searchable.

With the charrette library in place, the urban planning firm will then work with Durango University's webmaster to develop a website that offers information and updates on the Cool Campus Project, as well as provide opportunities for the public to participate through weblogs and electronic bulletin boards. Documents from the Cool Campus library would be made available to the public through this project website. The website will be accessible through a link on Durango University's homepage.

When this step is concluded, we will have developed a library of materials that can be accessed both locally and through the Internet. The Cool Campus website will also serve as a forum for public comment as well as an information clearinghouse.

Step Three: Host the Charrette at the Student Union, September 2008

In the Fall of 2008, we will host a weekend charrette that brings together stakeholders and any others who might be interested in the project. We expect about 100 people to attend, so we will reserve the Student Union's Chandler Ballroom and breakout rooms for the weekend. We will also order lunches and refreshments, so participants in the charrette can stay focused on the planning process.

At the Friday evening kickoff meeting, we will introduce the facilitators from Summers & Mondragon. The facilitators will explain the Cool Campus Project, discuss how the charrette will work, and make the Cool Campus library available to participants. We will then divide into design teams of six participants, allowing team members time to introduce themselves to each other.

On Saturday, each design team will develop its own plan for converting the campus to renewable energy sources. Experts from Summers & Mondragon and the Environmental Engineering Department will work with each team to explain technological abilities and limitations. They will also answer any questions that might arise in the design teams. The experts, however, will only serve as resources for the teams, not leaders. Our aim is to maximize the creativity of the design teams by offering guidance without limiting their ability to be innovative.

On Sunday afternoon, each team will have two hours to finish its plan and create a PowerPoint presentation. Then each team will present its plan to the assembly. Members of the audience will be allowed to ask questions, identify the strengths of each plan, and probe any weaknesses. The Sunday meeting

> **"Each design team will develop its own plan for converting the campus to renewable energy sources."**

Figure F: Solar panels could be installed on campus buildings.

SOURCE: Used with permission of New Bohemia Solar Project.

will be videotaped, and the facilitators from Summers & Mondragon will take close notes on the proceedings. At the end of this meeting, all the plans will be submitted by the design teams.

Our expectation is that the design teams will develop plans that incorporate a variety of renewable energy sources, such as wind, solar, and geothermal (Figures F and G). We also expect them to offer ideas for conserving energy and improving public transportation such as introducing hybrid vehicles (Figure H). The design teams will be asked to develop plans that have both long-range and short-term features: (1) a long-range plan that eliminates or offsets all greenhouse gases produced on campus, and (2) a short-term plan that allows us to make immediate changes that will help us conserve energy and reduce our emissions of greenhouse gases.

"Ultimately, the aim of the charrette will be to draw on the collective creativity of the participants."

Ultimately, the aim of the charrette will be to draw on the collective creativity of the participants. Charrettes used for urban planning have been shown to bring out more creativity and knowledge than would be gathered by an urban planning firm alone. Moreover, charrettes like this one bring more stakeholders into the planning process, encouraging increased buy-in and less resistance to change. The community participates in the planning process, fostering a sense of identity and cooperation.

When this step is completed, we will put copies of the designs and a podcast of the Sunday meeting on our website. We will also write a progress report to the Tempest Foundation that highlights the events of the weekend.

Step Four: Presentation of the Strategic Plan, October 2008

Using the plans from the charrette, Summers & Mondragon will develop a comprehensive Cool Campus Strategic Plan for converting the campus to

Figure G: Wind farms could be an excellent source
of electricity for Durango University.

SOURCE: Used with permission of Sandia National Laboratories.

renewable forms of energy. They will also identify any limitations that might keep us from achieving the goals discussed in the charrette.

At a Saturday meeting one month after the charrette, Summers & Mondragon will present the draft of their Cool Campus Strategic Plan to the participants of the charrette. They will explain their version of the plan and solicit feedback from the audience. These proceedings will be videotaped, and all comments will be recorded.

Figure H: Hybrid busses reduce emissions and would offer
a reliable and safe way to travel to and around campus.

SOURCE: Used with permission of General Motors.

Our goal for this meeting will be to reach consensus among stakeholders. If the charrette process is successful, the participants in the charrette will rally around the plan because they helped create it. When this meeting is over, we will put a copy of the design, as well as a podcast of the meeting, on the Cool Campus website. We will write a progress report to the Tempest Foundation that illustrates and discusses the plan developed by Summers & Mondragon.

Step Five: Finalizing the Plan, December 2008

Using the comments from the meeting, Summers & Mondragon will then develop a final version of the Cool Campus Strategic Plan. The full version will be sent to President Wilson within two months. Then, the final plan will be submitted by President Wilson to the university's Board of Regents for consideration.

> **"The purpose of the Cool Campus Strategic Plan will be to provide a blueprint for converting the campus to renewable energy sources."**

The purpose of the Cool Campus Strategic Plan will be to provide a blueprint for converting the campus to renewable energy sources while minimizing the campus's emissions of pollution and greenhouse gases. Upon approval by the Board of Regents, the Cool Campus Strategic Plan will be used to guide all future decisions about building and renovating the campus. All campus budgeting, construction, and renovation decisions will be required to satisfy the guidelines described in the Cool Campus Strategic Plan.

We will present the Cool Campus Strategic Plan to the Tempest Foundation at its January 2009 meeting. At that point, we can answer any questions about our plans for implementing the plan.

Dissemination

One of our goals is to establish a path that other universities can follow. For this reason, we will disseminate our plan through a variety of venues, including the Cool Campus website, national conferences, and a variety of publications. The website will make the Cool Campus Strategic Plan available to anyone who requests it. That way, other universities can use it to help themselves but their own charrettes and develop their own strategic plans. Meanwhile, at conferences, our administrators and faculty will present the results of the charrette. These conference presentations will lead to publications in academic journals and magazines.

The Tempest Foundation will be prominently mentioned on our website and in any printed materials related to this project. At conferences and in articles, the Tempest Foundation will be warmly thanked for its support of this project.

Assessment

To assess the program, we will retain two outside evaluators who are experts in urban planning and renewable energy. We will submit their credentials for consideration and approval by the Tempest Foundation. Funds from the grant will be used to pay their expenses and an honorarium of five hundred dollars each.

The evaluators will observe all aspects of the Cool Campus Project and have full access to any participants, meetings, and materials. When the project is completed, the evaluators will write a report to the Tempest Foundation that discusses their impressions and their appraisal of our efforts.

Qualifications of the Cool Campus Team

Durango University is an ideal setting to undertake this revolutionary transformation to renewable energy. Located in southwestern Colorado, our campus has access to a variety of alternative forms of renewable energy, including solar, wind, and geothermal energy. We also have a forward-thinking administration that is committed to converting the campus to renewable energy. We want to be a positive role model for the nation.

> **"Durango University is an ideal setting to undertake this revolutionary transformation to renewable energy."**

Biographies of Key Personnel

The project leaders for the Cool Campus Project will be Professor George Tillman and Vice President Anne Hinton. Key support will be provided by Diane Smith, a partner at Summers & Mondragon, and Gina Sanders, a Durango University research librarian.

- Professor George Tillman, Ph.D., is the John Connell Chair of Environmental Engineering. He has worked on geothermal energy issues for twenty-two years. He has authored or co-authored fifty-four articles on renewable energy and has worked with several small towns in Colorado to incorporate renewable energy into their energy grids. In 2003, Dr. Tillman was awarded the Environmental Engineer of the Year Award by the Colorado Environmental Protection Agency. He has been a principal investigator on $6.2 million of grants in renewable energy research.

- Dr. Anne Hinton is the vice president for Physical Facilities at Durango University. Before taking this position, she was dean of the College of Management. She is a specialist in international management and entrepreneurship. Her most recent book is *Managing Diversity: A Guide to Entrepreneurship*, which was published in 2005. She is a leading expert in fostering creativity in diverse teams of people.

- Diane Smith is a partner with Summers & Mondragon, an urban planning firm located in Santa Fe, New Mexico. Ms. Smith has facilitated twenty-three urban planning charrettes and has worked with numerous cities on urban renewal, including Albuquerque, Chicago, Toledo, Santa Fe, and Santa Barbara. Summers & Mondragon has been a leading firm in using "New Urbanism" to reconceptualize commerce and transportation and make cities more pedestrian-friendly and less congested.

- Gina Sanders is a senior research librarian at the Laura Vasquez Library on the Durango University campus. She has worked with many departments and local groups to gather information on technology issues. Her specialty is assembling information into electronically accessible formats. Her work with the Durango University e-Library won a Top Innovator Award from the National Librarians Council.

Curriculum vitae for the project leaders are included with this grant application.

Other faculty and staff members will also be assigned to this project. Durango University is the home of one of the leading environmental engineering departments in the nation. Our five faculty members and their graduate students will serve as resources for the community and the charrette. Meanwhile, staff members will be involved in developing the website for the charrette and assembling the library of documents and materials.

Background on Durango University

"Since its founding in 1912, the university has had a long history of environmental leadership in the region."

Another strength is Durango University itself. Since its founding in 1912, the university has had a long history of environmental leadership in the region. It was one of the first universities in the Southwest to develop an environmental engineering program. The program began in our Mining Engineering Department in 1958, drawing leaders in environmental engineering to its faculty. In 1970, the department was renamed Environmental Engineering to reflect environmental conservation as its primary mission.

Past Grants at Durango University

The university has received a variety of grants from government sources and foundations. Recently, the National Science Foundation awarded the Environmental Engineering Department a $1.2 million grant to research opportunities for using geothermal energy in remote mountain communities. A $2.3 million Department of Energy grant was awarded to the Electrical Engineering Department for research into solar energy. The U.S. Department of Education also awarded Durango University a $780,000 grant to develop an educational program on global warming that could be used in high schools throughout the United States. We have received funding from private foundations for our efforts to address world poverty in mountainous areas throughout the world. The Geneva Foundation provided a $630,000 grant to one of our research teams to help improve access to electricity for people living in the Himalayas.

Durango University has a track record of success in environmental issues. To learn more about the university and its successful grant-funded projects, please visit http://www.DurangoU.edu and http://www.DurangoU.edu/research.

Conclusion: The Benefits of the Cool Campus Project

"With this strategic plan in place, we can start taking positive steps toward strengthening our community and addressing the causes of global warming on our campus."

Let us conclude with a discussion of the costs and benefits of the Cool Campus Project. We are requesting $54,530 from the Tempest Foundation to help us develop the Cool Campus Strategic Plan. With this strategic plan in place, we can start taking positive steps toward strengthening our community and addressing the causes of global warming on our campus. Our itemized budget is enclosed, and we believe that cost-sharing with the Tempest Foundation is an important part of our contribution toward the project.

The benefits of the Tempest Foundation's support for the Cool Campus Project will be well worth the investment:

■ The Cool Campus Project will allow us to begin converting our campus to renewable energy sources from the grass roots up. The charrette will draw from the knowledge, wisdom, desires, and experiences of the community, while encouraging people to participate in the transformation process.

■ The Cool Campus Project will generate and cultivate an ongoing dialogue about energy conservation and sustainable lifestyles, which will build a sense of unity and cooperation on our campus.

- The Cool Campus Project will provide a prototype that other universities can follow to convert their campuses to renewable energy and a carbon-neutral status.

- The Cool Campus library will be accessible worldwide through the Durango University website, offering a comprehensive resource on issues related to global warming.

- The Cool Campus Project will be supported by our Environmental Engineering program, which has a track record of success in energy-related projects.

The most significant benefit of the Tempest Foundation's investment will be the development of a comprehensive strategic plan that will guide the conversion of our campus to a carbon-neutral status. We can then centralize the Cool Campus Project in our campus planning and take bold steps toward doing our part to solve global warming.

We believe the Cool Campus Project at Durango University will provide a way forward into the future—a future that is sustainable and environmentally sound. When the Cool Campus Project is completed, Durango University will have demonstrated that energy independence and sustainability are not only possible but highly advantageous. Today, our society no longer has the luxury to wait for others to take the lead on issues of global warming. At Durango University, we believe we can take steps right now that will help all of us to solve the global warming problem.

Thank you for your time and consideration. We look forward to hearing from you about this request for a grant. If you have any questions, comments, or suggestions for improvement, please feel free to contact George Tillman, professor of Environmental Engineering, at (970) 555–1924 or Anne Hinton, vice president for Physical Facilities, at (970) 551–1823. We appreciate your willingness to consider our request.

> **"We believe the Cool Campus Project of Durango University will provide a way forward into the future—a future that is sustainable and environmentally sound."**

Appendix A: The Cool Campus Project Budget

The start-up expenses for the Cool Campus Project will be modest, and Durango University is committed to sharing the costs with the Tempest Foundation. The major costs will include hiring an urban planner to organize and facilitate the charrette. We will also ask the Tempest Foundation for funding to promote the charrette, provide supplies, support expenses and honoraria for reviewers, and fund travel for project leaders. Minor costs will include items such as funding for phone calls, postage, and materials for disseminating the results of our project.

Durango University will cost-share by paying the salaries of project leaders and participants, purchasing food and refreshments for the charrette, and providing equipment and space. We will also calculate as in-kind contributions the time of volunteers and our webmaster. Table A shows our budget and how we arrived at the costs for this phase of the Cool Campus Project.

(*continued*)

Table A: The Budget

Item	Tempest Foundation	Durango University
Project Leaders' Salaries and Benefits		
George Tillman (20 percent time)		$20,650.00
Anne Hinton (10 percent time)		14,120.00
Major Participants' Salaries and Benefits		
Diane Smith, urban planner	$12,000.00	
Gina Sanders, librarian (10 percent time)		6,800.00
Staff and Assistants		
3 facilitators	10,000.00	
5 research assistants (50 percent time)	11,450.00	
Clerical assistance (100 hours @ 15.00/h)	9,000.00	3,000.00
Volunteers (200 hours @ 15.00/h)		
Services and Facilities		1,500.00
Rental of ballroom in student union		2,550.00
Room at library to house materials		540.00
Projector rental		450.00
Podcasting equipment rental		200.00
Space on server for website		
Materials		
Supplies for charrette	430.00	
Promotional materials	980.00	4,000.00
Food and Refreshments		
Travel and Housing Expenses		
Project leaders	3,200.00	
Urban planners	3,000.00	
Evaluators	2,000.00	
Communications and Dissemination		
Phone	230.00	
Postage	310.00	
Documentation	930.00	
Evaluation		
Honoraria for 2 evaluators	1,000.00	(waived)
Indirect Costs (F&A)		$53,810.00
Total Costs	$54,530.00	

References

Durango Universtiy, *Annual Report*. Durango, CO: Durango University, 1990–2006.

Intergovernmental Panel on Climate Change (IPCC), "Climate Change 2007: The Physical Science, Summary for Policymakers." 1 February 2007. 2 April 2007 Science, http://ipcc-wg1.ucar.edu/Wg1/docs/WG1AR4_SPM_Approved_05Feb.pdf.

James, Susan. *Analysis of Young Power Plant*. Durango, CO: Durango University, 2005.

Office of the Mayor (Seattle). "U.S. Mayors Climate Protection Agreement," 16 February 2005. 2 April 2007 http://www.seattle.gov/mayor/climate.

Philips, Thomas. *History of Durango College*. Durango, CO: Durango University Press, 1993.

Union of Concerned Scientists. "Cars and Trucks and Global Warming." 4 April 2007 http://www.ucsusa.org./clean_vehicles/vehicles_health/cars-and-trucks-and-global-warming.html.

References

Aristotle. (1991). *On rhetoric.* G. Kennedy (trans.) New York: Oxford UP.

Arnheim, R. (1964). *Art and visual perception.* Berkeley: University of California Press.

Bernhardt, S. (1986). Seeing the text. *College Composition and Communication, 30,* 66–78.

Burke, K. (1954). *A grammar of motives.* Berkeley: U of California P.

Burton, D. (1998). *Technical writing style.* Boston: Allyn and Bacon.

Cicero. (1986). *On oratory and orators.* J. Watson (trans.). Carbondale, IL: Southern Illinois UP.

Donnelly, R. (1984). *Guidebook to planning.* New York: Van Norstrand Reinhold.

Eastman, R. (1978). *Style.* New York: Oxford UP.

Haviland, S., and Clark, H. (1974). What's new? Acquiring new information as a process in comprehension. *Journal of Verbal Learning and Verbal Behavior, 13,* 512–521.

Jones, D. (1997). *Technical writing style.* Boston: Allyn and Bacon.

Koffka, K. (1935). *Principles of gestalt psychology.* New York: Harcourt.

Kostelnick, C., and Roberts, D. (1998). *Designing visual language.* Boston: Allyn and Bacon.

Laib, N. (1993). *Rhetoric and style.* Englewood Cliffs, NJ: Prentice Hall.

Lanham, R. (1991). *Revising business prose.* Boston: Allyn and Bacon.

Mathes, J. C., and Stevenson, D. W. (1976). *Designing technical reports.* Indianapolis: Bobbs-Merrill Educational Publishing.

Moore, P., and Fitz, C. (1993). Using gestalt theory to teach document design and graphics. *Technical Communication Quarterly, 2,* 389–410.

Penrose, A., and Katz, S. (1998). *Writing in the sciences.* New York: St. Martin's.

Ramsey, J., and Ramsey, I. (1985). *Budgeting basics.* New York: Franklin Watts.

Swales, J. (1984). Research into the structure of introductions to journal articles and its applications to the teaching of academic writing. In R. Williams, J. Swales, & J. Kirkman, (eds.), *Common ground: Shared interests in ESP and communication studies.* (pp. 77–86). New York: Pergamon.

Tufte, E. (1983). *The visual display of quantitative information.* Cheshire, MA: Graphics Press.

Vande Kopple, W. (1989). *Clear and coherent prose.* Boston: Scott, Foresman.

White, J. (1988). *Graphic design for the electronic age.* New York: Watson-Guptill.

Williams, J. (1990). *Style.* Chicago: U of Chicago P.

Williams, R. (1994). *Non-designer's design book.* Berkeley, CA: Peachpit.

Index